THE
National ⚾ Pastime

BASEBALL IN THE SPACE AGE

Houston Since 1961

EDITED BY CECILIA TAN

Published by
The Society for American Baseball Research

THE NATIONAL PASTIME

Copyright © 2014 The Society for American Baseball Research

Editor: Cecilia Tan
Design and Production: Lisa Hochstein
Cover Design: Lisa Hochstein
Fact Checker: Clifford Blau

Front cover images:
Courtesy of the Houston Astros: *Larry Dierker, uniform jersey*
National Hall of Fame Library, Cooperstown, NY: *Astrodome exterior, commemorative ticket*
Bob Busser Creative Vision 360 (www.ballparks.phanfare.com): *Astrodome interior*

ISBN 978-1-933599-65-6 print edition
ISBN 978-1-933599-66-3 ebook edition

The Society for American Baseball Research, Inc.
4455 E. Camelback Road, Ste. D-140
Phoenix, AZ 85018
www.sabr.org
Phone: (800) 969-7227 or (602) 343-6455

Contents

Introduction

This issue of *The National Pastime* is dedicated to baseball in Houston since 1961. For the past several years, each annual issue of *TNP* has centered on the geographic area of SABR's summer convention site. Since the convention moves around, that has given us great range: Philadelphia, Minnesota, Southern California have hosted recent conventions and corresponding issues of *TNP* have been produced. But this is the first one that will have a time-limited component as well as a geographic one. Why? SABR's Houston chapter is releasing a book for the convention, too: *Houston Baseball: The Early Years, 1861–1961.*

Houston Baseball is a gorgeous hardcover book and will be given to each attendee of the convention. With the first hundred years of Houston baseball covered so thoroughly in that publication, it made sense to focus *The National Pastime* for this summer on the space age and the arrival of Major League Baseball in the region. So here we have a special issue centered almost entirely on the Houston Astros (né Colt .45s) and their two influential and iconic homes, short-lived Colt Stadium and the Astrodome.

The Houston MLB franchise has been around only slightly longer than I have, but the Colts/Astros have amassed more than their share of history in the five-plus decades since their launch. Friends in Texas always tell me that "everything is bigger in Texas," and that certainly applies to the role of the Astrodome in pop culture, and to the outsize personality of team owner Roy Hofheinz, who was one part P.T. Barnum, two parts George Steinbrenner, and all Texan.

If you weren't able to attend the convention in Houston, please enjoy reading this issue of *The National Pastime* as your virtual trip to "Space City" in the Lone Star State. Seventeen SABR members will be your tour guides. Happy reading!

Cecilia Tan
July 2014

Houston's Role in the Initiation of Sunday Night Baseball

Bill McCurdy

It is something of a minor irony that Houston, the city that brought totally covered stadiums and air conditioning to baseball and football, also became the place that pushed the envelope on the approval of baseball on Sunday nights. Like air conditioning, the concept was introduced for the safety and comfort of Houston fans, and its adoption came about as a quirk of fate. Sometimes, issues are simply born in the timing of things.

When Houston was approved for one of the two National League expansion club franchises in 1960, the city won the bid on three major points: (1) Houston's robust population growth; (2) the city's decades of historical support for high level minor league baseball; and (3) Harris County's promise that it would, in fair return, construct the first all-enclosed, air-conditioned stadium in the world as the new venue for play.

Here's that timing factor: The new domed stadium would take years to construct. The new Houston team would have to play their MLB home games in a temporary venue until their new earlier-than-Star-Wars facility was ready to house games.

In fact, the whole space-age "Astros" theme did not even exist in 1962, the year of the club's debut. If it did, it was on the back-burner in the mind of the late Judge Roy Hofheinz, the P.T. Barnum-like visionary leader of the ownership group, the Houston Sports Association (HSA).

TIMING

In 1962, Judge Hofheinz was emerging from the difficult and expensive negotiation of the AAA minor league territorial rights from the Houston Buffs of the American Association. The deal included usage rights to the 11,000-seat Busch Stadium in Houston if the new National League team decided to remain there and handle the expense of any enlargements.[1] Busch Stadium had a covered main grandstand. Adding bleachers down the lines and behind the outfield walls could have expanded capacity to 20,000-plus, but the Judge didn't want that option.[2]

He wanted Houston NL fans to be on site to witness the new domed stadium grow from a cavernous hole-in-the-ground into what would be dubbed the "Eighth Wonder of the World." So he built a temporary venue, Colt Stadium, reflecting the name he had chosen from fan suggestions for the new club, the Houston Colt .45s. Colt Stadium was located on the northwest corner of the paved concrete parking lot that would live on in service to the covered colossus, once it was built. At the time, Houston fans thought that the "Houston Colt .45s" would be the city's permanent MLB identity, and that the domed stadium would be known as Harris County Domed Stadium.

Colt Stadium had a capacity of 33,000, but it offered no protection from the sun or rain.[3] Fans attending day games had to go against the JFK zeitgeist of avoiding headwear or have their blood and other bodily juices boiled to the temperature of tea.

Some referred to Colt Stadium as "The Sizzler" because of the guaranteed double roast that fans got from the direct sun and reflected heat from the seats, sidewalks, and parking lot pavement. Some wore ball caps despite any admiration for President Kennedy. It made sense under the dire circumstances.

What didn't make sense is what began to happen as June of 1962 moved into one of the hottest Houston summers on record. Fans at Colt Stadium were not simply placed in positions of inconvenience and mild discomfort; they literally were placing their lives at risk during day games.

Timing again. I have memories of profuse sweat running down my face, soaking my clothes, rendering me unable to drink enough lemonade and water to quench my boundless thirst; why am I here? Looking to the southeast from the highest row on the first base side of the stands was exhilarating. There sat the mammoth hole in the ground that would become the grand, air-conditioned palace that one day soon would be our salvation. What a dreamy thought that was on very hot days.

Timing. Its appearance and meaning suddenly became lucidly obvious: I believe this juxtaposition of hellish torment and the promise of heavenly climate-control was intentional. But the record-breaking heat of that summer was beyond Judge Hofheinz's influence. What could fans do in the meanwhile for relief?

Major League Baseball still had a policy against baseball on Sunday nights in 1962. It may have been grounded in the old blue laws in some cities that had formerly banned any baseball on Sundays, but it seems to also have had ties with that day's status as a fairly universal MLB "getaway day." The schedule makers apparently feared that a Sunday night game could jeopardize a visiting team's ability to reach their next destination in time to start a new series on Monday. Of course, one has to wonder: "Would the schedule makers have been equally upset by the idea of a Wednesday night game, if the visitors were set to start a new series elsewhere on Thursday?"

We have found no definitive answer to the complete truth in this matter of the old Sunday night game ban.[4] We may only observe that baseball is often reluctant to change longstanding policies. Early in the 1950s, St. Louis Cardinals' owner Fred Saigh had requested permission to play a make-up game on Sunday night, but was flatly refused. Commissioner A.B. "Happy" Chandler may have done it as much for personal enmity as any belief in the Sunday night ban.[5]

Commissioner Ford C. Frick could not so easily ignore the need for Sunday night baseball in Houston. Many fans at day games in Houston were suffering such severe effects from heat that they had to be transported by ambulance to the Texas Medical Center nearby.

Timing.

The dome was still almost three years away, and no one knew for sure when the world's first large air-conditioned domed stadium would actually be ready for use.

And though the summer of 1962 was one of the hottest on record, the reality is that summer sizzles in Texas. Night baseball had saved the minor league game in Houston from 1930 forward. Daylight baseball could have turned into the iceberg of heat for the city's titanic major league future, if people started dying during their wait for domed stadium relief. The weekend that turned the corner, moving it from concern to action on the Sunday night baseball problem, was the weekend of June 9–10. The Colt .45s faced the Dodgers. The teams were scheduled to play a day game on Saturday and a daylight double header on Sunday.

I chose to attend the Saturday 1:00 PM game despite the heat-induced delirium I'd experienced two weeks earlier. By noon the temperature at Colt Stadium had risen to 88 degrees with the humidity checking in at 88 percent. These figures undoubtedly rose throughout

the game, if the number of heat stroke cocktails served up to the soaking-wet, mostly hatless crowd was any indication. Over the course of the Colt .45s 13–1 slaughter of the Dodgers, the stadium medical staff saw numerous people with heat stress issues and at least six of them were taken from the ballpark to the Texas Medical Center with clear symptoms of full-blown heatstroke.

When the score hit 11–1 after five innings, Dodgers manager Walt Alston pretty much threw in the towel in an effort to save the health of some of his valuable starters. He removed Maury Wills, Jim Gilliam, and John Roseboro as a group.[6]

None of the players on either side were injured that day, but all dragged their bodies around the field as though they could drop at any moment from the sheer weight of added water in their baseball uniforms.

Saturday was bad, but the worst would come Sunday.

The dawn of Sunday, June 10, 1962, broke like any other summer day in Houston. A red ball of fire rose from the eastern horizon and began to climb into the sky. Houstonians would only feel the morning dew as it transformed into humidity. Anyone moving about outdoors would break their first sweat prior to 8:00 AM. Predictably, the doubleheader turned into an all-around disaster for Houston. The Colts lost both games by scores of 9–3 and 9–7, the fans got sick from the heat in record numbers, and none of the players or umpires came through the fire without casualty. Here's how the Associated Press reported the events at the "Skillet":

While Dodgers Show Class, Heat Shows Dome Vital

Houston (AP) – The Houston Colts demonstrated, unintentionally, the benefits of their proposed domed stadium while losing both ends of their first home doubleheader to the Los Angeles Dodgers yesterday.

The Harris County emergency corps treated 78 people for heat prostration as 33,145–30,027 of them paid—fans jammed into the multi-colored temporary Colt Stadium to see the league-leading Dodgers win, 9–3 and 9–7.

Jocko Conlon, the second base umpire, had to leave after the fourth inning of the first game because of the heat.

Don Drysdale, a 216-pounder, gave up 12 pounds of weight to the 90 degree temperature, but his six-hit performance was backed by a 17-hit

Dodger assault on six Houston pitchers in the first game.

Joe Moeller jumped to a 9-1 lead in the second game, but the Dodger righthander ran into a bases loaded home run by Don Buddin, Colt Shortstop, and he had to call in Ron Perranoski to preserve the victory.

Harris County is building an air-conditioned stadium with a permanent plastic dome as the home of the Colts. Excavation work is nearing completion. Fans sitting on the top row yesterday could see, across the parking area, the huge hole—725 feet wide and 26 feet deep.

Financial problems have delayed the opening of the multipurpose structure, however, until 1964, at the earliest. Original estimates called for a $15 million (dollar) expenditure, but county officials learned last month the structure will cost more. They now are trying to determine just how much more and where the additional funds can be found.

Several hundred fans had to be turned away yesterday as Houston had its first capacity crowd. The 30,027-paid shoved official attendance for the first 31 home dates to 502,308, a 16,203 average that is well above the 11,000 pre-season forecast of Colt owners.

Drysdale has reason to remember June 10. He won his tenth victory against three defeats. In six previous seasons with the Dodgers, the earliest Drysdale won his tenth game was on July 11, in 1959.

While Drysdale lost 12 pounds, Houston sustained an injury that could hurt.

Roman Mejias, the right fielder who has hit 16 home runs, injured his right arm while leaping for John Roseboro's double in the eighth inning of the first game. The 30-year old Cuban got a single in the first game to hit safely in 16 consecutive games but was held hitless by Moeller and Perranoski (in Game Two).

"I couldn't even use the arm in the second game today," he said. The arm was to be examined today.[7]

Houston General Manager Paul Richards put forth an immediate appeal to the Commissioner's Office and to the other National League clubs for permission to lift the ban on Sunday Night Baseball in Houston for as long as the team continued to play outdoors for the health and safety of fans, players, and staff.[8]

The answer came at a meeting of National League clubs in Chicago on July 31, 1962.[9] Every NL club and the Commissioner approved a time-limited removal of the ban in Houston for one season, starting in 1963, on Sunday games played after June 1. For the balance of 1962, from August 1 forward, Houston also was given permission to start their Sunday games at 4:00 PM.

Why the Sunday night game ban wasn't removed immediately or completely was not explained to the public. We are left to assume either more research is needed to find this answer or that in baseball even unanimous agreement on the need for it still results in a glacial pace of change. In that same meeting, NL President Warren Giles and the other clubs severely chastised Cubs owner P.K. Wrigley for his refusal to install lights at Wrigley Field in the interest of boosting attendance.[10]

In subsequent public statements, Commissioner Frick made it clear that while he was in full sympathy with Houston's plight, he still looked with disfavor upon any baseball that was played on Sundays due to competition with religious services, but he was consoled that the ban had been lifted in Houston for only one year and that by 1964 the move into the dome would preclude further need for Sunday night baseball.[11]

"The commissioner was looking at the clock a little differently from me in the summer of 1962," Tal Smith now says. "As the club's supervisor of the Dome's construction activities, there were plenty of times that I had to hope we could be in there by 1965. Nothing was certain, but Ford Frick simply put the matter to rest in his own mind and held onto the belief that we would be playing indoors by 1964.

"The potential for a big misunderstanding on construction completion was always there," Smith adds, "but fortunately for all concerned, it never happened."[12]

Frick also made it clear that the Houston exception came with a proviso that before a Sunday night game could be scheduled, the visiting teams and all players would be asked each time to approve it.[13]

THE EFFECT OF SUNDAY NIGHT BASEBALL ON ATTENDANCE

A brief tabular look at how Sunday baseball attendance at Colt Stadium in Houston fared over the course of the 1962 and 1963 seasons does not appear

NATIONAL BASEBALL HALL OF FAME LIBRARY, COOPERSTOWN, NY

Umpire Jocko Conlon had to leave the June 10 game in the fourth inning because of the heat.

to show a significant increase in attendance on Sunday nights from June 9, 1962, forward. Here is how the attendance and game results played out for Houston over this two-year period of changing rules on night baseball, starting after June 1, 1963:[14]

Table 1.

1962 Houston Attendance for Sunday Day Game Baseball Only

Date	Opponent	Result	Score	Record	Gate
APR 22	Phillies	Lost	3–4	0–1	13,130
APR 29	Braves	Won	3–2	1–1	21,050
MAY 13	Giants	Lost	2–7	1–2	19,879
MAY 27	Pirates	Lost	2–7	1–3	11,793
JUN 10	Dodgers	Lost	3–9	1–4	G1/DH
JUN 10	Dodgers	Lost	7–9	1–5	30,027
JUL 01	Reds	Lost	1–6	1–6	6,666
JUL 15	Cubs	Won	5–4	2–6	G1/DH
JUL 15	Cubs	Lost	1–4	2–7	6,907
JUL 22	Cardinals	Lost	1–3	2–8	8,685
AUG 12	Braves	Won	8–5	3–8	4,902
AUG 19	Cubs	Lost	3–4	3–9	4,543
SEP 09	Mets	Tie*	7–7	3–9–1	3,630
SEP 23	Giants	Lost	3–10	3–10–1	9,623

The Mets and Colts had agreed to start no inning beyond 7:00 PM due to getaway day travel arrangements. When time expired, the two clubs were tied after eight. Since it was the Mets' last scheduled trip to Houston, National League Secretary Fred Flag said the game would be resumed in New York on September 20. The game was not completed due to a rain that cancelled a regularly scheduled contest on September 19 in New York between the same clubs. The rained-out game was

moved to September 20 and Houston won two by 7–2 and 5–4. The teams never got around to completing the 4–4 tie that also had been re-scheduled from September 13 in Houston for completion after eight.

Of interest to superstitious fans: Note above the results and attendance for Sunday, July 1, 1962. The Colt .45s lost their sixth home Sunday game of the season to the Reds by a score of 6–1 before a crowd of exactly 6,666. Anyone have any non-scientific ideas as to who may have been working this Sunday heat job?

Sunday night baseball began on June 9, 1963 with these results:

Table 2.

1963 Houston Attendance for Sunday Day and Night Games

Date	Opponent	Result	Score	Record	Gate
APR 14	Dodgers	Won	5–4	1–0	10,180
APR 28	Reds	Won	3–2	2–0	9,569
MAY 12	Cubs	Won	2–1	3–0	4.910
MAY 19	Pirates	Lost	0–5	3–1	8,847
JUN 09	Giants	Won	3–0	4–1	17,437
JUN 30	Cardinals	Won	1–0	5–1	10,856
JUL 07	Braves	Lost	0–4	5–2	9,665
JUL 28	Cardinals	Won	8–2	6–2	6,552
AUG 04	Dodgers	Lost	0–4	6–3	14,237
AUG 25	Cardinals	Won	3–1	7–3	7,234
SEP 08	Cubs	Won	2–1	8–3	6,533
SEP 22	Phillies	Won	2–1	9–3	3,493
SEP 29	Mets	Won	13–4	10–3	3,899

The Colts pulled their best Sunday crowd of the season on June 9, the first time the doors opened for a Sunday night game. The peak is followed by a general decline into a low attendance pattern befitting the bottom-feeder production of an uncompetitive, second-season expansion club. Nevertheless, the temporal shift reduced the threat of heatstroke to nearly nil. Now all the fans had to do was to survive attacks by the night-feeding mosquitoes.

By the end of the 1963 season, it became obvious that ongoing dome construction would require the Colt .45s to play another season at their temporary venue. By late November, the 1964 schedule was announced: Houston would be playing 77 of 81 home games at night. The National League club owners had extended their permission for the entire 1964 season.[15,16]

As baseball club owners awoke to the fact that there was no significant opposition from religious groups to Sunday night baseball, everybody but the daylight-bound Cubs jumped onto the bandwagon.

"Baseball had to change," Tal Smith says. "The whole world was changing all around us. Once we got

COURTESY OF THE HOUSTON ASTROS

Colt Stadium: Houston's fiery first MLB home (1962–64). The large hole in the upper background is the cradle of the Astrodome: Eighth Wonder of the World (1965–99).

into the Astrodome, we had no health need for Sunday night baseball, obviously, but we sometimes played at night, if television wanted us for a late game. Back in our first season [1962], baseball was already waking up to the fact that it had major competition from other leisure time activities—and that home television, without question, was the biggest competitor we faced—along with the growing fan interest in pro football and pro basketball.

"We had to get television all the way on our side, and that meant being available in prime time when television wanted us there.

"As more and more teams got into the business of playing some Sunday night baseball, it made sense that one of the big sports networks (sic) would come along, as ESPN did, and build a weekly game telecast by that brand name."

"The Houston Colt .45s helped knock down a wall against Sunday night baseball," Tal Smith concluded, "but they also knocked down a wall that was going to fall anyway, in time. "That wall had to fall. Baseball's survival of the changing landscape depended upon it."[17]

By April 15, 1990, Sunday Night Baseball on ESPN, featuring Jon Miller and Joe Morgan as the play-by-play/analyst combo, had sprouted wings that still fly to this day.[18] ∎

Notes

1. Personal interview with Tal Smith February 4, 2014.
2. Personal interview with Tal Smith, February 4, 2014. Smith was Special Advisor to the Sugar Land Skeeters and long-time former president and general manager of the Houston Astros.
3. Wikipedia entry on Colt Stadium: http://en.wikipedia.org/wiki/Colt_Stadium.
4. Personal interview with Tal Smith, February 4, 2014. Tal Smith believes that the ban on Sunday night baseball had its unwritten roots in baseball's historical attempt to avoid conflict with Sunday church services, whenever possible.
5. John P. Rossi, *A Whole New Game: Off the Field Changes in Baseball*, (Jefferson, NC: McFarland and Company, 1999) 80.
6. George Lederer, *Long Beach* (CA) *Independence Telegram*, June 10, 1962.
7. Associated Press, *Corpus Christi Times*, Monday, June 11, 1962, 17.
8. Interview with Tal Smith, February 4, 2014.
9. *Official Baseball Guide for 1963*, (St. Louis: The Sporting News) 147.
10. Ibid, *Official Baseball Guide for 1963*, 146–7.
11. Associated Press, *Joplin Globe*, August 1, 1962, 8.
12. Tal Smith Interview, February 4, 2014.
13. Ibid, *Joplin Globe*.
14. *Baseball Almanac*; all data and explanatory sub-footnote information in these two charts is derived from the same Internet Database identified here.
15. Associate Press, "Colts Schedule 77 Night Games," *Lubbock Avalanche Journal*, November 19, 1963, 16.
16. "Houston Colt .45s will play 30 of first 41 Games on Home Field," *Mainland Times*, Galveston, TX, 15.
17. Tal Smith Interview, February 4, 2014.
18. "Sunday Night Baseball," Wikipedia, Google, Internet Search Engine.

Movies, Bullfights, and Baseball, Too

A Sports Stadium Built for Spectacle First and Sports Second

Eric Robinson

"Houston Astrodome or Bust"
—Tagline for *Bad News Bears in Breaking Training*

The Astrodome was born in spectacle, a very Texan sort of spectacle, tied to the state's historical heritage and fascination with its own cowboy mythos. Yet even within the western milieu, the first modern dome celebrated innovation, hailing the feasibility of large-scale domes, the invention of Astroturf, and the most advanced scoreboard of its day. The building played host to a number of pop culture and exhibition events as significant as any of the baseball or football games played there.

On January 3, 1962, the seven Harris County commissioners, many wearing holsters and cowboy hats in the style popularized by men such as Vice President Lyndon Baines Johnson, stood on a small platform to perform the groundbreaking. The "Harris County Domed Stadium" was to be built on drained swampland. The men walked to the edge of the podium and, rather than use shovels, fired Colt .45 six shooters into the ground to break the first dirt.[1] This homage to 1800's frontier Texas launched the project but it would quickly take on a more forward-looking moniker, capturing the excitement of the space race. The new NASA manned spacecraft center being built in the south part of Houston would soon put American astronauts on the moon.[2] This spectacular dichotomy of Texas western imagery and space-age technology became part of the Astrodome's attraction.

The opening of the Astrodome occurred on April 9, 1965, with an exhibition game against the New York Yankees. The Astros, who changed their name from the Colt .45s in the offseason, won the exhibition 2–1 on a bloop single hit by Nellie Fox in the 12th inning.[3,4]

Mickey Mantle led off the game for the Yankees and hit the second pitch he saw from pitcher Dick Farrell, and in the fifth inning he hit a 400-foot home run to center field, giving the crowd what they wanted to see.[5]

However, to most attending that night, the game itself was irrelevant. The real attraction was the first indoor stadium. The ceremonial first pitch was thrown by Lyndon Johnson, the first time the opening pitch of a new stadium was made by a President of the United States.[6] Following Johnson's ceremonial pitch, 21 astronauts threw out 21 pitches, and later the "Gemini Twins" Gus Grissom and John Young joined the president and Texas Governor John Connally in the presidential suite.[7]

As for the players themselves, Mantle got lost in the service area beneath the Astrodome trying to find the clubhouse. He had planned to sit out the game due to injuries until he heard that President Johnson was in attendance and that he was slated to "be the first man to bat first in the baseball Taj Mahal of the Southwest."[8,9]

Ross Moschitto commented that the Dome was "like an opera house." Wordsmith Jim Bouton found it "fantastic—no, indescribable—no, science fiction." Steve Hamilton was more concerned by the practical concerns of a major league ballplayer, asking, "Is it all right to chew tobacco here?"[10]

The Astrodome itself was crafted out of the hubris of Judge Roy Hofheinz. The anticipation for the opening had been building ever since Hofheinz stormed into the National League meeting in Chicago in 1960 concerning expansion and impressed the owners with his plans for a domed stadium, on the strength of which they awarded him and Houston one of the two available franchise slots (the other going to New York).[11] Hofheinz was a character described as a "collaboration between Horatio Alger and Sinclair Lewis" while Texas author Larry McMurtry described him as "echt-Texas."[12,13]

Hofheinz was born on April 10, 1912, and graduated from high school at the age of 16.[14] Following his father's death in a truck accident he started promoting dance bands in East Texas to support his family.[15] While doing this he attended law school at night, passing the bar at age 19.[16] He was elected as a representative to the state legislature at age 22, and at 24 he became the youngest man elected county judge of a major county.

Instead of using shovels, Judge Roy Hofheinz and other officials fire six-shooters at the ceremonial ground-breaking.

He spent 1948 running his friend Lyndon Baines Johnson's successful senatorial bid, and at the age of 40 became Houston's mayor.[17]

The Astrodome, and later the Astrodomain, was controlled by Judge Hofheinz beginning with his proposal to the National League owners in 1960, construction from 1962–65, and in the stadium's daily operation until his health began to fail him in the 1970s. During construction the stadium acquired the nickname "Can-Do Cathedral"[18] for overcoming obstacles such as multiple lawsuits and funding problems and still being completed six months early.[19]

Judge Hofheinz had installed many personal touches—most notably a three-story apartment above right field that he spent a significant amount of time living in.[20] It featured a matching set of hand-carved six-foot high Thai temple dog statues, a gold-plated phone, and a 12-foot desk with black marble top that faced three televisions.[21] And this was all before a guest actually entered the doors to the apartment. In addition to seats viewing the stadium, the apartment had a one-lane bowling alley, the Tipsy Tavern bar, velvet toilet seats, a personal movie theatre, a three-hole putting green, and a barbershop.[22] Comedian Bob Hope, a friend of Hofheinz, described its style as "early King Farouk."[23]

The indoor stadium was officially christened the Harris County Domed Stadium. However, this name was rarely used and everyone from Judge Hofheinz, the media, and the public simply referred to it as the Astrodome.[24] Evangelist Billy Graham is often credited with coining the "Eighth Wonder of the World" epithet during his ten-day crusade in late November 1965; however, the Texas media had already been calling the Dome the "Eighth Wonder" back in April.[25] *The New York Times* described the stadium prior to Opening Day by saying, "It stuns the eye with such dazzling splendor that even the natives, experts at the use of superlatives, find themselves groping for words in trying to describe this Eighth Wonder that has been created by their imagination, ingenuity and oil-soaked money," and "this is a reluctant concession to chronology" since the "first seven on the tabulation have been wonders for centuries, but the Astrodome will not be formally opened until tomorrow night."[26]

Between its opening in April of 1965 and December 28 of that same year, 402,712 people paid the $1 admission to tour the Astrodome.[27] By the following year the Commerce Department's Travel Service named it the country's third most popular tourist attraction, following only the Golden Gate Bridge and Mount Rushmore.[28,29] When these tourists, whether from across the country or across Houston, came to visit the Astrodome, their tour would be led by a young woman. She would seat the group in a section facing the field and begin by saying, "Welcome to the Astrodome. You are now seated in the world's largest room." The tour guide would then pause for several seconds to let the significance weigh on the assembled.[30]

The size and scale of the first domed stadium prompted write-ups from newspapers, magazines, and trade journals. The dome itself is "a steel trussed lamella-type trussed roof structure" that covers an area over nine acres and has an outer diameter of 710 feet while on the inside it is nearly half a mile around the outer concourse.[31]

The stadium radiated from second base out and directly above second the roof rose as high as 18 stories (202 feet), more than enough height for a young Bud Cort to soar in a homemade flying machine in the 1970 Robert Altman film *Brewster McCloud*.[32] It also had the world's largest parking lot, holding 30,000 cars, and over 45,000 deep-cushion "first class" theatre-style chairs arranged in continuous tiers of orange, red, and royal blue or as they described it on the tours, "vivid, zippy colors."[33]

High above the seats where most fans sat, the Astrodome was the first stadium to feature luxury boxes, 53 of them, called Skyboxes.[34] Two sets of stands on the field level were attached to tracks powered by motors to allow for the playing field to adjust from baseball to football.[35] At 120 feet, the dugouts were the longest in baseball. As Hofheinz stated, "People like to go home and say they had seats behind the dugout. We can get 65 percent of our seats behind the dugout."[36] Hofheinz understood attracting crowds through spectacle. As he said at the end of 1965, "Our best advertisement is word of mouth, and that's what we get when people come here and then go back to Timbuktu and brag about having been at the Taj Mahal."[37]

Hofheinz's approach led to criticisms over the years. In a New York Times travel piece from 1974, Gary Cartwright described the scale of the Astrodome as "confusing size and opulence with grandeur."[38] Architectural historian Stephen Fox described it as "one of the great monuments of American hubris in the 1960s in this kind of sense of no limits."[39]

One feature of the Astrodome that was worthy of hubris, size, and opulence was the stadium's scoreboard, which stretched across most of the outfield. It cost $2 million to construct and was described officially in the stadium's tour book as "easily the world's largest," "an electronic marvel," "giving patrons… more information, faster, than any visual display ever before seen," and gave it size as "474 feet" long and "more than four stories high."[40,41] When an Astro hit a home run, the scoreboard would light up with an animation that featured snorting bulls, exploding six-guns, a cowboy whirling a lariat, dancing stars, and an unfurled Texas flag.[42] After attending a game in 1965, author Larry McMurtry stated that "the game's true function was to provide material for the man who operated the screen."[43] What McMurtry did not know was that the scoreboard required six operators.[44]

The centerpiece of the scoreboard, both literally and figuratively, was the Astrolite.[45] It was a TV-style light screen that was the world's largest screen at the time.[46] Located directly in center field the Astrolite had a "seemingly endless repertoire of animated light pictures, story-board cartoons, or often simple one-word commands."[47] These commands were typically along the lines of "Charge" and "Olé." However, after using the giant screen to broadcast commands such as "Kill the Umpire" and "We Wuz Robbed" the team's

management received a reprimand from the league president.[48,49]

The Astrolite is a prime example of Hofheinz's naming convention, always space-related or incorporating the word Astro. Inside the Astrodome a visitor could eat at the Skyblazer Restaurant, Countdown Cafeteria, the Astrodome Club, or Domeskellar.[50] This naming convention extended to the ownership group's other business venture, the Astrodomain.[51] A visitor from out of town could stay at the Astroworld Hotel, Astrodome Motor Inn, Holiday Inn–Astroworld, or Howard Johnson's Motor Lodge–Astroworld.[52] The Astroworld Hotel even featured the "two-level 'Minidome Room' nightclub that duplicates in miniature the Astrodome, even to a scoreboard" which sounds like a perfect venue to unwind after spending all day at a convention in the Astrohall convention center.[53] For the kids there was Astroworld, an amusement park that was modeled to be become the Disneyland of the South, something it didn't quite attain. If the kids were too distracted to watch the game, they could find themselves (provided their parents were friends with Judge Hofheinz) in the Astrotot Theater, Circus Room, and Playroom.[54]

Despite all its size and technological feats, "the Dome had only one relatively minor defect: it wasn't very useful for playing baseball."[55] This led to the creation of the one still-used item from the Astrodomain with an Astro- name: Astroturf. The ceiling was built with 4,596 clear Lucite tiles to provide sunlight for the grass—Tiffway Bermuda grass tested at the Texas A&M College Experimental Station.[56] There was little prior thought to how the Lucite tiles would magnify the sunlight and affect the outfielders.[57] Fly balls would disappear somewhere around the dome's third tier. Complaints began as early as the first exhibition game against the New York Yankees.

DuPont sent the Astros ten dozen baseballs that had been dyed yellow, orange, and cerise, as well as several shades of sunglasses to be issued to the players.[58] Some outfielders began to wear chest protectors and batting helmets while they were in the field. Eventually the Astros painted over the Lucite which presented a new problem: the grass could not survive without sunlight. The outfield became a mess of dead grass, patched areas, and sawdust.[59] Chemical company Monsanto Industries—somewhat ironically also the creators of the infamous defoliant Agent Orange—pitched a new synthetic playing surface called ChemGrass to Hofheinz.[60]

As the story goes, in early 1966 Monsanto sent a top salesman, armed with charts, drawings, renderings, and more. The salesman was nervous, and after he completed his pitch Hofheinz remained quiet. The salesman added 10 minutes' worth of details before stopping again. Hofheinz was once again quiet. The salesman tried for 15 more minutes to add every previously unmentioned detail, sales hook, and more. When he was done Hofheinz asked "What'd you say it cost?" to which the salesman replied "$800,000." After a long pause Hofheinz replied, "Funny thing. That's just exactly what I was thinkin' of charging you to let you call it Astroturf."[61]

Whether Hofheinz's encounter with the nervous salesman was true or a tall tale has been lost to history but the team did get the plastic surface free in exchange for letting Monsanto have the name Astroturf. On April 18, 1966, the Astrodome had an Astroturf infield. By July 16 the Astros were playing their first games on a field that was completely covered in Astroturf. In 1970 five outdoor stadiums, Comiskey Park, Candlestick Park, Busch Stadium, Veterans Stadium, and Riverfront Stadium, became the next to install the artificial "grass," which resembled a very short-pile shag rug.[62] Many stadiums and playgrounds followed as well as the backyard of television's Brady Bunch house.

The appearance of Astroturf in the backyard of *The Brady Bunch* wasn't the only time the Astrodome or an aspect of it appeared on a television or theater screen. Throughout the 1970s, the dome was used as a setting for both popular sports comedies and forgettable television movies. The first and perhaps most interesting movie to prominently feature the Astrodome as a setting was Robert Altman's *Brewster McCloud*, which was released in 1970.

The movie was Altman's first release following his surprise hit *M*A*S*H* and in his review from December 1970, Roger Ebert described the film as "difficult," "it may not have a narrative," and concluded the review by saying, "I'm not sure it's about anything."[63] And these observations were from a review that gave it 4.5 out of 5 stars. The plot is about an owlish young man named Brewster McCloud, played by Bud Cort, who lives in the depths of the Astrodome mechanical level. Under the guidance of a fallen angel (maybe) named Suzanne, McCloud builds a hand-powered flying machine. He also has interactions with a hot shot detective, a National Anthem-singing Houston socialite, and an elderly millionaire, but the supporting character that attracts the most attention is Shelly Duvall in her debut as Suzanne, a perky Astrodome tour guide who fancies herself an aspiring race car driver.

Current Sony Pictures Classics co-president Michael Barker wrote of growing up in south Dallas and how the movie "was highly anticipated in Texas because it was the first movie made in the Astrodome, that great

modern Texas landmark" and that they realized while watching the film that "we are definitely not in the Texas of John Wayne."[64] The Astrodome itself played a prominent role in the movie, with many scenes set and filmed there: the socialite sings "The Star Spangled Banner" with a marching band behind her; Shelly Duvall gives the Astrodome tour to a group of tourists; numerous cat-and-mouse sequences as Brewster evades Dome security. In the spectacular closing, Brewster soars through the stadium in his flying machine with the authorities in pursuit, then crashes midfield while a large circus troupe enters through the center field gate and performs around the wreckage. The film's premiere was held inside the Astrodome itself, with VIP seats on the actual turf.

The next film to feature the Astrodome was 1971's *Evel Knievel* starring George Hamilton as the famous stuntman and motorcycle-jumper. The movie incorporated footage of Knievel's real-life appearance at the Astrodome. On January 9, 1971, Knievel twice jumped 13 cars, breaking the record for an indoor motorcycle jump.[65] The attendance for the two jumps totaled 99,000.

Also at the Astrodome, three years and one month later, the record Knievel had set was broken by Debbie Lawler, a 21-year-old petite blonde whose fans called her "The Flying Angel." On the February 3, 1974, episode of *ABC's Wide World of Sports*, Lawler jumped a total distance of 101 feet over 16 Chevrolet pickup trucks.[66]

In 1974 a movie entitled *The Lord of the Universe* was released to document the Millennium '73 event that was hosted at the Astrodome by the teenage Guru Maharaj Ji, the prophet and leader of the Divine Light Mission religious group that many critics argued was a cult.[67] The film details the preparation for the Millennium '73 event, the devotion of the group's followers, and their attempts to get close to the guru to gain "knowledge." The film also gave screen time to critics including Abbie Hoffman, hare krishnas, and Houston-area Christian churches. The Divine Light Mission spent an estimated $1 million to rent the Astrodome from November 8 through November 10, 1973, and another estimated $500,000 on promotion for the event.[68] Their advertising slogan was "Love is Free, Truth is Free, Admission is Free." The Astrodome appealed to their astrological leanings from the very name Astrodome (and the Astrohall and Astroland Hotel). The guru they viewed as the celestial king was staying in the Celestial Suite, and the accents on the water faucets were swans, which the guru took to be his personal symbol. Premies, as the members of the group were called, spoke beforehand of how the event would be "the most important event in human history" and how "by November 15 the Astrodome will physically separate and fly from this earth" due to the power of the meditation within. Alas, this did not happen; the Houston Oilers were able to play a game the next day against Cleveland in an Astrodome still firmly planted on the same reclaimed swampland as before.

Millennium '73 expected 100,000 attendees each day, but ended up with an estimated 20,000 for the entire event.[69] *The Lord of the Universe* ends with a telling shot, beginning with the elaborate center-field stage

Hofheinz shows off an artist's rendering of plans for the massive Astrodome scoreboard.

on which the guru sat and then panning out until the stage is dwarfed by the Astrolite and scoreboard. The massive screen showed the Astros usual in-game fireworks display accompanying the guru's message. A sparse crowd straggles through the outfield, and the stadium seats are nearly empty. The image was symbolic of the huge financial loss that began the organization's decline.

There were two baseball-related releases in 1977. *Murder at the World Series* is a long-forgotten "movie of the week" television movie that premiered on March 20, 1977, on ABC.[70] Bruce Boxleitner plays a revenge-minded pitcher cut from the Astros who pulls a series of kidnappings to hurt the Astros' chance to beat the Oakland A's. This would be the only time, imagined or real, that a World Series was filmed in the Astrodome. One critic described it as a "violent version of *Nashville* in which everyone is dull, mostly incompetent and associated with the Astros."[71] However that July a movie was released that better encapsulates the appeal of the Astrodome.

A surprise box office hit in 1976 was *The Bad News Bears*, a comedy in which the hard-drinking Walter Matthau manages an oddball collection of scrappy misfits on a Little League team. The sequel came out the following summer, part of a plan instituted by new Paramount executive Michael Eisner to turn the company's struggles around. Eisner's strategy was releasing movies with demonstrable money-making potential that could be made cheaply, movies which producer Don Simpson referred to as having to have a "cheeseburger heart."[72]

The Bad News Bears in Breaking Training definitely had a cheeseburger heart. The movie had most of the team returning from the original, with the exception of the three most recognizable characters. Walter

Matthau did not return as manager, Tatum O'Neal did not return as the girl pitcher, and Jeffery Louis Star had to replace Gary Lee Cavagnaro as Engelberg after Cavagnaro lost too much weight to play "the fat kid" in the year since the previous filming. This go round, the Bears are invited to play an exhibition game against a Houston team at the Astrodome. They take a long road trip from Southern California in a stolen van to get there, facing obstacles along the way, while the Bears' star player and resident cool kid Kelly Leak reconnects with his father.

Though a line is tacked on about the winner getting to go to Japan (to set up the next sequel), the goal of the team is not to win a championship, not to beat a league rival, not even to get to play where the Houston Astros play, but to just get the chance to play an exhibition game in the Astrodome. This premise is displayed on the film's advertisement and lobby posters, in which a banner hanging from the side of the team's stolen van reads: "HOUSTON ASTRODOME OR BUST."

There is a moment when, after driving all night, the team arrives in Houston and Leak wakes up the team so they can take in the Dome. Following some "oohs" and other excited comments, the Bears simply look at the stadium in awe. Later in the movie, following a difficult moment, Leak stands in his hotel room and opens a curtain, revealing the Astrodome to the camera and the audience.

The movie climaxes with a scene that potentially haunts Bud Selig. The Bears-Toros game is called because of time, so the scheduled Astros game that night can begin. As the Little Leaguers file off the field, an assortment of Houston Astros (including Bob Watson, J.R. Richard, Cesar Cedeño, and manager Bill Virdon) walk out in the vibrant mid-70s tequila sunrise uniforms. But feisty Bears shortstop Tanner Boyle refuses to leave the field. Bob Watson, the only Astro with a speaking part, notices and says, "Hey, let the kids play."[73] This chant is picked up first by the Bears manager, then the players, and eventually the whole Astrodome crowd is chanting "Let them play!" This same chant erupted at the 2002 All Star Game in Milwaukee after Selig called the game off, tied 7–7 after 11 innings.

When it was not being used for baseball or football games or as a film set, the Astrodome hosted many other events and spectacles including rodeos, conventions, circus acts, to the first mid-air car crash. The first large non-sport event was a 10-day Billy Graham "Crusade for Christ" which began on November 19, 1965.[74] President Lyndon Baines Johnson and Texas Governor John Connally were among the 61,000 who attended Graham's opening night, setting an attendance record for the Astrodome that stood for years.[75] The attendance for the 10-day event exceeded 600,000 and Graham sent a mixed message to Houston, declaring that the Dome was "a tribute to the boundless imagination of man" and also that "most Houstonians will spend an eternity in hell."[76]

In its debut year of 1965, the Dome also hosted such diverse events as a boat show, a polo match, and a bloodless bullfight starring the legendary Spanish matador El Cordobes. The bloodless bullfights caught on and became a bit of a fad in mid-'60s Houston.[77] As the Astrodomain expanded with the Astrohall and the various hotels, the number of conventions increased significantly. This expansion, especially the Astrohall, brought to the Astrodome what would be the longest running tenant of the stadium—not the Astros, but the Houston Livestock Show and Rodeo, who first used the venue on March 6, 1966, and returned every February/March through 2002.[78]

The rodeo became as well known for the nightly concerts as for the rodeo competition itself. Elvis Presley played a six-show stand at the Astrodome in 1970 with over 200,000 fans attending, and when he returned on March 3, 1974, Elvis set his single-show attendance record with 44,175 concert-goers. His previous single-concert record had also been set at the Astrodome, in 1970.[79] On February 26, 1995, Tejano star Selena set a new Astrodome event attendance record at 61,041. This performance would be one of the singer's last concerts prior to her murder.[80] The final Houston Livestock Show & Rodeo concert would also be its largest, with 68,266 fans witnessing George Strait in his 16th performance at the Astrodome on March 3, 2002.[81]

One other sort of spectacle set an attendance record that lasted just shy of 11 months. On April 1, 2001, the World Wrestling Federation held the WrestleMania X-Seven, headlined by local wrestler Stone Cold Steve Austin and drew a crowd of 67,925.[82] The first time the Astrodome hosted wrestling was when legendary local promoter Paul Boesch booked the arena in 1981 for two events headlined by the popular local wrestler Chief Wahoo McDaniel, one match against Dory Funk Jr. and later that summer against Professor Boris Malenko.[83]

That was not McDaniel's first appearance in the Astrodome: on October 6, 1968, he was a middle linebacker for the Miami Dolphins. The Oilers had spent their early years playing at Rice Stadium, but had moved to the Dome that year. However, in 1974 when Super Bowl VIII was played in Houston, the game was held at Rice Stadium, which had 20,000 more seats. The first national sporting event to come through was in November of 1966 when Muhammad Ali defeated the local Cleveland "Big Cat" Williams by knockout in the third round.[84] That night set the indoor boxing attendance record that stood for 25 years with a crowd that was 35,460 strong and grossed $461,290 which almost set the record for gross revenue at a boxing event.[85] The most infamous boxing match at the Astrodome took place in December of 1982. Larry Holmes pummeled Tex Cobb in a mismatched affair that left Cobb bloodied. *Sports Illustrated* said the beat-down belonged "in the Alamo," not the so-called Eighth Wonder of the World.[86] The fight is also known for ringside announcer Howard Cosell vowing afterwards to never call another boxing match again in his career—a vow that he kept.[87]

The Astrodome hosted a 1968 game that many consider to have popularized college basketball and an NCAA Final Four Championship Tournament that was described as the most "odd" ever.[88] In the "Game of the Century," Kareem Abdul-Jabbar (then known as Lew Alcindor) and UCLA faced the University of Houston, led by stars Elvin Hayes and Don Chaney.[89] UCLA at the time was riding a 47-game win streak and were the defending NCAA champions. The hometown UH beat UCLA by a score of 71–69 that January night in front of 52,693 fans. The contest received more national media attention than any prior college basketball game.[90]

Inspired by the success of that game, the NCAA choose the Astrodome to host the 1971 NCAA Final Four Basketball Championship.[91] However a decision was made to place the court in the middle of the Dome yet have no floor seating around it. The placement created a vast expanse, a disconnect between the crowd and the action on the court, and a barren look on television.[92] UCLA won the championship but officially only two teams are recognized as participating in the games. Later sanctions against Western Kentucky and Villanova, due to each team having players associated with professional agents, vacated the teams from the official NCAA record of the event.[93]

The sporting event hosted at the Astrodome that most etched itself into the memory of popular culture, though, was the exhibition tennis match on September 20, 1973, between female champion Billie Jean King and self-proclaimed "male chauvinist" Bobby Riggs in an event that was dubbed "The Battle of the Sexes."[94] Riggs had already been inducted into the International Tennis Hall of Fame and had won multiple championships in his career. However, his last championship had come almost 25 years prior to the match and he was 26 years older than his opponent, who was in the prime of her career. The 30,492 in attendance that night—still the largest attendance for a single tennis match in the United States—witnessed King carried Cleopatra-style into the Dome by members of the Rice University track team wearing togas, and Riggs arriving in a rickshaw pulled by a bevy of scantily clad women.[95] An estimated 50 million people in the United States and another 40 million worldwide watched as King soundly defeated Riggs, leaving the brash man depressed for a considerable time afterwards.[96] In addition to the prize money for the match, King scored a symbolic victory for women in sports, the effects of which are still felt today. Her performance made her an icon in the world of female athletics.[97]

Through the 1980s and '90s the Astrodome began to lose some of its luster, as the newness wore off and newer domes, some of them even larger, began to pop up in New Orleans, Seattle, Indianapolis, Pontiac, Michigan, and elsewhere. National events suited to the domes spread to other cities and the Dome relied more on its core tenants of the Astros, Oilers, and Houston Livestock Show and Rodeo. In 1992, the Republican National Convention was held there. Judge Hofheinz had been hoping for a presidential convention ever since the Astrodome was built, and had even included a Presidential Suite in the design, with rugs featuring the presidential seal as part of the décor. During the time of the RNC, the Astros were forced to take a 26-game road trip, per the Secret Service's request.

Citing the by-then outdated stadium and the dilapidated field conditions that had forced NFL officials to cancel a preseason game, the Houston Oilers left not just the Astrodome but Houston altogether and relocated to Tennessee for the 1997 season. In 2000 the Astros themselves left the Dome to begin play at Enron Field, now named Minute Maid Park. The Houston Livestock Show and Rodeo followed them in 2003. Concerts and high school football games were still held in the Dome for a while, but the presence of the newer and larger Reliant Stadium hurt the Dome significantly and in 2006 it was officially closed.

But in the months prior to that closing in 2006, the Astrodome managed to be a part of the national news one last time. Part of a large humanitarian effort by the city of Houston and the state of Texas, the Dome was the destination for 500 buses carrying refugees from New Orleans in the wake of Hurricane Katrina. On the morning of August 31, 2005, two days after the hurricane had made landfall, the convoy left the New Orleans Superdome, which had been severely damaged in the hurricane. More than 25,000 people were living in the Astrodome through September while they sought more permanent housing solutions.[98]

As of this writing, the city of Houston is still trying to determine what to do with the Astrodome. Few people refer to it as the Eighth Wonder of the World anymore and in comparison to Reliant Stadium next door it looks a bit drab. When asked about the Dome's status in the pantheon of classic buildings, Neil deGrasse Tyson, astrophysicist and head of the Hayden Planetarium said, "When you're in the present, you cannot judge what will become a wonder of the world, that's to be judged by generations that follow. Here we are, ready to level the Astrodome, and the Pyramids are still standing."[99]

However, even if the Harris County Domed Stadium is torn down at some point in the future, the mark the Dome leaves on pop culture and American history will not be so easily erased. Between movies, historic events, and the Dome's historic firsts, while it might not match the Pyramids on the scale of world wonders, the Astrodome leaves us with a hell of a lot more memories than the Seattle Kingdome ever provided. ∎

Notes

1. Claude Charlier, "After a While, Nothing Seems Strange in a Stadium with a 'Lid,'" *Smithsonian*, January, 1988.
2. "The Houston Astrodome Overview," Housing the Spectacle, Dome Case Studies, www.columbia.edu/cu/gsapp/BT/DOMES/HOUSTON/ intro.html, Date accessed February 10, 2014.
3. Dene Hofheinz Mann, *You Be the Judge* (Houston: Premier Printing Company, 1965), 81.
4. Joseph Durso, "Astros Down Yanks 2–1, in First Major League Game Played Under Roof," *The New York Times*, April 10, 1965.
5. Ibid.
6. Ibid.
7. Adam Chandler, "The Sad Fate (but Historic Legacy) of the Houston Astrodome," *The Atlantic*, November 8, 2013, www.theatlantic.com/ entertainment/archive/2013/11/the-sad-fate-but-historic-legacy-of-the-houston-astrodome/281269/, Date accessed February 18, 2014.
8. Ibid.

9. Al Reinert, "Greetings From the Eighth Wonder of the World: Happy Birthday, Dear Astrodome, Happy Birthday to You," *Texas Monthly*, April 1975.
10. Durso, op. cit.
11. Mann, *You Be the Judge*, 80.
12. Reinert, op. cit.
13. Larry McMurtry, *In a Narrow Grave: Essays on Texas* (New York: Simon & Schuster, 1968) 109–17.
14. Mann, *You Be the Judge*, 13.
15. Reinert, op. cit.
16. Ibid.
17. Ibid.
18. Chandler, op, cit.
19. Ibid.
20. Mickey Herskowitz, "Dome Hits 30," *Houston Post*, April 9, 1995.
21. Ibid.
22. Ibid.
23. J. Michael Kennedy, "7 Floors Decorated in 'Early Farouk': Hofheinz's Gaudy Suite in Astrodome Being Razed," *Los Angeles Times*, March 18, 1988, http://articles.latimes.com/1988-03-18/news/mn-1682_1_fred-hofheinz, Date accessed February 18, 2014.
24. "In Texas, Where Everything is Big, Houston Stadium is the Greatest," *The New York Times*, December 6, 1994.
25. Robert Lipsyte, "The Astrodome Caps a Profitable Year," *The New York Times*, December 31, 1965.
26. Arthur Daley, "Ball Park, Texas Style," *The New York Times*, April 9, 1965.
27. Lipsyte, op. cit.
28. Chandler, op. cit.
29. Reinert, op. cit.
30. Ibid.
31. Louis O. Bass, A.M., "Unusual Dome Awaits Baseball Season in Houston," *Civil Engineering—ASCE*, January 1965.
32. Ibid.
33. Reinert, op. cit.
34. Ibid.
35. Bass, op. cit.
36. Reinert, op. cit.
37. Lipsyte, op. cit.
38. Gary Cartwright, "There's More Texas than Technology in the Houston Astrodome," *The New York Times*, April 7, 1974.
39. Jim Yardley, "Last Innings at a Can-Do Cathedral," *The New York Times*, October 3, 1999.
40. Herskowitz, op. cit.
41. Reinert, op. cit.
42. Herskowitz, op. cit.
43. McMurtry, op. cit.
44. Cartwright, op. cit.
45. Ibid.
46. Ibid.
47. Reinert, op. cit.
48. Cartwright, op. cit.
49. Reinert, op. cit.
50. McMurtry, op. cit.
51. Cartwright, op. cit.
52. Cartwright, op. cit.
53. Ibid.
54. Ibid.
55. Reinert, op. cit.
56. Bass, op. cit.
57. Dan Epstein, *Big Hair and Plastic Grass* (New York: Thomas Dunne Books, 2010), 48–50.
58. Durso, op. cit.
59. Reinert, op. cit.
60. Epstein, op. cit.
61. Reinert, op. cit.
62. Epstein, op. cit.
63. Roger Ebert, "Brewster McCloud," rogerebert.com, www.rogerebert.com/reviews/brewster-mccloud-1970, Date accessed February 20, 2014.
64. Michael Barker, "BREWSTER MCCLOUD; Faves, Hot and Cold," *The New York Times*, May 4, 2008.
65. Stuart Barker, *Evel Knievel Life of Evel* (New York: St. Martin's Press, 2004), 95, 286.
66. Steve Mandich, "The Daredevil is a Woman," stevemandich.com, www.stevemandich.com/evelincarnate/debbielawler.htm, Date accessed February 21, 2014.
67. Thorne Dreyer, "God Goes to the Astrodome," *Texas Monthly*, January 1974.
68. Ibid.
69. Ibid.
70. Tom Keiser, "Sportsflicks: Taxi Driver (Of the Bullpen Car)," *The Classical*, October 30, 2013, http://theclassical.org/articles/sportsflicks-taxi-driver-of-the-bullpen-car, Date accessed February 21, 2014.
71. Ibid.
72. Josh Wilker, *Deep Focus: Bad News Bears in Breaking Training* (Berkeley: Soft Skull Press, 2011).
73. Ibid.
74. "Graham to Open Crusade in Houston's Astrodome," *Ocala Star-Banner*, November 19, 1965.
75. LBJ Hears Graham—Universal Newsreels, Internet Archive, www.archive.org, https://archive.org/details/1965-08-30_LBJ_Hears_Graham, Date accessed February 23, 2014.
76. Cartwright, op. cit.
77. J.R. Gonzales, "Dome of the Month: Bullfighting Under the Roof," *Houston Chronicle*, April 30, 2012.
78. Jim Saye, "Show and Rodeo—The Houston Livestock Show and Rodeo: A Historical Perspective," *Houston History Magazine*, January 2011.
79. Craig Hlavaty, "When Elvis Presley Came to Houston," *Houston Chronicle*, August 16, 2013.
80. "Houston Livestock Show & Rodeo—16 Years Later," Selena Legend, http://selenalegend.com/selena-live-at-the-houston-livestock-and-rodeo-show-16-years-later/, Date accessed February 23, 2014.
81. Saye, op. cit.
82. "WrestleMania X-7," *Pro Wrestling History*, www.prowrestlinghistory.com/supercards/usa/wwf/mania.html#17, Date accessed February 23, 2014.
83. G. Neri, "Wahoo! The Incredible Adventures of Chief Wahoo McDaniel: Wrestling Superstar," *Hunger Mountain—The VCFA Journal of the Arts*, http://www.hungermtn.org/wahoo-the-incredible-adventures-of-chief-wahoo-mcdaniel-wrestling-superstar/, Date accessed, February 23, 2014.
84. Bert Randolph Sugar, "Greatest Knockouts: Ali vs. Williams," espn.com, September 28, 2006, http://sports.espn.go.com/sports/boxing/news/story?id=2606152, Date accessed February 23, 2014.
85. Ibid.
86. Pat Putnam, "He Took it All and Would Not Fall," *Sports Illustrated*, December 6, 1982.
87. John Spong, "Randall "Tex" Cobb," *Texas Monthly*, September 2001.
88. Mike Lopresti, "Houston's Last Final Four: One Dome, Two Asterisks, and UCLA," *USA Today*, March 13, 2011.
89. David Barron, "UH—UCLA Classic Played 43 Years Ago Elevated the Game," *Houston Chronicle*, January 20, 2011.
90. Ibid.
91. Lopresti, op. cit.
92. Ibid.
93. Ibid.
94. Selena Roberts, *A Necessary Spectacle: Billie Jean King, Bobby Riggs, and the Tennis Match that Leveled the Game* (New York: Crown Publishers, 2005).
95. Ibid.
96. Ibid.
97. Ibid.
98. USA Today website, http://usatoday30.usatoday.com/news/nation/2005-08-31-astrodome_x.htm.
99. Chandler, op. cit.

Wooing Women Fans

The Houston Astros

Will Flaherty

Although the earliest of American baseball clubs in the mid-1800s were organized as exclusively male social organizations, spectators were soon drawn to their games, and plenty of women were among them. The Knickerbocker Base Ball Club would often draw female spectators to its grounds at Elysian Fields in New Jersey. The New York Giants sponsored the first recorded Ladies' Day in 1883 by offering female fans discounts on admission, concessions, and souvenirs, beginning a tradition that would spread league-wide and last for decades. When their husbands and significant others were overseas fighting in World War II, female fans helped keep professional baseball alive by attending games as well as participating in female professional leagues like the All-American Girls Professional Baseball League, made famous by the film *A League of Their Own*.[1]

But by the early 1960s, teams began to notice declining attendance of women. Surveys conducted in 1951 by the New York Yankees and New York Giants indicated that their fanbases were only 10 percent female. The Boston Red Sox garnered similar findings in a 1957 survey.[2] Although the established eastern teams may have shared this trend, baseball's westward expansion during the 1950s and 1960s provided opportunities for franchises to take a different approach with fans—both male and female—hungry for Major League-caliber baseball.

Few franchises in this westward expansion attempted to cater to female fans like the Houston Astros. Established in 1962 as the Houston Colt .45s and led by eccentric owner Judge Roy Hofheinz, Houston's entry in the National League employed a variety of marketing strategies to attract female fans to ballgames. The opening of the Astrodome in 1965 brought both the games and fans indoors for the first time, revolutionizing both how the game was played by players and enjoyed by spectators. This project will take an in-depth look at the ways the Hofheinz-era Astros (1962–76) attempted to draw female fans.[3]

"HOUSTON, WE HAVE A TEAM"

As new population centers in the country's western half grew, Major League Baseball followed. Boston lost the Braves to Milwaukee in 1952, and 1954 marked the departures of the Athletics from Philadelphia to Kansas City and the Browns from St. Louis to Baltimore, but this westward trend was firmly established in 1958 when the New York Giants and Brooklyn Dodgers relocated to San Francisco and Los Angeles.[4] Soon the larger question was not if the league would expand westward, but where, and a group of investors in Houston made sure that the Lone Star State's biggest city was first in line for a new team.

With a recorded history of baseball dating back to an 1861 match between the Houston Stonewalls and the Galveston Robert E. Lees, the Bayou City had a hardball heritage that long predated the arrival of the major leagues.[5] The Houston Buffs of the Texas League were the minor league affiliate of the St Louis Cardinals for over 30 years, and Hall of Famers Joe Medwick and Dizzy Dean were among the future Cardinals stars to pass through Houston. Beginning in 1928, the Buffs played at an eponymous stadium situated two miles south of the current site of Minute Maid Park. Commissioner Kenesaw Mountain Landis lauded Buff Stadium as one of the best minor league parks in the nation. Its mission-style architecture included modern trappings such as air-conditioned ladies' restrooms.[6]

The Buffs drew well at the box office, but the smothering heat and humidity of Houston summers often made outdoor baseball an unpleasant endeavor for fans. One loyal fan was an influential lawyer who would often escape the office to attend day games, enjoying strawberry snow cones as he braved the heat and the mosquitoes. A visionary who had a long string of successes in business and politics, including stints as mayor of Houston and Harris County Judge, Roy Hofheinz thought long and hard about alleviating the uncomfortable conditions for baseball fans. He would settle on an idea that would consume his wealth and energies for nearly the rest of his life. Hofheinz not only wanted to bring big-league baseball to Houston, he wanted to bring it indoors, into climate-controlled, air-conditioned comfort. The idea for the Astrodome was born.[7]

With the help of businessmen George Kirksey and Craig Cullinan and the financial backing of oilman R.E. "Bob" Smith, Hofheinz championed the construction of a publicly financed, domed stadium as the centerpiece of Houston's bid for a Major League franchise. Hofheinz consulted geodesic dome inventor Buckminster Fuller about the feasibility of building a domed baseball stadium (feasible so long as sufficient money was available, Fuller said) and commissioned a $35,000 scale model of the stadium to be shown at the October 1960 National League owners meetings in Chicago. On October 17, 1960, the owners accepted the expansion bids of Houston and New York, awarding the Hofheinz-led Houston Sports Association (HSA) a National League franchise to begin play in April 1962.[8]

THE COLT .45s AND "COLORFUL" COLT STADIUM

Because construction delays pushed back the opening of the Harris County Domed Stadium well beyond April 1962, the newly named Houston Colt .45s needed a home. Buff Stadium was mentioned as a temporary fix, but Hofheinz instead built a 33,000 seat auxiliary stadium on the northwest corner of the 240-acre domed stadium site.[9] Intimately involved in the details of the new stadium, Hofheinz went to extreme lengths to make the stadium fan friendly, with a particular emphasis on elements he believed would make it appealing to women. Instead of the green common in older stadiums, Colt Stadium's seats boasted a vibrant spectrum of colors: red or burnt orange for the lower boxes, chartreuse and turquoise alternating in the upper grandstand. In March 1962 *Sports Illustrated* described Colt Stadium as "the most colorful baseball park in either league."[10]

Though the color scheme allowed ushers to efficiently seat incoming fans (each ticket was color-coordinated by section), Hofheinz also hoped that it would "please the ladies," according to Robert Reed's history of the Colt .45s, *A Six Gun Salute*. "Men don't care, as long as the overall tone is pleasant and clean. Baseball has to stimulate the wife and family interests," Hofheinz stated.[11]

Seeking to turn games into social events, Hofheinz commissioned a private stadium club to be built under the first-base bleachers, reserved for season ticket holders who purchased a $150 membership. Called the Fast Draw Club and decked out in gaudy 1890s-era Western décor, the club offered the stadium's only full bar and provided well-heeled fans a refuge from the heat and full meals served by waitresses costumed in period attire. The club proved popular before and after Colts games and such private clubs are now ubiquitous in ballparks and arenas.[12]

Hofheinz also paid extraordinary attention to the attire and appearance of stadium staffers. Hofheinz made the novel decision to hire female "usherettes" and he commissioned Houston fashion designers Evelyn Norton Anderson and Iris Stiff to design costumes for stadium employees. Called "Triggerettes," the 150 usherettes wore blouses and skirts that featured blue stripes, orange piping, and a special hat bearing the team logo. Parking lot attendants wore white jumpsuits with gaudy orange Stetsons, while ticket takers were dressed in 1880s-era outfits, replete with striped blazers and pillbox hats.[14]

TRAINING DAY: JUDGE

As the finishing touches were being put on Colt Stadium in the early months of 1962, fans began to show up by the thousands on weekends to get a peek at the progress. In an attempt to capitalize on the swelling fan interest, HSA Executive Vice President George Kirksey invited fans to tour the nearly complete ballpark on March 17. Over 8,000 fans showed up, such a success that the event was repeated the following three weekends. When the final open house drew an estimated 30,000 fans, a local department store held a fashion show for ladies to show "what the lady baseball fan should wear to Colt Stadium this summer."[15] Colt Stadium merchandise kiosks stocked numerous products specifically aimed at them, including aprons ($2), scarves ($1.50), garters ($1.50), and ladies' sun hats ($2).[16]

The franchise also introduced the "Miss Colt .45" beauty pageant. Coordinated by the team's radio affiliates, each participating station in Texas and surrounding states sent one college-aged representative to compete. Photographs show contestants posed in swimsuits by the pool of the ritzy Shamrock Hilton, and finalists were presented at a game with the winner announced in front of the stadium crowd.[17] A University of Houston freshman named Rocky Renee was the winner of the first contest in 1962, and she and the "Miss Colt .45s" who followed made appearances at games and other events in the Houston area on behalf of the team and sponsors. Male fans were the more ardent supporters of the pageant, and even the Colt .45 players themselves didn't miss out on chances to get photographs with the winners.[18] But pageants and beauty shows drew a female following of their own, and the surfeit of contestants shows that the Miss Colt .45 program helped drum up female fan interest.

The Colt .45s adopted the longstanding league practice of holding a "Ladies Night" at the ballpark by offering discounts to selected games, but Hofheinz went a step further by reserving a special press box for female journalists called "The Hen Coop," with the goal that the articles written by these women would draw female fans to Colt Stadium. Team employee Virginia Pace was given a crash course in baseball rules and staffed the "Hen Coop," answering all baseball questions from the lady journalists—even some as elementary as "Why isn't there a fourth baseman?" When the team hit the road, Pace traveled around town to lecture on the game to a variety of women's groups, with one talk at a Houston hotel drawing a 1,300-person crowd.[19]

The special treatment of female journalists seemed to pay dividends as journalists like the Houston *Chronicle*'s influential society columnist Maxine Mesinger glowed about the gameday experience at Colt Stadium. "It's a wonderful, colorful spot depicting the old-time saloons of the gay '90s, with bartenders and waitresses in the Fast Draw Club costumed in that period," Mesinger wrote. "What a thrill to stand on the top tier and look out over what will be the new domed stadium. The whole thing is nothing short of fabulous for our town."[20]

But as Mesinger's column alluded, Colt Stadium was a temporary building. The stadium offered no shade to fans and was often inhospitably hot. Mosquitoes were such a nuisance that players routinely stepped out of the batter's box to battle swarms. None of these nuisances would plague their new home. The Astrodome would prove to be revolutionary not only for the simple fact that baseball would be played indoors, but also that fans would now enjoy an unprecedented gameday experience.

THE EIGHTH WONDER OF THE WORLD

On the blue level, where our most expensive boxes are, we experimented for a week to determine what light looked best on ladies' makeup and clothes. Listen, every day here will be ladies day.

—Roy Hofheinz discussing the Astrodome in the April 12, 1965 edition of *Sports Illustrated*.[21]

When the $37 million, taxpayer-financed Astrodome opened in April 1965, it was a palace to the game of baseball with extravagances seen in no previous stadium. The stadium's primary scoreboard cost $2 million and spanned 474 feet of outfield wall; whenever an Astro player hit a home run, it erupted in an elaborate "40-second spectacular."[22] The stadium's air conditioning supplied 6,600 tons of cooling and was monitored by a specially engineered central computer nicknamed "The Brain," designed and built by Honeywell at a cost of $330,000.[23]

In addition to these costly infrastructure frills, Hofheinz spared no expense in perfecting the appearance of the Dome's interior, again with an eye toward appealing to women and families. He catered to the needs of female fans in large part because market research indicated 42 percent of the team's radio and TV audiences were female.[24] As with Colt Stadium, Hofheinz commissioned colorful seats for the Astrodome. Lipstick red, coral, burnt orange, terra cotta, black, purple, gold, bronze, and blue seats "provided an explosion of color throughout the stadium."[25]

"We did a lot of research before choosing the colors," Hofheinz told the *Houston Chronicle* on April 4, 1965. "We made sure that each color complemented the complexion and clothing of women."[26]

On the same day, the *Houston Post* printed a full article on the design intricacies. Titled "A Touch of Midas in Décor, Too," the article previewed the Dome's opening in "what promise[d] to be the most colorful sports show of the year." Arguing that "Décor-conscious women, who are decidedly more interested in pop art than they are pop flies, probably will be more enthralled with the offstage drama than they are with the doings on the diamond," the article described the design specifications in exquisite detail. The private Astrodome Club featured plush carpeting in an Aubosson or Torginol pattern with "ornate golds, deep reds, and blacks," while the walls featured enormous Toulouse-Lautrec murals hung in "baroque gold frames." The Trail Blazer Room on the sixth level boasted specially commissioned paintings featuring trailblazers in history "from the time of the wagon masters through the ages of the automobile and space ships," while the Skydome club included a large mural of the starscape complete with planetarium lighting effects. But to assuage any fears of readers that felt such trappings were out of place at a baseball stadium, the *Post* noted that "there are old fashioned concession stands that will dispense peanuts, popcorn, and Cracker Jacks for old fashioned folks who still remember with nostalgia that old refrain 'Take Me Out To The Ballgame.'"[27]

Much of this elaborate décor was installed in the Dome's series of clubs, restaurants, and private boxes. Drawing upon the success of the Fast Draw Club at Colt Stadium, Hofheinz included no fewer than five restaurants in the Astrodome with a combined seating capacity of 3,280.[28] Each catered to a different stadium niche and two of the clubs—the Skydome Club and

Judge Roy Hofheinz in front of the Astrodome. Hofheinz was intimately involved in determining the dome's design and amenities.

the Astrodome Club—were open to season ticket holders year-round, even when there was no game. These private clubs were a place to see or be seen in Houston, and for many fans they were an attraction apart from the action on the field.[29]

Perhaps the most elaborate of Hofheinz's design details was incorporated into the stadium's 53 Skybox suites that ringed the upper level. Hofheinz successfully pushed for the inclusion of these private boxes that were not in the original blueprints because he envisioned, accurately, that he could sell them for a great windfall. The Judge was a world traveler who had seen a similar arrangement of private boxes at the Roman Coliseum during a visit to Italy. For $15,000 a season, well-heeled individuals or corporations could purchase a box complete with its own TV, radio, stock ticker, bar, refrigerator, and restroom. According to an April 1965 *Sports Illustrated* feature on the new stadium, "Ladies can freshen up by taking only a step to the private room, and those faint from peering down at the miniature game below can lie down and watch it on TV."[30] But the décor inside these boxes was even more remarkable. Inspired by his numerous trips around the world, Hofheinz gave each box a unique theme—"Old South," "French Riviera," "Beauvais," "Ramayana,"—with each individually designed to meet its appointed theme, again with the main goal of suiting female tastes.[31]

"Believe me, it is quite a job when you have to come up with 53 different color schemes, trying to make each club unique," Hofheinz said. "It took us two weeks alone to get the right color of blue. Many blues would give ladies a pasty-looking complexion."[32]

The dome's roof made inclement or uncomfortable weather inconsequential, and the air conditioning itself was a major draw for a wide fan base that included women. But other enhancements in fan comfort that playing indoors allowed were also a major selling point for female fans. Unlike the usual uncomfortable wooden seats or backless bleachers, each of the Astrodome's 45,000 seats was upholstered and padded. This selling point appeared in team advertisements which noted, "For the first time in sports history you can watch a baseball game from deep-cushioned, foam-padded, nylon-upholstered chairs."[33]

"Women will go to the ball game now because there will be no wind to whip their hairdos, no rain to ruin their dress and no sun to turn them red," Hofheinz told the *Chronicle*. "The Astrodome will get a promenade of best-gowned, best-looking and most-influential women ever collected."[34]

Sure enough, when the stadium opened its doors on April 9, the details of what women wore to the Astrodome was one of myriad news stories that dominated the headlines of Houston's two daily newspapers. *Chronicle* fashion editor Beverly Maurice penned an article headlined "Silks, Linens and Hats at Fashionable Game," that detailed the "white silk sleeveless jacket suit over a black blouse" worn by the wife of HSA founding shareholder Craig Cullinan and the outfit of Mrs. Dotty Hines (wife of real estate magnate Gerald Hines), "a blue-green tussah dress to complement her tennis tan."[35] The *Post* did not indulge in quite the same level of detail in its related story, but it did note that "most of the women, however, were decked out in spring finery of vibrant colors. Some of them would have looked out of place at an ordinary ballpark, but they harmonized beautifully with Friday night's mad mood."[36] Attending an Astros game soon became a full-fledged social event, with the well-heeled in skyboxes and average fans in the stands alike wearing their finest to the ballpark.

But fans weren't the only well-dressed individuals in the ballpark. The Astrodome boasted a full corps of carefully costumed usherettes. Called "Spacettes" (a name that seemingly was closely derived from the "Triggerettes" of the old park), the 300-person usher group wore outfits of "quilted gold lame trimmed in a royal blue velvet and accented in orange" in a feminine nod to an astronaut's suit.[37] Hofheinz again relied upon Evelyn Norton Anderson and Iris Stiff to design the ballpark's uniforms and gave the two designers a blank check to purchase whatever materials they needed. Stiff estimated that the usherette outfits would have retailed for $200, and she told *Chronicle* Fashion Editor Beverly Maurice that she "was not working on a budget." The end results of their work were a staggering 53 different outfits for the stadium's variety of staffers, from groundskeepers to cocktail waitresses. Anderson likened the design job to "costuming a dozen operas—Wagenerian scale!"[38]

Once the costumes were complete, the job of administering the Astrodome's Spacette program fell to 22-year old Sharon Wilhoit. A Triggerette at Colt Stadium, Wilhoit was named Director of Usherettes and was in charge of selecting and training the stadium's usher corps. Each Spacette completed a 10-hour finishing course from the John Robert Powers School on speech, personality, poise, and grooming, and Wilhoit personally interviewed the majority of applicants to the program. Wilhoit, a Colt Stadium veteran, was ecstatic about the Astros' new home. "Working conditions in the stadium should be a lot better. We had trouble with our hairdos before in the humidity," she told the *Post*. "Our hairdos will stay now, and our appearance in general should be much improved."[39]

AT HOME IN THE DOME: PROMOTIONS AND SPECIAL EVENTS

Based on its novelty and growing recognition alone, the Astrodome drew sellout crowds in 1965, despite the home team's dismal 65–97 record. The Astrodome drew 2,151,470 fans in 1965, easily besting the team's best attendance mark in Colt Stadium by over 1 million.[40] In a press release highlighting the promotions surrounding Fan Appreciation Day on the final home date of 1965, the Astros noted that the expected season attendance total of 2,150,00 fans would be "the third highest total in National League history." Even if that boast was inaccurate—the Dodgers had drawn more than 2.15 million fans in five of their first eight seasons

in Los Angeles—there was little doubt that the new stadium was an unabashed success with fans.[41]

Something else of note in that same press release was that, in addition to fan giveaways and prize contests, the first 5,000 ladies in attendance received a free carnation. Female-specific giveaways and promotions were not random but the norm at the Astrodome, and an in-depth look at the team's voluminous press release archives reveals fascinating details about some of the promotions and other events the Astros used in efforts to market to female fans.[42]

Continuing a tradition begun at Colt Stadium, the Astros proclaimed each Wednesday home game in the Astrodome "Ladies Night," with all ladies receiving a $1.00 discount on any seat in the stadium. The press release announcing the first Ladies Night, an April 28 tilt against the New York Mets, pulled out all the stops as it shilled the ticket promotion:

This ladies night, the first of 11 such events planned for the Astrodome this year, features a $1 reduction on tickets for ladies. It's an obvious attempt to appeal to a woman's intuition to never pass up a bargain.

Many thousand women already this spring have found the Astrodome a new kind of entertainment gathering spot. They've found it clean, comfortable and a place where they can dress up or dress casually and feel "at home' while enjoying a baseball game.

The gentler sex not only has added to the color, but to the enormity and enthusiasm of Astrodome crowds, which thus far this year have averaged more than 30,000 per game.

The Mets are a fitting team for the season's introduction of baseball to the ladies. This year, in addition to gentleman Casey Stengel, there are many other Metropolitans of charm, not the least of whom are veterans Warren Spahn, and, of course, Lawrence Peter Berra, known even to the ladies as Yogi.[43]

Ladies nights at the Astrodome would become a mainstay of the team's first decade indoors. A press release as early as 1967 described the $1 discount for ladies on Wednesdays as "customary," and the practice would remain in place for the duration of Judge Hofheinz's ownership of the team.[44]

As the newness and novelty of the Astrodome

slowly began to wear off in 1966 and attendance softened to 1,872,108, Hofheinz decided to expand on his program of Ladies Day with a little help from his own family. On April 19, Dene Hofheinz Mann, the Judge's daughter, was named "Social Director of the Astrodome," with primary job responsibilities of "handling women's activities at the Astrodome such as special promotions for ladies, fashion shows, publicity and social life in and about the stadium." Her new supervisor, VP of Public Relations Bill Giles, said in a press release, "The Astros have managed to create a large following among the women due to the Astrodome's comfort, colorful surroundings and exciting atmosphere, and Dene will concentrate on creating more interest and enthusiasm from the feminine set." At age 23, Dene Hofheinz Mann was already a published author after having written a biography of her father, *You Be The Judge*, and she was well versed in Houston's elite social circles, as one might expect due to her father's prominence in the city.[45]

Although it is difficult to ascertain the exact role that Mrs. Hofheinz Mann had on promotions for women, press releases from the 1966 season show a significant spike in events for women at Astros games, typically piggy-backed onto Wednesday Ladies Night. Before the June 8 game against San Francisco, a "Wednesday Warm-Ups" program was held in the Astrodome's Domeskeller restaurant, with two Astros players making an appearance at the restaurant to sign autographs and answer questions. On July 6, a special fashion show preceded another Ladies Night game against Atlanta. Also added to the promotional slate in 1966 were family-oriented promotional nights. Saturday, July 23 was "Meet The Astros Family Night," with all Astros players, wives, and children introduced on the field prior to the game. Three days later was "Family Night" against the Mets, with all children accompanied by a parent receiving a $1.50 ticket discount. Additionally, the largest immediate family in the ballpark would receive a color TV set.[46]

Dene Hofheinz Mann would soon leave Houston to pursue what would turn out to be a successful career as a singer and songwriter, but the Astros still relied on targeted promotions to draw female fans after her departure. With attendance dropping to 1,348,303 in 1967 came the emergence of promotions like "Runs for the Astros." On the heels of a 3–11 start to the season and a 10-game losing streak that saw Houston outscored 54–23 by its opponents, the Astros offered a $1 ticket reduction for their April 27 game against St. Louis to any "lady fan" who brought a "stocking" with a "run" in it. The countless pairs of ruined pantyhose must have

done the trick to snap the team out of its hex, as the Astros defeated Bob Gibson and the St. Louis Cardinals by a 6–4 final score. Another regular promotion for women during this period was the distribution of flowers, with women receiving Orchid corsages on Mothers Day in 1966 and on Easter Sunday in 1968.[47]

Player meet-and-greets for women would appear intermittently from 1966 until 1970, when the Astros held them before eight of nine Ladies Night games. Typically featuring Astros players, the events in the Domeskeller were advertised as "baseball clinics" for female fans. At least 13 different Astros were advertised on press releases to appear at these clinics, including pitcher Larry Dierker, outfielder Jimmy Wynn, and second baseman Joe Morgan. The events often included some sort of special programming in addition to autographing and question-and-answer sessions, like the playing of the 1969 MLB season highlights film before a May 20 home game against the Reds or the hosting of a special coffee held on August 12 for ladies with the Astros players' wives. At the final such meeting on September 30, there was even the awarding of "Favorite Player of the Year" honors, per the vote of female attendees at the event.[48]

The 1971 season saw the unveiling of the Astros' new "Orange Crush" jerseys, with orange caps and orange jersey lettering, but the players in the Astrodome weren't the only team employees to get a uniform update. In keeping with style shifts for women at the turn of the decade, new uniforms for the Astrodome Spacettes were unveiled for a May 14 game against the Cardinals. Debuting the "Age of Aquarius look in fashion for Astros baseball fans," the outfits included "the popular new feminine fashion, 'Hot Pants,' with a radiant sun orange side slit wrap skirt, bordered in cosmic yellow," along with a yellow leotard with a "stand up Astronaut collar" and calf length boots made of "brilliant yellow crinkled vinyl." The press release announcing the new uniforms noted that the "'Spacette look,' and the 'Orange Crush' create a galaxy of color meant to blast-off the 'old' from the Astrodome, and take the Astros straight up to reach the stars." But some older female styles still prevailed at the Astrodome for at least one night—as part of "Old Fashioned Night" on April 23 against Montreal, the first 5,000 ladies attending would receive black Astros garters. The promotion went along with beer served at the "old fashioned" price of five cents, and a Dixieland band was on hand for a pre-game performance.[49]

But the 1970s also saw the continued growth of feminist movements in America, and before long the long-standing tradition of Ladies Night would come

COURTESY OF THE HOUSTON ASTROS

Roy Hofheinz (sans glasses, center) shows Colt Stadium to some representatives of Carrier Corp., the providers of the Astrodome's air conditioning system.

under fire. In 1972, a man filed suit against the New York Yankees charging the team with discrimination because he had to pay full price for a ticket to a "Ladies Night" game while women received a discount. The New York City Commission on Human Rights agreed with the plaintiff, ruling that "the stereotyped characterizations of a woman's role in society that prevailed at the inception of 'Ladies Day' in 1867 have ceased to be relevant in a modern technological society where women and men are to be on equal footing as a matter of public policy." The Commission issued a non-binding decision mandating the end of Ladies Night discounts, to which the Yankees complied.[50]

Although the New York court decision did not apply to the Astros, nor did the team discontinue its tradition of Ladies Night on Wednesdays, the influence of changing attitudes concerning Women's rights and equality could be seen in a humorous 1974 press release advertising a special pregame softball game between Astros players and their wives:

Has Womens' Lib finally invaded the previously sacrosanct National League for-men-only Astrodome territory? Heaven forbid. 'Tis sadly true!

Now, at last, the true story of the Houston Astros can be told. They have, indeed, underestimated the power of a woman and have yielded to a command challenge. This woman, in particular, is vivacious young Tamy Metzger, bride of the Astros 1973 MVP Roger Metzger.

Tamy, it seems, was a little tired of Roger grabbing all the Metzger sports page headlines, and she figured out that the other members of the Pinchitters Club (Astros wives) might very well feel the same.

So, they have challenged their own husbands to a duel-to-the-die finish on the softball field at the Astrodome...calling themselves the Astros Better Halves, and gaily clad in orange jerseys (bearing their own names and borrowing their husbands' official team numbers), navy blue knit shorts, white sneakers and Astro orange caps and sox, the wives take the field in a baseball tug-o-war guaranteed to outclass the Bobby Riggs-Billie Jean King tennis match in derring-do for the final and ultimate authoritative decision on which sex shall prevail!![51]

The Astros maintained specific promotions for women into the 1970s even as such marketing tactics were coming under fire elsewhere. In 1973, the team held a "Cash Scramble" for women after a Ladies Night matchup with Atlanta. According to the press release for the event, 100 women were selected from the audience to come down on the field after the game. Once the contestants were assembled, 850 one-dollar bills and three 50-dollar bills would be dropped from the Astrodome's catwalks and "the fun will be on as the ladies scramble for whatever they can get. No limit!" The event seemed to be somewhat rooted in the common practice at area rodeos of a calf scramble, where dozens of contestants attempt to catch a calf released into the rodeo arena for a prize. An Astrodome scoreboard advertisement for the Cash Scramble proclaimed that "If you thought the rodeo calf scrambles were exciting, you haven't seen anything until you witness the cash scramble...1,000 dollars of bills to be dropped from the top of the Astrodome with 100 anxious ladies waiting below— Wednesday, May 16!!!"[52]

Throughout the team's first decade in the Astrodome, one of the steadiest promotions geared towards women was the "Miss Astro" contest. A natural progression from the "Miss Colt .45" pageant, the contest was an annual promotion held with much fanfare,

24

The "Astros Better Halves" prepare to play their husbands under the Dome.

typically near the end of the season. Contestants were nominated from across the Astros TV and Radio network, which spanned portions of five states, and flown into Houston for the final competition. The contest was quite elaborate, as the itinerary for the 1970 contest shows. Arriving in Houston on Thursday, contestants (who usually numbered in the 30s) had a jam-packed weekend. First came a Friday pregame presentation at home plate, followed by interviews with judges in the Astrodome Skyboxes. At 9:00 the next morning, the women competed in the Swim Suit Competition at the adjacent Astroworld Hotel pool. That night was dinner with judges at the hotel. Finally, the winner was crowned in an on-field ceremony before Sunday's game. "Miss Congeniality" and a pair of runner-up honors were awarded before the new Miss Astro was named.[53]

Judged on "charm, intelligence and personality, as well as beauty," Miss Astro honorees would make public and social appearances on behalf of the team throughout the year. In addition, the Astros offered a full four-year college scholarship to the winner. Judge Hofheinz noted in a press release announcing the 1970 contest that "the Miss Astro contest extends the benefits of baseball, our national pastime, to eligible young ladies who desire opportunities in higher education. We believe it to be an unparalleled experience for all and take pride in the academic achievement of our former contestants."

In some years there were additional prizes. Take for example Miss Astro 1973, Camille Dowden of El Campo, Texas. In addition to her college scholarship,

she received "a $1,000 diamond ring, an expense-paid trip to Mexico, a $500 wardrobe, a modeling course, a real estate course, and a radio."[54]

The team would often mention the achievements of past contestants and winners in press releases. The announcement for the 1970 contest noted that of previous winners, four had already completed their college degrees, and two later finished as runners-up in the Miss Texas Pageant. The same release also mentioned the movie contract secured by a former contestant from Corpus Christi—Ms. Farrah Fawcett.[55]

HOFHEINZ'S HOUSE OF CARDS COLLAPSES

As much of a visionary as he was, Roy Hofheinz was also a divisive figure who alienated many around him. HSA President Craig Cullinan, who had worked on bringing baseball to Houston years before Hofheinz became involved, decided to sell his stake in the team in late 1962 due to the "autocratic control" that Hofheinz began to assume over the team's operations. Cullinan remembered an early conversation with the Judge where Hofheinz offhandedly remarked that the Astros would eventually be only a small portion of a much larger entertainment business portfolio that he hoped to build. The idea that a championship team was not the Judge's primary motive deeply concerned Cullinan to the point that he and six other part-owners sold their stakes in the team to R.E. "Bob" Smith. Cullinan's fears of Hofheinz's inflated ambitions would prove to be prescient, because in his desire to build an empire, the Judge would lose almost everything.[56]

Not long after Cullinan sold his stake in the team, a split between the previously unassailable partnership of Hofheinz and Smith would give Hofheinz total control of the Astros, but would end up saddling him in what would become a crushing debt. Although Smith's buyout of the other shareholders gave him a 63 percent ownership stake in the team, he had long delegated day-to-day decision making responsibilities to Hofheinz. But Smith, too, would soon be turned off by Hofheinz's controlling style. On May 12, Smith made a stunning announcement—he wanted out. Smith gave Hofheinz a month to exercise an option that would sell all but 10 percent of his stake in the HSA to the Judge for $7.5 million. Hofheinz would buy out Smith to become the majority owner of the HSA, but the move was highly leveraged, with the Judge financing $5.5 million of the purchase price by obtaining loans and mortgages against his various real estate and business holdings.[57]

From that point on Hofheinz fought an uphill battle against creditors. But in an attempt to build his dream entertainment empire, Hofheinz only increased his debt load. He purchased a controlling stake in the Ringling Bros. and Barnum & Bailey Circus in 1967 in a $10 million deal before plowing into one of his biggest ventures yet—Astroworld. At a cost of approximately $25 million, Hofheinz built a 56-acre theme park across the freeway from the Astrodome, with the goal of turning the "Astrodomain" into a Disney World-like tourist hub. Along with the park, Hofheinz subsequently began construction on an $18 million motor-hotel complex for the Astrodome and Astroworld. Both the park and the hotels opened in the summer of 1968.[58]

Although little was known publicly about the situation, high interest rates combined with a recession began to create significant debt service problems for Hofheinz by 1970. According to HSA Vice-President Jack O'Connell, Hofheinz would "never pay anything down on the principal, but [he'd] pay interest or borrowed the interest and extended his note. With interest rates going up, it became pretty tough. We were carrying a lot of raw land on our books." In May 1970, Hofheinz suffered a stroke that paralyzed the left side of his body and kept him in a wheelchair for much of the remainder of his life. Hofheinz survived and regained some of his health, but his credit problems only worsened. Contingent on accepting a long-term financing package of $38 million dollars from a group of creditors led by Ford Motor Credit Company and General Electric Credit Company, Hofheinz stepped down as the day-to-day president of the Astrodomain Corporation in 1972, but still influenced operations as the

chairman of the board. But continued high interest rates on his debt payments meant that Hofheinz had nowhere near the cash flow necessary to service his debt, and by 1976 it was all over. On September 23, 1976, a press release announced that GE Credit and Ford Credit had purchased the Astros from Hofheinz. The release stated, "Judge Roy Hofheinz' imagination and drive created this complex for Houston and without him it would never have happened." Although the House that Roy Built still stood as the Home of the Astros, things would never be quite the same without Judge Roy Hofheinz at the helm of the team.[59]

CONCLUSION: A WHOLE NEW BALLGAME

Through his nearly 15 years at the helm of the Houston Astros, Roy Hofheinz burnished a reputation as a marketer and businessman not quite seen before in the game. In its preview article of the brand-new Astrodome, the *Houston Post* argued that "as a promoter, Hofheinz makes Bill Veeck look like a peanut butcher suffering from the financial shorts."[60] Hofheinz's marketing panache was clear and evident in the ways he catered to female fans. From early on, he realized the significance of drawing female fans out to the ballpark, and the measures he took at Colt Stadium to draw a wide fanbase aided that goal substantially. The opening of the Astrodome was revolutionary and groundbreaking in its own right, so much so that *Sports Illustrated* highlighted Hofheinz and the Astrodome in its 40th anniversary issue as one of the four major catalysts of changes in sports since the magazine's founding in 1954. The Astrodome, in the words of Roy's son and former Houston mayor Fred Hofheinz, opened up Astros baseball specifically, but sports in general to a much wider audience than ever before, including women:

> Enormous new markets opened up, and the Dome was part of that: If you were to go to a Houston Buffs minor league game, you would have seen the die-hard fans, the people who kept scorecards and read the box scores every morning. That guy was in the minority at the Dome. At the Dome the wives came. The Children came. Suddenly it was a whole new milieu of fans. The Dome greatly broadened sports' appeal for these people. In Houston it became a social event to go to the Astrodome. Women went to the Astrodome in heels![61]

The Astrodome's groundbreaking fan frills combined with Hofheinz's unique gift for promotion and marketing created a marketing dynamo that changed the way baseball was presented to female fans. That legacy remains strong today, as Commissioner Bud Selig's 2000 Initiative on Women and Baseball concluded that "women are the key to reaching families" and that "marketing to women will grow the game's fan base," tenets that were core to Hofheinz's marketing strategy back in 1962.[62]

Though the Astros have since moved from the Astrodome to newer, swankier digs downtown with more of the luxury boxes and other revenue-generating amenities that Hofheinz pioneered 40 years earlier, the Astrodome still stands intact as an aging monument to the successful efforts of Hofheinz and others to bring baseball to Houston and make the game attractive to a universal fan base, including women. ■

Notes

1. Jean Hastings Ardell, *Breaking into Baseball: Women and the National Pastime* (Carbondale, IL: Southern Illinois University Press, 2005), 29, 31.
2. Ibid., 39
3. Hofheinz was forced by poor health and crippling debt to sell the Astros to his creditors in 1976.
4. Bill James, *The New Baseball Historical Abstract* (New York: Free Press, 2001), 240–41.
5. Robert Reed, *A Six-Gun Salute: An Illustrated History of the Colt .45s* (Houston: Gulf Publishing Co., 1999), 1.
6. Ibid., 9.
7. Dene Hofheinz Mann, *You Be The Judge* (Houston: Premiere Printing Company, 1965), 79.
8. Edgar W. Ray, *The Grand Huckster: Houston's Judge Roy Hofheinz, Genius of the Astrodome* (Memphis: Memphis State University Press, 1980), 257, 262; Reed, *A Six-Gun Salute*, 41; Reed, *A Six-Gun Salute*, 37.
9. Ray, *The Grand Huckster*, 272.
10. Roy Terrell, *Sports Illustrated*, "Fast Man With A .45," March 26, 1962, 34.
11. Reed, *A Six-Gun Salute*, 74.
12. Ray, *The Grand Huckster*, 281.
13. Archival photograph of Fast Draw Club, Houston Astros Baseball Club Archives, Houston, TX.
14. Reed, *A Six-Gun Salute*, 74.
15. Reed, *A Six-Gun Salute*, 81.
16. Archival photograph of Colt .45s Merchandise Stand, HABC Archives, Houston, TX, date unknown (1962–65).
17. Archival photographs of Miss Colt 45 contest, HABC Archives, 1964.
18. Reed, *A Six-Gun Salute*, 82.
19. Ray, *The Grand Huckster*, 282.
20. Ray, *The Grand Huckster*, 280.
21. Liz Smith, *Sports Illustrated*, "Giltfinger's Golden Dome," April 12, 1965, 56.
22. Everett Groselcose, *Wall Street Journal*, "Baseball's Big Top: Houston Astros Open Fancy Enclosed Park," April 9, 1965, 1.
23. Ray, *The Grand Huckster*, 302.
24. *Houston Chronicle*, "Designers kept the gals in mind," *Texas Magazine*, April 8, 1965.
25. Ray, *The Grand Huckster*, 299.
26. *Houston Chronicle*, "Designers kept the gals in mind," *Texas Magazine*, April 8, 1965.
27. *Houston Post*, "A Touch of Midas in Décor, Too," April 4, 1965.
28. *Houston Chronicle*, "Five Restaurants Under Dome," April, 4 1965.
29. Smith, *Sports Illustrated*, "Glitfinger's Golden Dome," April, 12 1965, 52, 58.
30. Smith, *Sports Illustrated*, "Glitfinger's Golden Dome," April, 12 1965, 56.
31. Ray, *The Grand Huckster*, 299.
32. *Houston Chronicle*, "Designers kept the gals in mind," *Texas Magazine*, April 8, 1965.
33. Ray, *The Grand Huckster*, 299.
34. *Houston Chronicle*, "Designers kept the gals in mind," April 8, 1965.
35. Beverly Maurice, *Houston Chronicle*, "Silks, Linens and Hats At Fashionable Game," April 10, 1965.
36. Bob Cargill, *Houston Post*, "Like…a Foreign Country," April 10, 1965, A1, A3.
37. Teddye Clayton, *Houston Post*, "Spacettes Will Sparkle Under Dome," April 4, 1965.
38. Beverly Maurice, *Houston Chronicle*, "'At Home' in the Dome," April 4, 1965.
39. Clayton, *Houston Post*, "Spacettes Will Sparkle Under Dome," April 4, 1965.
40. Houston Astros, *2008 Houston Astros Media Guide* (Tempe, AZ: Ben Franklin Press, 2008), 331.
41. Baseball-Reference.com, "Los Angeles Dodgers Attendance, Stadiums and Park Factors," www.baseball-reference.com/teams/LAD/attend.shtml, accessed August 3, 2008; Astros Press Release 65–262, Houston Astros Baseball Club Archives, September 30, 1965.
42. Astros Press Release 65–262, Houston Astros Baseball Club Archives, September 30, 1965.
43. Astros Press Release 65–97, HABC Archives, September 30, 1965.
44. Astros Press Release 67–117, HABC Archives, May 4, 1967.
45. Astros Press Release 66–109, HABC Archives, April 19, 1966.
46. Astros Press Release 66–139, HABC Archives, June 2, 1966; Astros Press Release 66–162, HABC Archives, June 24, 1966; Astros Press Release 66–177, HABC Archives, July 20, 1966.
47. Lisa Gray, *Houston Chronicle*, "What Dene Remembers," www.chron.com/disp/story.mpl/metropolitan/gray/4934096.html, July 1, 2007; Baseball-Reference.com, "1967 Houston Astros Schedule, Box Scores and Splits," www.baseball-reference.com/teams/HOU/1967_sched.shtml, accessed August 3, 2008; Astros Press Release 67–110, HABC Archives, April 26, 1967; Astros Press Release 66–112, HABC Archives, April 25, 1966; Astros Press Release 68–92, HABC Archives, March 27, 1968.
48. Astros Press Release 70–58, HABC Archives, May 1966; Astros Press Release 70–82, HABC Archives, August 5, 1970; Astros Press Release 70–102, HABC Archives, September 21, 1970.
49. Astros Press Release 71–80, "Astrodome Spacettes Take a Giant Step For Fashion," HABC Archives, May 11, 1971; Astros Press Release 71–69, HABC Archives, April 16, 1971.
50. Vered Yakovee, *Entertainment and Sports Lawyer*, "Spotlight on 'Ladies Night' Promotions," Volume 24, Number 4, Winter 2007.
51. Astros Press Release 74–93, HABC Archives, July 1, 1974.
52. Astros Press Release 73–106, HABC Archives, May 3, 1973.
53. Astros Press Release 70–91, HABC Archives, August 26, 1970.
54. Astros Press Release 70–91, HABC Archives, August 26, 1970; Astros Press Release 72–128, HABC Archives, August 13, 1972.
55. Astros Press Release 70–91, HABC Archives, August 26, 1970.
56. Reed, *A Six-Gun Salute*, 203–4.
57. Ray, *The Grand Huckster*, 318–21.
58. Ray, *The Grand Huckster*, 366–67, 370, 372–73.
59. Ray, *The Grand Huckster*, 407, 452, 457–8, 462, 567; Astros Press Release 76–88, HABC Archives, September 23, 1976.
60. Mickey Herskowitz, *Houston Post*, April 8, 1965.
61. Steve Rushin, *Sports Illustrated*, "At Home in the Dome," August 16, 1994, 47.
62. MLB Properties, Inc., "Commissioner's Initiative on Women and Baseball" (Washington, D.C., July, 2000), 5.

The Colt .45s and the 1961 Expansion Draft

Stephen D. Boren and Eric Thompson

On October 10, 1961, the National League held the expansion draft to provide players for the Houston Colt .45s and the New York Mets. While the American League had held a seemingly similar expansion draft on December 14, 1960, the National League draft had the following distinctions:

- It was held earlier in the year.
- There were three distinct price levels for draftable players.
- It was less cumbersome to implement.
- There were different draft selection requirements.
- It was held before the Rule 5 Draft.

As in the 1960 American League draft, the eight established National League teams were required to name 15 available players on their 40-man roster—including seven players from their 25-man roster.[1] The due date for the National League lists was September 20 for the draft that would occur on the day after the 1961 World Series ended, more than two months earlier than the American League draft had taken place in 1960.

In the previous AL draft, all the players in the expansion pool were available for $75,000 each to the new teams. However, the National League draft had three prices for players: $50,000, $75,000, and $125,000. Each expansion team was required to select 16 players: two from each established team's available player list at $75,000 (regular phase), then at most eight players, one from each established team at $50,000 (optional phase) from the players remaining. At that point, in a major departure from the AL system, each established team was to submit two additional names from their August 31 active roster: "premium players." From this list of 16, each expansion team was required to choose four players at $125,000 each (premium phase), and no established team could lose more than one premium player.

If an expansion team purchased the maximum number of players—16 at $75,000 each, eight at $50,000 each, and four at $125,000 each—the total cost would be $2.1 million. That cost represented the team's entry fee into the National League and was equal to the amount paid by the AL expansion teams for 28 players at $75,000 each. While these prices for players do not seem high in 2014, they were quite pricey in 1961 even after discounting the entry fee involved. The consumer price index was 29.9 in 1961, compared to 233.5 in 2013.[2] Adjusting 1961-dollars to 2013-dollars at a rate of $7.81, would yield prices of $585,750, $390,500, and $976,250.[3] The sale of players was a financial bonanza to each of the eight established teams.

The American League had required that each new team draft ten pitchers, followed by two catchers, six infielders, four outfielders, and then six players unrestricted by position. The NL draft did not have any position requirements. In the AL draft no established team was supposed to lose more than seven players and an expansion team could take no more than four players from any established team. Unfortunately Joe Cronin forgot about these requirements while he conducted the AL draft and the selections needed to be rearranged after the draft was seemingly over because the Tigers and Indians had lost eight players each![4] The NL draft did not make this mistake.

While these differences were significant, the most significant distinction was the date of the draft. The AL draft was held more than two months after the season ended. Thus before the 1960 American League expansion draft, the lists of available players had not been distorted by any of the following roster changes:

- Retirements (e.g. Ted Williams)
- Unconditional releases
- Sale and optioning of players to minor league teams
- Promotion of prospects
- Addition of players taken in the Rule 5 Draft held on November 28

After the 1960 season ended but before the 1960 draft, the Cleveland Indians had released Jack Harshman and sold Billy Moran to the International League, the Orioles had released Jim Busby, Del Rice, and Dave

Philley, the Yankees had released Jim Hegan, and the White Sox had released Bob Rush and Mike Garcia and dropped Don Ferrarese, Jake Striker, Frank Barnes, and Al Worthington.[5,6] With only eight days between the end of the season and the NL draft, no roster modifications by any of the eight established National League teams had yet taken place.

The greatest inequity of the NL expansion draft was that few blue chip minor league prospects were included on the 40-man rosters. Most promoted their top minor leaguers on October 17, 1961, seven days after the draft and the last day to modify the 40-man roster before the Rule 5 and Rule 3 Drafts. These players had been exempt from the expansion draft in October and now were protected in late November as well. A partial list of these prospects appears in Table 1.[7]

Meanwhile, many "deadwood" players promoted in September to be showcased for the expansion draft, but not taken, were then shuffled off the 40-man roster to make room for superior minor league talent.

The list of players made available for the NL expansion draft appears in Table 2 on the following page.[8]

The general managers in Houston and New York, Paul Richards and George Weiss, were not happy with the players made available. Richards commented, "I figured the lists of players would be bad, but they're worse than I thought they would be."[9]

Thirty of the available players were 31 or older. Nineteen had eight years or more of major league experience including many with correspondingly high salaries. Of the 120 available players, 23 were rookies who ended their baseball careers without ever appearing in a single major league game—19 additional players never played

at the major league level after 1961. Twenty-one were journeyman players who had spent seven or more seasons in the minor leagues.

At the AL expansion draft there were five coin tosses, one for each position category. At the NL expansion draft there was one coin toss with the winner selecting to go first in the regular-optional phase or the premium phase. The Colts won the coin toss and elected to go first in the regular-optional phase.

The Colts decided that shortstop Ed Bressoud of the Giants was the best player available and selected him. He had been the backup to Jose Pagan and played in only 59 games the past season while hitting a mere .211. On November 26 he was traded to the Red Sox for the erratic Don Buddin, another shortstop. After 40 games in 1962, Buddin was hitting .163 and was sold to the Tigers. They did well with their second pick, Bob Aspromonte, who had a successful career with Houston. Incidentally, his brother Ken had been selected by the Senators and traded to the Angels at the draft table in the AL expansion draft.[10] Their third pick was light-hitting shortstop Bob Lillis, who did have a long Houston career as a player, coach, and manager.

Fourth and fifth picks, Dick Drott and Al Heist, were both from the Cubs and were both busts. Drott was called to eight months of active military duty on November 2 and appeared in only six games.[11] Heist was on the disabled list for a month, played in only 27 games, and batted only .222.[12] In 1963, Drott went 2–12 in his final year in the majors. Heist was in the minors all season.

Sixth pick Roman Mejias was a power hitting success in 1962 for the Colts and became one of their most

Table 1. Select Players Promoted after the 1961 National League Expansion Draft

Braves (17)	A	B	Dodgers (14)	A	B	Giants (13)	A	B	Pirates (11)	A	B
Menke,Denis	4	13	McMullen,Ken	1	16	Perry,Gaylord	4	22	Bailey,Bob	1	17
Azcue,Joe	6	11	Richert,Pete	4	13	Mota,Manny	5	20	Veale,Bob	4	13
Blasingame,Wade	1	10	Moeller,Joe	1	8	Cardenal,Jose	1	18	May,Jerry	1	10
Charles,Ed	9	8	Nen,Dick	1	6	Lanier,Hal	1	10	Lamabe,Jack	6	7
Garrett,Adrian	1	8	Shirley,Bart	1	4	Tartabull,Jose	4	9	Woods,Ron	1	6
Aaron,Tommie	4	7	Brumley,Mike	5	3	Phillips,Dick	8	4	Elliot,Larry	4	4
Jimenez,Manny	4	7	Burright,Larry	5	3						
Ribant,Dennis	1	6	Smith,Jack	6	3	**Reds (11)**	A	B	**Cardinals (9)**	A	B
Uecker,Bob	6	6	Smith,Richard	5	3	Rojas,Cookie	6	16	Beauchamp,Jim	4	10
Samuel,Amado	4	3				Pavletich,Don	3	10	Whitfield,Fred	4	9
						Ruiz,Chico	4	8	Duliba,Bob	7	5
Cubs (10)	A	B	**Phillies (9)**	A	B	Ellis,Sam	1	7	Wicker,Floyd	1	4
Koonce,Cal	1	10	Hamilton,Jack	5	8				Toth,Paul	5	3

Number in parentheses indicates the total number of prospects promoted by the team.
Players listed played three or more years in the major leagues after 1961.
A = years played in Organized Baseball through 1961
B = years played in the major leagues after 1961

popular players. In 1962, Mejias led the team in batting, home runs, runs batted in, runs scored, hits, and stolen bases. After the season he was traded to the Red Sox for the reigning AL batting champion, Pete Runnels. Unfortunately, Runnels lost his batting eye when he joined the Houston team and was released in early 1964.

Seventh pick George Williams, like Drott, was called to active military duty soon after the draft.[13] Williams played in only five September games for the Colts in 1962, played in the minors in 1963, and was sent to the Cardinals after the season. Eighth pick Jesse Hickman never played in a major league game

Table 2. Players Made Available for the 1961 National League Expansion Draft

Cubs

	Age	A	B	C	
Pitchers					
* Brewer,Jim	24	6	2	15	
Burwell,Dick	21	3	2	0	X
Carlander,Wayne	20	2	0	0	
* Drott,Dick	25	8	5	2	H
Wright,Mel	33	12	4	0	X
Catchers					
Bales,Walter	23	2	0	0	X
Thacker,Moe	27	10	3	2	
Infielders					
* Bouchee,Ed	28	8	6	1	N
* Drake,Sam	27	5	2	1	N
McKnight,Jim	25	7	1	1	
* Roach,Mel	28	7	7	1	
Outfielders					
Bishop,Lou	20	2	0	0	X
* Heist,Al	34	12	2	1	H
Mathews,Nelson	20	3	2	4	
* McAnany,Jim	25	7	4	1	

Reds

	Age	A	B	C	
Pitchers					
Alex,Harvey	21	2	0	0	
Davalillo,Vic	25	4	0	16	X
Fodor,Marv	20	3	0	0	X
* Johnson,Ken	28	9	4	9	H
* Jones,Sherm	26	8	2	1	N
Nunn,Howie	26	8	2	1	
Pena,Orlando	28	7	3	11	
Rippelmeyer,Ray	28	7	0	1	X
Catchers					
* Johnson,Darrell	33	13	5	1	
* Zimmerman,Jerry	27	10	1	7	
Infielders					
* Gernert,Dick	33	12	10	1	H
Hopke,Fred	24	6	0	0	X
Alvarez,Rogelio	23	6	1	1	X
* Chacon,Elio	25	6	2	1	N
Outfielders					
* Bell,Gus	33	15	12	3	N

Dodgers

	Age	A	B	C	
Pitchers					
Chittum,Nelson	28	6	3	0	X
* Craig,Roger	31	10	7	5	N
* Golden,Jim	25	8	2	2	H
Tillotson,Thad	21	2	0	2	
Valdes,Rene	32	10	1	0	X
Warren,Rick	22	5	0	0	X
Catchers					
* Sherry,Norm	30	10	3	2	
Infielders					
* Aspromonte,Bob	23	6	3	10	H
* Hodges,Gil	37	17	16	2	N
* Larker,Norm	31	13	4	2	H
Norris,Al	24	6	0	0	X
Plumlee,Ralph	22	2	0	0	X
Wallace,Gene	28	8	0	0	X
Outfielders					
Brodsky,Sheldon	25	7	0	0	X
* Windhorn,Gordie	28	10	2	1	X

Braves

	Age	A	B	C	
Pitchers					
* Antonelli,Johnny	31	12	12	0	X
Botz,Bob	26	7	0	1	X
MacKenzie,Ken	27	5	2	4	X
Morehead,Seth	27	10	5	0	X
Overby,Dennis	20	3	0	0	X
Roof,Paul	19	2	0	0	H
Catchers					
Ranew,Merritt	23	5	0	5	H
Roof,Phil	20	3	1	14	X
* Taylor,Hawk	22	5	3	8	
* White,Sammy	33	12	10	1	X
Infielders					
* Boyd,Bob	42	12	9	0	X
* Mantilla,Felix	27	10	6	5	N
Outfielders					
* Chrisley,Neil	30	11	5	0	X
* DeMerit,John	25	5	4	1	N
McDonald,Wayne	23	2	0	0	X

Phillies

	Age	A	B	C	
Pitchers					
Culp,Ray	20	3	0	11	
Gomez,Ruben	34	13	8	2	X
Gruber,Bruce	19	2	0	0	
Hickman,Jesse	22	2	0	2	H
* Lehman,Ken	33	14	5	0	X
* Roberts,Robin	35	14	14	5	X
Catchers					
Coleman,Clarence	24	6	1	3	N
* Kenders,Al	24	6	1	0	X
Infielders					
Allen,Dick	19	2	0	15	
* Herrera,Pancho	27	7	3	0	
Sadowski,Bob	24	7	2	2	X
Williams,George	22	4	1	2	H
Outfielders					
* Smith,BobbyGene	27	9	5	2	N
* Valo,Elmer	40	21	20	0	X
* Walters,Ken	28	8	2	1	

Pirates

	Age	A	B	C	
Pitchers					
Jackson,Al	26	7	2	8	N
* Labine,Clem	35	17	12	1	X
* Mizell,VB	31	11	8	1	
Raydon,Curt	28	9	1	0	X
* Shantz,Bobby	36	17	13	3	H
Umbricht,Jim	31	7	3	2	H
Catchers					
Plaskett,Elmo	23	5	0	2	
Infielders					
Housley,Norm	19	2	0	0	
* Logan,Johnny	34	15	11	2	
* Nelson,Rocky	37	17	9	0	X
Outfielders					
* Christopher,Joe	26	7	3	5	N
Mejias,Roman	31	9	6	3	H
Mitchell,Henry	25	7	0	0	X
* Moryn,Walt	35	14	8	0	X
Powers,John	32	11	6	0	X

Giants

	Age	A	B	C	
Pitchers					
Choate,Don	23	6	1	0	X
Daviault,Ray	27	9	0	1	N
Denton,Richard	22	2	0	0	X
Feldman,Ed	20	2	0	0	
Fisher,Eddie	25	4	3	12	
* Jones,Sam	36	12	9	3	H
* Loes,Billy	32	12	11	0	X
* Zanni,Dom	29	11	3	4	X
Catchers					
Dietz,Dick	20	2	0	8	
* Landrith,Hobie	31	13	12	2	N
Infielders					
* Bowman,Ernie	26	6	1	2	
* Bressoud,Eddie	29	10	6	6	H
* Marshall,Jim	30	12	4	1	X
Peterson,Cap	19	2	0	8	
Outfielders					
Weekly,Johnny	24	6	0	3	X

Cardinals

	Age	A	B	C	
Pitchers					
* Anderson,Craig	23	2	1	3	N
* Cicotte,Al	32	12	4	1	X
McDaniel,Kerry	18	1	0	0	
Stark,Clint	19	2	0	0	
Wakefield,Bill	20	1	0	1	
Catchers					
* Cannizzaro,Chris	23	6	2	11	N
Herrera,Roberto	22	6	0	0	
Infielders					
* Lillis,Bob	31	9	4	6	H
Marx,Gerry	19	2	0	0	
* Schoendienst,Red	38	20	17	2	X
Outfielders					
Hickman,Jim	24	6	0	13	N
Kolb,Gary	21	2	1	6	
Landrum,Don	25	8	3	5	
* Olivares,Ed	23	5	2	0	H
* Taussig,Don	29	11	2	1	H

Age = age on December 31, 1961
A = years played in Organized Baseball through 1961
B = years played in the major leagues through 1961
C = years played in the major leagues after 1961
* indicates player was on active roster on 31 August 1961.
H indicates palyer was selected by Houston Colts.
N indicates player was selected by New York Mets.
X indicates player was no longer on team's 40-man roster
   by 17 October 1961.

with the Colts. It is very likely that Paul Richards mistook him for Jim Hickman, who was also available in the expansion draft. It wasn't the first time a GM made such a mistake: The St. Louis Browns took Garvin Hamner in the 1947 minor league draft, thinking that they were selecting his brother Granny.[14] Ninth pick Merritt Ranew was a backup catcher for one season, then was traded away and spent most of his career in the minors. Their 10th pick Don Taussig hit only .200 in 16 games, but the Colts received part of their investment back when the Braves drafted him in the minor league phase of the 1962 Rule 5 Draft.

Their 11th pick Bobby Shantz started three games on the mound for the Colts before being traded to the Cardinals for Carl Warwick and John Anderson on May 7, 1962. Warwick became the Colts' regular center fielder for 1962. Since the Washington Senators had selected Shantz in the 1960 AL expansion draft, Shantz bore the distinction of being the only player selected in both drafts.[15]

Their 12th pick was Norm Larker, who had lost the 1960 batting title by making an out in his final plate appearance. However, he hit only .263 for the Colts and was traded after the 1962 season. Their 13th pick, Sam "Toothpick" Jones, never pitched for the Colts. Jones was quickly traded on December 1 to the Tigers for Bob Bruce and Manny Montejo. Bruce pitched in the Colts starting rotation for five years. Jones won only four games during the remainder of his career. Their 14th pick was Paul Roof, who never played major league baseball, although his brothers Phil and Gene did. Again, perhaps he was mistaken for Phil who was also in the draft.

Their 15th pick was Ken Johnson who was a decent pitcher for Houston for several seasons during his 13-year major league career. His main claim to fame was pitching a nine-inning no-hitter for the Colts on April 23, 1964, but losing the game 1–0 when he and Nellie Fox made errors in the ninth inning. Their 16th pick, Dick Gernert, hit .208 in 10 games and was quickly released on May 17, 1962.

Their 17th pick and first $50,000, optional pick was Ed Olivares. Olivares was on the disabled list during the entire 1962 season and never played again in the majors.[16] Eighteenth pick Jim Umbricht pitched effectively out of the bullpen for two years before he, unfortunately, died of cancer in 1964. Nineteenth pick Jim Golden was back in the minors in 1963 and traded for Nellie Fox after that season.

Golden was the last optional pick taken in the draft because Weiss and Richards refused to spend any more money. By leaving eleven optional choices unused, the Mets saved $300,000 and the Colts $250,000 on the anticipated $2.1 million expected expenditure by each team. Both general managers intended to use that money to develop their teams: Weiss to purchase retreads at his own price, Richards to acquire and develop young talent.

At that point a representative from each established team made known the identity of their team's two premium players. Table 3 shows the 16 premium players, two from each established team, made available for the NL expansion draft.[17]

The premium player choices were marked by the presence of three "bonus babies" from the mid-1950s. Those three, Bob L. Miller (Cardinals), Joey Amalfitano (Giants), and Jay Hook (Reds), were the first three players taken in the premium phase. Since the Mets chose first in the premium phase, Miller and Hook became Mets. The Colts took Amalfitano with their first premium pick. Their original teams actually turned a tidy profit when they received $125,000 each! On the humorous side, when Amalfitano discovered that he had been purchased for that princely sum, he said, "I'll have to go out and get another life insurance policy. I'm worth more than I thought."[18] Amalfitano

Table 3. Premium Players Made Available for the 1961 National League Expansion Draft

Cubs	Pos	Age	A	B	C		Reds	Pos	Age	A	B	C		Dodgers	Pos	Age	A	B	C	
Ashburn,Richie	OF	34	16	14	1		Henry,Bill	P	34	14	8	8		Farrell,Turk	P	27	9	6	8	H
Zimmer,Don	INF	30	13	8	4	N	Hook,Jay	P	25	5	5	3	N	Neal,Charlie	INF	30	12	6	2	

Braves	Pos	Age	A	B	C		Phillies	Pos	Age	A	B	C		Pirates	Pos	Age	A	B	C	
Cimoli,Gino	OF	32	13	6	4	X	Green,Dallas	P	27	7	2	6		Leppert,Don	C	30	7	1	3	
Spangler,Al	OF	28	6	3	10	H	Walls,Lee	OF	28	11	7	3	N	Smith,Hal	C	31	13	7	3	H

Giants	Pos	Age	A	B	C		Cardinals	Pos	Age	A	B	C
Amalfitano,Joey	INF	27	8	4	6	H	Miller,Bob	P	22	5	4	13	N
LeMay,Dick	P	23	4	1	2		Sawatski,Carl	C	34	15	9	2	

Age = age on December 31, 1961

A = years played in Organized Baseball through 1961

B = years played in the major leagues through 1961

C = years played in the major leagues after 1961

* indicates player was on active roster on 31 August 1961.

H indicates palyer was selected by Houston Colts.

N indicates player was selected by New York Mets.

X indicates player was no longer on team's 40-man roster by 17 October 1961.

lasted only one season with Houston but enjoyed a long career as a major league coach and manager.

Their second premium pick, Dick "Turk" Farrell, was an all-star pitcher for the Colts, and was their jewel of the draft. Their third premium pick, Hal W. Smith, was their regular catcher in 1962 and their third string catcher the next season, before he was released. Their final premium pick, Al Spangler, was a regular outfielder for three seasons before being traded away. Spangler had the distinction of being the final player taken in the NL expansion draft as well as the last player to bat in an eight-team National League. The regular, optional, and premium choices made by the Colts and Mets appear in Table 4.[19]

After the draft, Paul Richards had changed his tune. Richards was quoted, "I was frightened a week ago when I did some talking, but had I known that we would get the team we did, I never would have opened my mouth."[20]

George Weiss saw much work ahead saying, "We did as well as we expected to do, maybe a little better, but please don't think this will be our starting club on opening day. We plan to purchase many more players and have some deals in mind."[21]

When the Colts and Mets left eleven optional choices at $50,000 each untaken, the players shown in Table 5 were still available who went on to play at least five years at the major league level after 1961.[22]

Passing over Vic Davalillo is understandable since he had been a pitcher in the Reds' organization through the 1961 season rather than an outfielder, the position he played throughout his 16-year major league carer. However, infielder Dick Allen became NL rookie of the year in 1964 and AL Most Valuable Player in 1972. In 1961, Allen was in his second year in Organized Baseball and had batted .317 with 21 home runs and 94 runs batted in as a second baseman at Magic Valley in the Class C Pioneer League. Allen finished his major league career with a .292 average and 351 home runs.

Also untaken was Eddie Fisher, a highly regarded 25-year-old pitcher in the Giants' farm system who had posted a record of 47–28 with a 3.23 ERA in his four minor league seasons. Fisher became the main piece in the Giants' November 30, 1961, trade with the White Sox for Billy Pierce and Don Larsen. Fisher followed with twelve successful years in the AL posting an 80-61 record with a 3.25 ERA. He was AL Fireman of the Year in 1965.

Other noteworthy names included Robin Roberts, Jerry Zimmerman, Jim Brewer, and Ray Culp. The Colts and Mets left some experienced talent and potential talent untaken.

The National League kicked off their first season as a ten-team league in 1962. The Houston Colts managed to duplicate the Los Angeles Angels' feat of 1961 by

Table 4. Regular, Optional, and Premium Draftees of the Colts and Mets

Houston

REGULAR SELECTION PHASE ($75,000 each)

	Player	Pos	Team	Age	A	B	C
1	Eddie Bressoud	INF	Giants	29	10	6	6
3	Bob Aspromonte	INF	Dodgers	23	6	3	10
5	Bob Lillis	INF	Cardinals	31	9	4	6
7	Dick Drott	P	Cubs	25	8	5	2
9	Al Heist	OF	Cubs	34	12	2	1
11	Roman Mejias	OF	Pirates	31	9	6	3
13	George Williams	INF	Phillies	22	4	1	2
15	Jesse Hickman	P	Phillies	22	2	0	2
17	Merritt Ranew	C	Braves	23	5	0	5
19	Don Taussig	OF	Cardinals	29	11	2	1
21	Bobby Shantz	P	Pirates	36	17	13	3
23	Norm Larker	1B	Dodgers	31	13	4	2
25	Sam Jones	P	Giants	36	12	9	3
27	Paul Roof	P	Braves	19	2	0	0
29	Ken Johnson	P	Reds	28	9	4	9
31	Dick Gernert	1B	Reds	33	12	10	1

OPTIONAL SELECTION PHASE ($50,000 each)

	Player	Pos	Team	Age	A	B	C
33	Ed Olivares	OF	Cardinals	23	5	2	0
35	Jim Umbricht	P	Pirates	31	7	3	2
37	Jim Golden	P	Dodgers	25	8	2	2

PREMIUM SELECTION PHASE ($125,000 each)

	Player	Pos	Team	Age	A	B	C
2	Amalfitano,Joey	INF	Giants	27	8	4	6
4	Farrell,Turk	P	Dodgers	27	9	6	8
6	Smith,Hal	C	Piates	31	13	7	3
8	Spangler,Al	OF	Braves	28	6	3	10

New York

REGULAR SELECTION PHASE ($75,000 each)

	Player	Pos	Team	Age	A	B	C
2	Hobie Landrith	C	Giants	31	13	12	2
4	Elio Chacon	INF	Reds	25	6	2	1
6	Roger Craig	P	Dodgers	31	10	7	5
8	Gus Bell	OF	Reds	33	15	12	3
10	Joe Christopher	OF	Pirates	26	7	3	5
12	Felix Mantilla	INF	Braves	27	10	6	5
14	Gil Hodges	1B	Dodgers	37	17	16	2
16	Craig Anderson	P	Cardinals	23	2	1	3
18	Ray Daviault	P	Giants	27	9	0	1
20	John DeMerit	OF	Braves	25	5	4	1
22	Al Jackson	P	Pirates	26	7	2	8
24	Sammy Drake	INF	Cubs	27	5	2	1
26	Chris Cannizzaro	C	Cardinals	23	6	2	11
28	Clarence Coleman	C	Phillies	24	6	1	3
30	Ed Bouchee	1B	Cubs	28	8	6	1
32	Bobby Gene Smith	OF	Phillies	27	9	5	2

OPTIONAL SELECTION PHASE ($50,000 each)

	Player	Pos	Team	Age	A	B	C
34	Sherman Jones	P	Reds	26	8	2	1
36	Jim Hickman	OF	Cardinals	24	6	0	13

PREMIUM SELECTION PHASE ($125,000 each)

	Player	Pos	Team	Age	A	B	C
1	Miller,Bob	P	Cardinals	22	5	4	13
3	Hook,Jay	P	Reds	25	5	5	3
5	Zimmer,Don	INF	Cubs	30	13	8	4
7	Walls,Lee	OF	Phillies	28	11	7	3

Table 5. Players Not Taken in 1961 National League Expansion Draft

Player	Pos	Team	Age	A	B	C	Player	Pos	Team	Age	A	B	C
Davalillo, Vic	P	Reds	25	4	0	16	Dietz, Dick	C	Giants	20	2	0	8
Allen, Dick	INF	Phillies	19	2	0	15	Peterson, Cap	INF	Giants	19	2	0	8
Brewer, Jim	P	Cubs	24	6	2	15	Taylor, Hawk	C	Braves	22	5	3	8
Roof, Phil	C	Braves	20	3	1	14	Zimmerman, Jerry	C	Reds	27	10	1	7
Fisher, Eddie	P	Giants	25	4	3	12	Kolb, Gary	OF	Cardinals	21	2	1	6
Culp, Ray	P	Phillies	20	3	0	11	Roberts, Robin	P	Phillies	35	14	14	5
Pena, Orlando	P	Reds	28	7	3	11	Landrum, Don	OF	Cardinals	25	8	3	5

finishing in eighth place but with only a 64–96 record compared to the Angels' record of 70–91 in 1961. The Cubs, who lost 103 games, had the dubious distinction of finishing ninth, six games behind the Colts.

The Colts featured an everyday lineup of veterans. Norm Larker, Joey Amalfitano, Bob Lillis, and Bob Aspromonte covered the infield. Al Spangler, Carl Warwick, and Roman Mejias held down the outfield posts. Hal Smith was the regular catcher. All, except Warwick, were taken in the expansion draft. Dick Farrell, acquired in the expansion draft, and Bob Bruce, acquired from the Tigers in the December trade for Sam Jones, each won ten games. Don McMahon, purchased from the Braves on May 9, 1962, and Jim Umbricht, acquired in the expansion draft, anchored the bullpen.

The Colts had heavily invested in young talent. Waiting in the wings for the opportunity at the major league level were catcher Jerry Grote, outfielders Ron Davis and Rusty Staub, and pitchers Dave Giusti and Chris Zachary. The future looked bright for Houston. ■

Acknowledgement

Portions of the information used here were obtained free of charge from and is copyrighted by Retrosheet. Interested parties may contact Retrosheet at www.retrosheet.org.

References

Rules governing the American League expansion draft of 1960:
Baseball Guide and Record Book 1961. Compiled by J. G. Taylor Spink.
    Charles C. Spink and Sons Published, St. Louis, 1961. Pages 110–12.

Rules governing the National League expansion draft of 1961:
Baseball Guide and Record Book 1962. Compiled by J. G. Taylor Spink.
    Charles C. Spink and Sons Published, St. Louis, 1962. Pages 119–20.
Daniel, Dan. "N.L. Execs Okay Grab-Bag Plan in Marathon Huddle."
    The Sporting News, July 5, 1961, pages 5–6.

Statistical data for players included in all lists and for players drafted by Houston:
retrosheet.org and SABR minor league database included in baseball-
    reference.com
Description of 1962 Houston season compiled from retrosheet.org

Notes

1. The 25-man roster as of August 31.
2. www.bls.gov/cpi/tables.htm.
3. http://inflationdata.com/inflation/Inflation_Calculators/Inflation_
    Calculator.asp.
4. Letter of May 13, 1973, from Hal Keller, farm director of the Texas Rangers, to Cliff Kachline, historian of the National Baseball Hall of Fame, on file in the 1961 American League Expansion Draft folder in the A. Bartlett Giamatti Research Center at the National Baseball Hall of Fame, Cooperstown, NY.
5. www.retrosheet.org/boxesetc/1960/YM_1960.htm.
6. Edward Prell, "In the Wake of the News," *Chicago Tribune.* Part 4, 1, September 23, 1961.
7. List compiled from *BASEBALL,* Office of the Commissioner, Official Bulletin No. 23, November 14, 1961, 2–3.
8. List compiled from information in 1962 National League Expansion Draft folder in the A. Bartlett Giamatti Research Center at the National Baseball Hall of Fame, Cooperstown, NY.
9. Clark Nealon, "Colts Get Frick Okay to Set Up 40-Man Roster," *The Sporting News,* October 11, 1961, 15.
10. Letter of May 13, 1973, from Hal Keller, farm director of the Texas Rangers, to Cliff Kachline, the historian of the National Baseball Hall of Fame, on file in the 1961 American League Expansion Draft folder in the A. Bartlett Giamatti Research Center at the National Baseball Hall of Fame, Cooperstown, NY.
11. *BASEBALL,* Office of the Commissioner, Official Bulletin No. 26, December 20, 1961, 2.
12. *BASEBALL,* Office of the Commissioner, Official Bulletin No. 14, August 15, 1962, 3.
13. *BASEBALL,* Office of the Commissioner, Official Bulletin No. 23, November 14, 1961, 3.
14. http://en.wikipedia.org/wiki/Garvin_Hamner.
15. Shantz could not compare with former NBA player George Wilson. Wilson was selected in three NBA expansion drafts (May 1, 1967 by the Seattle Super Sonics from the Chicago Bulls, May 6, 1968 by the Phoenix Suns from the Seattle, and May 11, 1970 by the Buffalo Braves from the Philadelphia 76ers) www.basketball-reference.com/players/w/wilsoge01.html.
16. BASEBALL, Office of the Commissioner, Official Bulletin No. 8, April 25, 1962, 3.
17. List compiled from information in 1962 National League Expansion Draft folder in the A. Bartlett Giamatti Research Center at the National Baseball Hall of Fame, Cooperstown, NY.
18. *Milwaukee Sentinel,* October 11, 1961, 11.
19. List compiled from www.retrosheet.org/boxesetc/1961/10101961.htm.
20. Clark Nealon, "Colts Corralled Slick Infielders, Richards Chirps," *The Sporting News,* October 18, 1961, 7.
21. Bob Burnes, "Draft Gives Colts, Mets Solid Send Off," *The Sporting News,* October 18, 1961, 7.
22. List compiled from retrosheet.org.

Dick "Turk" Farrell

Houston's First All-Star

Ron Briley

Pitcher Dick "Turk" Farrell was selected in 1962 to represent the expansion Houston Colt .45s franchise at both All-Star Games. In the expansion draft to fill the rosters of the new clubs in New York and Houston, the Mets elected to go with veterans, while Houston built on youth. Under manager Harry Craft and general manager Paul Richards, they focused on pitching, drafting such promising hurlers as Ken Johnson from the Cincinnati Reds and Dick Farrell from the Dodgers, in addition to trading for Bob Bruce from the Detroit Tigers. Blessed with an outstanding fastball, Farrell also enjoyed a reputation for being somewhat of a character and loving the party life. Many observers thought Houston had made a mistake, but Farrell's work on the mound for the Colt .45s silenced his critics.

Richard Joseph Farrell was born April 8, 1934, in Boston, Massachusetts. His mother, Mary, immigrated to the United States from County Mayo in Ireland during her teens, while his father, Tom, often referred to as Turk, was a grave keeper at Holyhood Cemetery. The family struggled to make ends meet during the Great Depression and then confronted illness when two-year-old Dick was diagnosed with polio. He was in braces until age six. His left leg remained shorter than his right and he walked with a slight limp the rest of his life.[1]

The health problems of his youth did not prevent Farrell from becoming an outstanding athlete at St. Mary's High School in Brookline, Massachusetts, where he earned varsity letters in basketball, football, and baseball. He struggled academically, though, and was forced to repeat 11th grade. After graduation, Farrell signed a contract with the Philadelphia Phillies and used part of his $5,000 signing bonus to send his mother back to Ireland, where she saw her family for the first time in over twenty years. At age 19 he was assigned to the Schenectady Blue Jays of the Class A Eastern League. In two seasons at Schenectady, Farrell went 18–18 with a club that provided little offensive support. His 3.21 ERA in 40 appearances in 1954 earned him a promotion to the Triple A Syracuse Chiefs of the International League. Pitching as both a starter

and in relief, Farrell won 12 games at Syracuse. While trying to break into the Phillies rotation, Farrell spent the 1956 season with the Triple A Miami Marlins owned by Bill Veeck. Despite missing time with a broken ankle, he won 12 and posted a 2.50 ERA before joining the Phillies at the end of the season.

Although Farrell had worked hard to make the big leagues, he was perceived as a free spirit and practical joker. He reportedly nailed the shoes of the legendary Satchel Paige to the clubhouse floor in Miami. Other tall tales abound. One that is oft-repeated is that in Schenectady Farrell stuck limburger cheese in the glove of catcher Clint Courtney, who was noted for his avoidance of showers, and bet his teammates that Courtney would catch at least one inning before noticing the

A childhood bout with polio did not prevent Turk Farrell from becoming an outstanding National League pitcher.

smell. Unfortunately Courtney and Farrell did not actually play together in Schenectady. Another story has the 6-foot-4, 215-pound Farrell allegedly slugging Marlins teammate Ed Bailey for mocking his Boston accent. But Bailey did not play for the Marlins then. That such stories accrued to Farrell regardless of veracity only cements his reputation.[2]

Farrell enjoyed an outstanding rookie campaign in 1957, appearing in 52 games, winning 10 and saving 10. The following season, Farrell continued his excellent work and was selected for his first All-Star game appearance, in which he struck out four, including Ted Williams, in two innings. The Phillies, however, seemed to have overworked their young pitcher, who stumbled during the second half of the 1958 campaign, finishing 8–9 in 54 games with a 3.35 ERA and plagued with control problems. Control did not return in 1959, and Farrell was briefly demoted to the minor leagues. Farrell finished the season with the Phillies, going 1–6 (with 6 saves) and an ERA that soared to 4.74.

Farrell's disappointing performance was also blamed on extracurricular activities with pitching teammates Jack Meyer and Jim Owens who became known as the Dalton Gang. In April 1959 Farrell was fined $250 by Phillies manager Eddie Sawyer for "conduct unbecoming a major league ball player" after smashing a mirror with his fist in a Milwaukee bar following a poor outing on the mound.[3] In a profile for *Sports Illustrated*, Walter Bingham described the Dalton Gang as "hell-raisers" and "a wild bunch," who came from diverse backgrounds. Meyer was from an affluent New Jersey

family and attended such schools as Philadelphia's Penn Charter School and Wake Forest University, while Owens was profiled as the product of a broken home where his father encouraged drinking at an early age. Farrell, on the other hand, was depicted as coming from a respectable family but Bingham wrote that he was unpredictable, "big and tough, occasionally unfriendly, occasionally abusive." Following a record fine for Meyer early in the 1960 season for fighting and tearing up a Pittsburgh hotel room, Bingham concluded, "Unlike some of the storied hell-raisers of old, the members of The Dalton Gang aren't really good enough to be so bad. Perhaps the fine Jack Meyer must pay will shock him and his friends into a more moderate way of life. If not, members of the Dalton Gang probably will find themselves riding elsewhere, and separately."[4]

Farrell had little use for the Bingham article, but responded in a positive fashion both on and off the playing field. Displaying a sense of humor, Farrell described a visit to the Dalton Gang Hideout and Museum in Meade, Kansas, which led him to quip that the pilgrimage to the old stomping grounds "brought back memories" and encouraged him to reform the gang.[5]

Farrell returned to form in 1960 and enjoyed a fine season. The big right-hander pitched in 59 games, winning 10 and saving 11, with a 2.70 ERA—although the Phillies still lost 95 games.

When Farrell got off to a slow start the following season, the Phillies traded him to the contending Dodgers. A change of scenery, however, did not help

Turk Farrell was Houston's first All-Star. The popular pitcher made four All-Star rosters while with Houston, and one with the Phillies.

NATIONAL BASEBALL HALL OF FAME LIBRARY, COOPERSTOWN, NY

Farrell get back on track. In 50 appearances with the Los Angeles club, Farrell struggled with his control, his ERA rose to 5.06, and the Dodgers failed to win the pennant. According to Farrell, Dodgers general manager Buzzie Bavasi blamed him for the club's disappointing finish and falsely accused him of attempting to form another gang.[6] Thus, it was not surprising that the Dodgers failed to protect Farrell in the expansion draft.

Houston planned to use Farrell primarily in a starting role after picking up relief pitcher Don McMahon from the Braves. He joined the Colt .45s with a positive attitude, but maintained his reputation for individualism. Taking a more disciplined approach toward spring training, Farrell told reporters, "I want to trim down to about 210. I went on a self-imposed diet. One poached egg for breakfast, fruit salads and cottage cheese the rest of the day. No more steaks." He also insisted upon walking the two miles from the hotel to spring training facilities at Geronimo Park in Apache Junction, Arizona, every day. But Farrell found a way to make that trek a little more exciting by carrying a .22 caliber target pistol and shooting at rabbits along the way. Acknowledging that he was shut out by the rabbits, Farrell vowed to be more successful in hunting wild hogs. In addition, he reassured reporters that the Dalton Gang stories were exaggerated and that he and Jim Owens had reached an out-of-court settlement with *Sports Illustrated*.[7]

Houston manager Harry Craft was certainly appreciative of Farrell's talent, noting, "He's one of the few pitchers in baseball today who can overpower a hitter with his fastball."[8] Craft's approach to managing also seemed a good fit with spirited players such as Farrell. In a profile for the *Houston Chronicle*, Craft was described as being "hired because of his ability to get along with players of all kinds and get the most out of each." In support of this assessment, Craft proclaimed, "I don't believe in belittling a player or tearing him down. Have confidence in your players and win their respect and you've taken a great stride in the direction of building a winning club." Craft asserted that he would not allow gambling by the players as it encouraged dissension, but curfews after a day game would be at midnight or two hours after the conclusion of a night game. Concluding his interview, Craft told reporters, "I want my players in condition to play, but I will not treat them like they were children."[9]

Craft's style was a good match for Farrell, and the pitcher stayed out of management's doghouse, focusing on his work on the mound. The Colts opened the 1962 season in Houston with a three-game sweep of the Chicago Cubs. In the second game, Farrell combined with Hal Woodeschick for a 2–0 shutout. On April 13 Farrell had an opportunity to pitch against his old teammates in Philadelphia. He responded with an excellent game, striking out nine while allowing only two hits in six innings of work. But the .45s struggled offensively and lost the game, 3–2.

Farrell also got a pinch of revenge: On June 16, he allowed three hits while surrendering one run at Dodger Stadium. Houston, from whom little was expected, found themselves at the first All-Star game break in eighth place, ahead of the Cubs and Mets.[10]

Farrell was the only Houston player to be selected for the National League All-Star squad by Cincinnati Reds manager Fred Hutchinson. Hutchinson resolved to not use Farrell because the right-hander had lost both games of a doubleheader to the Reds on the weekend before the All-Star break. But Farrell did work in 1962's second All-Star game and surrendered a three-run home run to Rocky Colavito. Farrell asserted that he was surprised at his selection, considering his modest won-loss record of 5–8. The anemic victory total was the result of little hitting support: Farrell had posted an ERA of 2.46 with four saves while working as both a starter and reliever.[11]

Farrell's selection was also a surprise because many in Houston assumed that Cuban-born outfielder Roman Mejias, drafted by the Colts from the Pirates, would represent the franchise. Through games of July 2, Mejias led Houston with 19 home runs and 48 RBIs, and was hitting .311. When Hutchinson picked Richie Ashburn of the Mets and Johnnie Callison of the Phillies as reserve outfielders, a disappointed Mejias lamented, "How do you like dot [sic]? Well, nothing to do but jus' keep swinging."[12] Mejias refused to pin this oversight on racism, but the Cuban outfielder was often portrayed by the press in stereotypical fashion. For example, in referring to Mejias's language difficulties in being able to order food during his early days in the United States, reporter Mickey Herskowitz wrote in *The Sporting News* that the outfielder, who had a bit of the "gaucho" in him, had emerged as, "Houston's ham, eggs, bread, butter, milk, and poultry man."[13] Mejias, however, was not in a position to purchase too many heavy cholesterol breakfasts. He was only making $12,500. In the era of the strict reserve clause and weak player representation, Mejias could not expect any mid-season correction to his contract. In addition, Mejias was concerned about his wife and two young children in Cuba, observing, "There is not much food there, and I worry if they are eating properly."[14] Whether from worry or exhaustion, Mejias did slump

Farrell pitched 241⅔ innings for the Colt .45s in 1962, with 203 strikeouts and a 3.02 ERA, but was saddled with 20 losses.

during the second half of the season, and that winter he was traded to the Boston Red Sox for first baseman and Texas native Pete Runnels—a transaction that did not work out well for either club.[15]

Meanwhile, Farrell continued to pitch well, albeit in hard luck, and avoid controversy...at least until a radio interview on July 21 with St. Louis Cardinals broadcaster Harry Caray. He admitted that the day before he had attempted to get Stan Musial out with an illegal spitball, but the Cardinal great had connected for a base hit. The incident was reported to the National League office which refused to order a fine or suspension for a radio comment. Farrell apologized for raising such a ruckus with his confession, pointing out that many pitchers such as Lew Burdette of the Braves were guilty of employing the illegal pitch on a regular basis. Facing reporters in the Colts locker room, Farrell concluded, "The spitball isn't a pitch of mine. I don't throw the thing because I can't control it. It would be easy to load 'em up out there. The sweat pours down your arm and into your palms. I could load up, but I don't. I go to the resin bag all the time. The spitball is not part of my repertoire. I threw it to Musial just for fun." The final word on the mini-controversy was left

to Farrell's catcher Hal Smith, who, observing that the right-hander had fanned twelve Cardinal batters, proclaimed, "Farrell doesn't need the spitball, and you can quote me."[16]

Despite the hard luck defeats that eventually resulted in a 20-loss season, Farrell kept his cool for the most part. On September 2, however, *The Sporting News* reported that Farrell was tossed by umpire Lee Weyer for arguing balls and strikes in a game that the Colts lost to the Cardinals, 3–1. The lone run scored by Houston marked only the second time that the club had plated a runner in over 32 innings with Farrell on the mound.[17] Meanwhile, Willie Mays described Farrell as a good pitcher who was "bush" for plunking the Giants center fielder after he had struck home runs in two consecutive at bats against him. Said Mays, "He's too good a pitcher to do that. He doesn't have to do that. The guy was just trying to start something when there was no need to."[18]

Mays would have the last laugh: on the final day of the 1962 season he hit a home run off Farrell that propelled the Giants into a playoff with the Dodgers and saddled Farrell with his 20th loss of the season. A pitcher must be fairly good to earn enough appearances to lose 20 games. Researcher David Skelton notes that of the approximately 500 pitchers who have lost 20 games in a season, Farrell's earned run average of 3.02 remains the best since Hall of Famer Jessie Haines of the St. Louis Cardinals posted a 2.68 mark in 1920.[19] The Colts were last offensively in the National League, yet they finished in eighth place ahead of the Cubs and Mets, with a 64–96 record.

Farrell's contributions to the club's success were certainly appreciated by management. Manager Harry Craft made it clear that Farrell was one of the few Colts off limits for trade offers. Craft asserted, "I don't think any other team could afford to give us as much as we'd have to get for Turk. I'm not sure he'd be as valuable to another club as he is to us. We've had to use him both as a starter and reliever, and he has done just a marvelous job."[20] General Manager Paul Richards was full of praise for Farrell, noting that with a contender the right-hander would have won 20 games. "Farrell's development was one of the most encouraging things in our building program, and he's a major part of the nucleus around which we plan to build a championship team in the future." Farrell's efforts were also acknowledged by his teammates. Fellow starter Bob Bruce observed, "The slip pitch and curve have made Turk a new pitcher. He's got such a great fastball, he throws the slipper and keeps the hitters off balance."[21]

Farrell downplayed his partying image during his 1962 All-Star season in Houston, and he moved his young family to the Texas city following the season. In 1963, he won 14 and matched his previous season's ERA of 3.02. The following year, after a start which seemed to offer the promise of a 20-win season, Farrell finished 11–10, 3.27. In 1965 Farrell surrendered the first home run ever hit in the Astrodome to Mickey Mantle of the Yankees in an exhibition game. He was selected for his fourth and final All-Star game appearance, winning 11 games, but he was beginning to lose something from his fastball. Following the 1966 season when his ERA ballooned to 4.60, the Houston Astros were open to trading Farrell, and early in the 1967 season they dispatched the former staff ace back to Philadelphia where he continued to pitch through the 1969 season.

After being released by the Phillies, Farrell tried to make it back to the major leagues with a number of teams, finally retiring in 1971 after a stint in the Mexican League. Beyond baseball, Farrell found employment with the Houston-based construction company Brown and Root. While working with the company on an off-shore oil rig in the North Sea, Farrell was killed in a head-on automobile crash in Great Yarmouth, England on June 10, 1977 at age 43. Obituaries in *The New York Times* and *The Sporting News* emphasized Farrell's reputation as a member of the Dalton Gang rather than his impressive performance as the Houston franchise's first All-Star. Columnist Dick Young of the *New York Daily News* wrote, "Fans who followed the Phillies Dalton Gang in the late '50s were shaken by the news that Dick Farrell was killed in an auto crash in England. Turk was a charter member of that colorful team. His blazing fastball frightened batters. A foul ball off Farrell in the first inning of a relief appearance was considered a big achievement."[22] Farrell's reputation as a character and charter member of the Dalton Gang tended to overshadow the legacy of his pitching performance, but there is little doubt that Houston's first All-Star was always a competitor when on the mound, completing his 14-year career with 590 appearances, 106 victories, 83 saves, 1,177 strikeouts, and a 3.45 ERA. ■

Notes

1. For a biographical sketch of Farrell see David E. Skelton, "Turk Farrell," Bioproject, Society for American Baseball Research, http://sabr.org/bioproj/person/180d81d6 (February 19, 2014).
2. Robert Reed, *Colt .45s: A Six-Gun Salute* (Houston, Texas: Lone Star Books, 1999), 129.
3. "A Frolic with Farrell," *The Sporting News*, June 8, 1963, 28.
4. Walter Bingham, "The Dalton Gang Rides Again," *Sports Illustrated*, 12:24 (June 13, 1960), 24–6.
5. "A Frolic with Farrell," *The Sporting News*, June 8, 1963, 28.
6. Reed, *Colt .45s*, 128-9.
7. Zarko Franks, "Righthander Farrell Talk of Colt Camp," *Houston Chronicle*, February 25, 1962, section 8, 2.
8. Ibid.
9. "Craft Brings Out Best in Players," *Houston Chronicle*, January 21, 1962, section 8, 1.
10. Clark Nealon, "Mound Stars Firing Bullets for Colt .45s," *The Sporting News*, June 30, 1962, 10.
11. "Farrell First Houston Pitcher Selected on N. L. Star Squad," *The Sporting News*, July 14, 1962. 20.
12. Reed, *Colt .45s*, 112–13.
13. Mickey Herskowitz, ".45s Change Puny Attack with Miracle Man Mejias," *The Sporting News*, June 2, 1962, 23.
14. Zarco Franks, "Mejias's Season of Milk, Honey," *Houston Chronicle*, May 30, 1962, section B, 1.
15. For an overview of Mejias's 1962 season in Houston see Ron Briley, *Class at Bat, Gender on Deck, and Race in the Hole: A Line-up of Essays on Twentieth Century Culture and America's Game* (Jefferson, NC: McFarland & Company, 2003), 250–65.
16. Clark Nealon, "Farrell Drops Bomb in Spitter Confession," *The Sporting News*, August 4, 1962, 26.
17. "Farrell Thumbed from Hill after Beefing at Ump Weyes," *The Sporting News*, September 1, 1962, 15.
18. Bob Odem, "Farrell Good Hurler but He's Bush," *Houston Chronicle*, July 25, 1962, section C, 1.
19. David Skelton, "Turk Farrell," Bioproject, Society for American Baseball Research http://sabr.org/bioproj/person/180d81d6 (February 19, 2014).
20. Clark Nealon, "Ex-Hill Dud Brunet First Bullet Slants as Colt .45 Player," *The Sporting News*, September 8, 1962, 14.
21. Clark Nealon, "Farrell Rated Double-Barreled Dilly by .45s," *The Sporting News*, November 3, 1962, 7.
22. "Turk Farrell, 'Ex-Pitcher, Killed in Auto Accident," *The New York Times*, June 13, 1977; "Obituaries," *The Sporting News*, July 2, 1977, 34; and Dick Young, "Young Ideas," *The Sporting News*, July 2, 1977, 15.

The 1963 Pepsi Cola Colt .45s Baseball Card Set

Charles Harrison

This article investigates the 1963 Pepsi Cola Colt .45s Baseball Card Set, documents rarities, and identifies why certain of these cards are rare, drawing attention to this set that is obscure to all except the most sophisticated collectors.

In 1963 the Houston Colt .45s were relatively new to the baseball world and Pepsi Cola hoped to capitalize on the promotional value of that novelty. The company issued a set of 16 trading cards on relatively thin card stock. Each card measured $2\frac{7}{16}$ inches by $9\frac{1}{8}$ inches featuring a black and white picture of a Colt .45 player, a schedule, and ads in the form of tabs which are often cut off by collectors to make a more standard-sized card. These cards were distributed in the local Houston and Beaumont/Port Arthur area and possibly other local markets. This set has an American Card Catalog designation of F230-3 and was designed as an insert for six pack cartons of Pepsi Cola. They were free to kids who could talk their parents into buying Pepsi by the carton.

So why are some of these cards rarer than others? There is a clue to this in an article written by Mike Anderson which appeared in the April 12, 1985, issue of *Sports Collectors Digest* (SCD pages 144–5). Anderson states in his article that he was living in Beaumont, Texas in 1963, but there were cards he could never find in the Pepsi cartons. He eventually went to the distributor, where workers on the loading dock told him to go look in the dumpster. Pepsi relied on truck drivers to insert the cards into the cartons and the drivers found it much easier to just throw them away. If so, many more cards were printed than collected.

In the dumpster, Anderson found many copies of cards featuring 14 players, but not others—i.e. one Carl Warwick but no John Bateman. Assuming that this was common practice by distributors, all of these cards are likely relatively scarce, but not necessarily rare. It also suggests that not all of the cards were printed at the same time and some may not have ever made it to public distribution.

I have been able to find only two additional articles about this set after Anderson's. His was accompanied by a picture of Bateman, but it was not a picture of the 1963 Bateman Colt .45 card. The featured set in the May 1, 1987, *Sports Collectors Digest* price guide section (page 110) states that the Bateman was apparently not distributed publicly and declared its value at $300. No picture of the Bateman card appears in that article either.

In the October 1988 *Baseball Hobby News*, Lew Lipset's sale item number 26 is for a set of 15 of the 16 Pepsi Cola Colt .45 cards from Dick Reuss's collection. Bateman is the missing card.

Bert Randolph Sugar states on page 14 of *The Sports Collectors Bible* that this card is "not seen frequently." Today, most price guides acknowledge that the Carl Warwick card (one of which was found by Mike Anderson) is rare and the John Bateman card is extremely rare. When these cards occasionally come up for sale as a set, it is usually a set of 14 missing Warwick and Bateman, and once in a while, a set of 15 missing the Bateman.

I am often dismayed when I see modern day cards advertised for sale in publications or on auction sites described as "rare." The word is misused in the hobby as much as "great" is by sportscasters. A good example

Catcher John Bateman spent the first six years of his ten in the major leagues with Houston, 1963–68

PEPSI·COLA

JOHN BATEMAN
CATCHER

COLT .45s

JOHN BATEMAN
CATCHER

Bats right. Throws right. Hgt. 6-3.
Weight 200. Born: July 21, 1942

1962 Record

Modesto (Calif.)

G	AB	H	2B	3B	HR	RBI	SB	AVG
121	435	122	25	2	21	75	5	.280

Has played only one season of pro ball . . .
played in Arizona Instructional League
1962 . . . attended Lawton, Oklahoma high
school playing baseball, football and
basketball . . . played three years of
American Legion baseball.

This could be the rarest baseball card issued since World War II.

of a truly rare find is the U.S. Caramel (R328) number 16 which was unknown until recently. The famous T206 Wagner card can legitimately be described as rare.

In the case of the 1963 Colt .45s set, their rarity equalled obscurity, even for me, a serious collector. I spent my entire life between Bay City and the golden triangle and I was never aware of this set. I had been a serious collector 1951–56 and from about 1974 until the present. Even though it was the only regional set issued in the area where I lived most of my life, and despite how active in the hobby I was—subscribing to trade publications, attending shows—I had never encountered or heard of it. That was about to change.

I moved to Houston in February 1979, before the age of the Internet and smart phones, to find my new office building had a bulletin board. Eager to tap into the big city market, I put an ad on that board: "I buy baseball cards." I also advertised in local newspapers. It wasn't long before I had bought a small lot of about a dozen nice U.S. Caramels. They were very desirable cards and I thought a nice find. My ad remained up and about May a fellow contacted me and said he had a sack of cards he wished to sell. He brought me a small brown bag about the size of a typical lunch bag full of cards. I was very busy and quickly scanned the cards. They seemed to all be 1961–64 Topps and I guessed there were about 300. I bought them without going through the cards in detail. He said he had acquired them all in Houston. He also had a friend who had some cards and he would let him know about me. His friend had lived in Houston, but was now in the Dallas area.

I took the cards home and put them aside until the weekend. Upon a closer look, I found 24 cards that I had never seen before. They were 1963 Pepsi Cola Colt .45s without tabs. I was disappointed. While I knew nothing about the set, there was a lot of duplication with only four different players. I had one Carl Warwick, two J.C. Hartmans, 11 Ken Johnsons, and 10 John Batemans. Within a month, I found a dealer in a local flea-market who had several different cards from this set and he was willing to trade me 2-for-1 for my doubles. He promised to hold the cards for me until I returned with my cards in two weeks. I dutifully returned, cards in hand to trade, only to find he had sold them 30 minutes earlier to a 12-year-old boy. I was irritated that the dealer's word was not good, but since I was already there, I decided to tour the flea-market. I happened upon the boy who had bought the cards and offered to trade with him at two for one. He was tempted, but I was a grown man and he was afraid of me as I probably came on too strong out of frustration.

I put the cards away in June of 1979 and forgot about them for about six months. I was still unaware of the rarity of any of these cards or even how many were in the set. For Christmas my sister-in-law gave me a copy of *Sports Collectors Bible*. (This is now out of print. The last edition was likely published in 1984.) While thumbing through it at random, I opened to page 74 and began to read about the Pepsi regional set distributed in Houston. The phrase "not seen frequently and is very scarce" referring to the Bateman card caught my eye. It also estimated the value at that time at $275–350, similar to the Anderson article. This was the first clue that maybe I had made a good deal by purchasing the lot and also by not being successful in my trade efforts. Christmas that year was at my in-laws' home so I had to wait until that evening to see if my memory was good. When I got home I immediately went to check and was pleased to find I had 10 copies of the very rare Bateman card.

In 1985 the friend of the man I had bought the cards from said he had found a shoebox full of cards and wanted to know if I was interested. We agreed to a price without me seeing the cards and he mailed them to me. In this box of cards were two more Batemans which brought my total to 12. In the interim between 1979 and 1985 I had seen one more of these cards at a Houston baseball card shop. This brought the total different Batemans I had seen with my own eyes to 13, all in the Houston area. All 13 were without the tabs. I have never found another one or even a photo of one since in the following 29 years of active collecting. It seems very likely that my 12 were all from the same source because I got them from two friends.

I believe the Bateman card may be the rarest baseball card issued since World War II. I would not venture a guess as to what it is worth, but would say it is certainly not the $300 put forth in the 1980s. Generally cards, like houses, are priced on the basis of comparable recent sales and there are no recent sales that I know of. If a Bateman card with tabs were to surface, I would venture that it would certainly be the rarest card since the war. And how remarkable that such a "rare" card was issued right here in Houston. ∎

If any of you have or know of copies of this card I would appreciate you contacting me to help better establish the true number in existence. My contact information is as follows:

Charles Harrison
218 Haven Brook Lane, Richmond, Texas 77406
W: (713) 235–5110 / H: (281) 342–1434
email: charriso@bechtel.com

The details of the events I have outlined can be corroborated by a few individuals who were close to me and aware of the transactions, including wife Virginia, my son Brian, my cousin Vernon Harrison, and my friend Sam Cochran. Sam, Vernon, and Brian are also serious collectors. Each has laid eyes on the 12 that I owned, but none saw the 13th card which was sold to Will Weber. All 13 cards were without tabs and I have never seen or been aware of one with tabs. All 15 of the other cards in the set do exist with tabs. I would be very interested to know if anyone is aware of other Bateman cards from this set and if they have ever seen one with tabs. I would like to establish if any other examples exist so I can document how many exist. I would bet fewer than 20. It would be interesting to know if the 13 I am aware of were obtained by someone working for Pepsi or their printer and none were in fact ever released to the public.

At this time I still have 7 of my original 12. My son Brian has one so our family still has 8. I am not in contact with Will Weber, but suspect he still has his so that accounts for 9. What happened to my other 4? I sold one card to an Oklahoma dealer who bought it for a customer in Nebraska. I cannot remember the dealer's name and I never knew the customer's name. I traded two cards to Bill Heitman, a dealer/collector from California for, among other things, a 1952 Topps Mickey Mantle. (Editor's Note: The 1952 Topps Mickey Mantle is described by Professional Sports Authenticators as "the most valuable post-war sportscard." One in gem mint condition sold for $275,000 in 2001.) The last card was traded to a collector in the San Francisco area for, among other things, a Zeenut Joe DeMaggio (that is how it is spelled on the card).

Astros 1, Mets 0

Almost Three Games in One

John McMurray

T*he Sporting News* neatly summarized the April 15, 1968, game played at the Astrodome between the New York Mets and the Houston Astros in a classic headline: "24 Innings, Six Hours, One Run."[1] Surely fans who attended this Monday night game could not have anticipated that they were going to witness a total of 158 at-bats but only 22 hits, 23½ consecutive scoreless innings, and 39 participating players, three of whom had at least nine at-bats without a hit.

The Mets, managed by Gil Hodges, entered the early-season game with a record of 2–2, while Grady Hatton's Houston team was 4–1. Sophomore Don Wilson of the Astros was tasked with facing Tom Seaver, who was coming off a strong and often dominant rookie season for New York. Given the quality pitching matchup, the 14,219 fans in attendance may have anticipated a low-scoring affair.

The first inning was uneventful: Wilson, with Hal King as his catcher, set down Al Weis, Ken Boswell, and Tommie Agee in order.[2] Seaver then did the same, retiring Ron Davis, Norm Miller, and Jim Wynn. The second inning, however, was pivotal. Had things gone differently, the two teams might have avoided becoming the first teams to play at least 21 innings without scoring a run.[3] Though the top half of the inning was scoreless, it included the first hit, a two-out single from Mets first baseman Ed Kranepool before Wilson could retire the side.

In the bottom half of the second inning, Seaver ran into the only real trouble that he would experience in the ten innings that he pitched. After Rusty Staub had flied out to right field, King doubled to left. A wild pitch moved King to third. A *New York Times* account described the play that followed: "Bob Aspromonte hit a sharp grounder to second. Boswell fielded it cleanly, took his time, and threw accurately to the plate. King, however, slammed into [Jerry] Grote, and although the Mets' catcher fell, he made the tag and held the ball."[4] Julio Gotay then popped out to end the inning.

The missed opportunity for Houston would be the last time the team would get a runner to third base until the 22nd inning. The Mets also would get a runner to third three times without scoring (in the 12th, 17th, and 19th innings).

In the top of the third inning, the Mets got a runner into scoring position in an unconventional way. With two outs, Weis—playing at shortstop in place of Bud Harrelson, who was out with a sore arm—walked, and Boswell was then able to reach base on a wild pitch with two strikes.[5] With runners on first and second, Agee was unable to deliver, flying out to right field to end the inning. After going 0-for-10 in this game, Agee's batting average would fall from .313 to .192.[6]

Beginning with the bottom of the third inning, the two pitchers settled into a rhythm of retiring the side with relative ease or, as Vito Stellino described it,

In his second full season, Don Wilson had established himself as one of the National League's hardest throwers.

"matched scores for what seemed like forever."[7] Seaver retired the Houston batters in order in every inning from the third through the ninth. Wilson was less efficient, allowing a single to Art Shamsky in the fourth (and allowing him to reach second base on Wilson's own errant pickoff throw) before retiring the side.

Oddly, in a game remembered for its lack of offense, Wilson gave up a single to Seaver in the fifth before retiring the side. Kranepool hit a leadoff single in the seventh and was sacrificed to second base before failing to advance further, even as Wilson walked Seaver in the meantime.

In spite of these blips, the Mets were never again close to scoring against Wilson, except perhaps in the ninth inning, when Kranepool reached second base with two outs, though that rally too was snuffed out by Houston. Once Lee Thomas pinch-hit for him in the bottom of the ninth inning, Wilson was out of the game, having faced 36 batters, given up five hits, and made two wild pitches. He obviously did not give up a run.

Seaver continued into the 10th inning, retiring Miller and Wynn before giving up a two-out single to Staub. Hodges left Seaver in the game with a runner on first and two outs, and the manager's confidence was rewarded, as Seaver got King to hit a grounder which forced Staub at second to end the inning. As Joseph Durso noted in *The New York Times*, "Seaver…pitched ten innings this time, allowed no runs and only two hits—and still was 14 innings short of a decision."[8]

In the meantime, John Buzhardt was quietly efficient in relief of Wilson, retiring the side in order in both the 10th and 11th innings, departing only when Doug Rader pinch-hit for him in the bottom of the 11th. (Rader, alas, flied to right.) Ron Taylor came in to pitch the 11th, replacing Seaver, and allowed only a single in his one inning of work.

The Mets made things interesting in the 12th against Danny Coombs, who had replaced Rader. The left-handed reliever began the inning by striking out Ed Charles, but Jerry Grote and Al Weis each singled around a Phil Linz popup, putting runners on first and second with two out. Ken Boswell then singled to load the bases, but Agee grounded out to second, thwarting the rally. Wrote Durso after the game: "One of the haunting memories of the night for the Mets was the hitting of their 'big men,' Agee and Swoboda, who hit third and fourth. Between them they went 0 for 20, with nine strikeouts."[9]

Cal Koonce came in to pitch the bottom of the 12th inning for the Mets, but he had the shortest stint of the game (⅓ of an inning), giving up a single to Davis and retiring Miller on a sacrifice. Bill Short came in to

Grady Hatton's victory in this game was perhaps the highlight of his 1968 season, as he was replaced as manager by Harry Walker after 61 games.

put out that fire, yielding an intentional walk and then retiring both Staub and King. Coombs, having settled down after his bumpy entrance in the 12th, retired New York in order in the top of the 13th.

The bottom of the 13th inning offered more ups and downs. When Short gave up a single to Gotay and then walked Hector Torres, Hatton called on Dick Selma, who retired the only two batters he faced. Jim Ray took care of the Mets in order in the top of the 14th, while Al Jackson retired Miller, Wynn, and Staub on three groundouts to end the inning. Then both Ray and Jackson each retired the side again in order in the 15th.

After Ray retired the Mets in order (again) in the top of the 16th, Jackson received the benefit of good defense in the bottom of the inning. Torres reached base on a leadoff bunt single, and Ray attempted to sacrifice Torres to second. As Durso described it: "The Mets came up with the play of the night in the 16th. Hector Torres was on first base with Ray at bat in a bunting situation. So Hodges pulled the old Brooklyn shift. He called in Ron Swoboda from right field, gave him a first-baseman's mitt and stationed him on first. Ed Kranepool moved way in toward the plate to field the bunt. The outfield was left to Tommie Agee and Cleon Jones. After that, Ray struck out."[10]

Though Hatton may be faulted for not pinch-hitting for Ray with a runner on first in the 16th, Ray was likely the unsung hero of the game for Houston, pitching seven shutout innings and striking out 11 while allowing only two hits. The Mets touched him only for a double in the 17th inning, and, with a runner on third, Ray managed to get Harrelson to strike out on a squeeze attempt and then Weis to ground out.

After those struggles, Ray went on to strike out the side in the top of the 18th inning. The Astros, however, were unable to gain any traction against New York's Danny Frisella, who retired the Astros in order

Rusty Staub was a gritty player who broke in with Houston as a 19-year-old in 1963 and played the first six of his 23 big league seasons there. If only he had scored instead of being stranded on third in the 22nd inning.

in the 17th inning and gave up only a two-out single to New York in the 18th.

Another critical juncture occurred in the top of the 19th inning. Against Ray, who had been sailing along, Cleon Jones began the inning with a single and advanced to second on Kranepool's sacrifice. Ray then walked Charles intentionally. According to the account in the *Chicago Tribune*, "Grote struck out. But Jones and Charles were running on the pitch and stole second and third. Since he was now running out of players, Hodges let pitcher Danny Frisella bat for himself and he struck out."[11] The Astros were out of the inning, and Ray stayed on to pitch one last scoreless inning before lefty Wade Blasingame replaced him to start the 21st.

Frisella stayed in the game for the Mets and pitched effectively. In the 19th, he got out of a jam with runners on first and second with two out; in the 20th, he got out of the inning when Gotay was caught stealing as Torres stuck out; and in the 21st, Miller was caught stealing to end the inning. Frisella remained in the game until Don Cardwell pinch-hit for him in the top of the 22nd inning, after which Les Rohr came in to pitch for the Mets.

With the exception of some struggles in the 22nd inning, Blasingame pitched well—and well enough to earn the victory. He faced the minimum in the 21st, 23rd, and 24th innings, running into trouble only in the 22nd, when he retired Weis with Grote on second base and two out. For the Mets, Rohr had an uneven time, walking two (one intentionally) in the 22nd before striking out Gotay with Staub, the potential winning run, on third base with two out.

The game was decided in the bottom of the 24th inning. Norm Miller singled to start the inning (and,

surprisingly, got the only hit of the inning). Rohr then balked by "breaking his hands" accidentally, which moved Miller to second.[12] Jim Wynn was walked intentionally, putting runners on first and second. A groundout by Staub moved the two runners into scoring position. With one out, Rohr walked John Bateman intentionally to load the bases. Bob Aspromonte's grounder then went through Weis's legs at shortstop, allowing the winning run to score and ending the marathon game.

According to Durso: "It might have been a double play grounder ending the threat and putting everybody into the 25th inning. But the ball skidded off the chemical carpet known as the Astroturf and went right through Weis' legs into left field while Miller scored the only run of the night."[13] The *Tribune* account said, "When Norm Miller scored from third, he gleefully jumped on home plate and was mobbed by his teammates and Manager Grady Hatton."[14]

The *Washington Post* noted the next day that "Weis had played brilliantly for 23 innings, but he sank to his knees from sheer exhaustion as the ball went through his legs. 'I just plain blew it,' said Weis."[15]

Weis, as Stellino noted, was playing out of position when he made his critical error, as he was typically a second baseman who was forced to play shortstop due to Harrelson's injury.[16] Still, there was no denying that Weis's error was the game's consequential play.

"Baseball's longest night was filled with moments of humor, drama, dullness, and frustration—but, most of all, it was a nightmare for Al Weis," commented Stellino.[17]

Accounts vary regarding the number of fans there when the game ended at 1:37 AM, six hours and six minutes after it began; estimates range from 1,000 to

3,000 fans remained.[18] According to the *Tribune*, "The few fans who remained were noisy to the end despite a Texas state law which forbids the sale of liquors after midnight. Houston officials announced they were cooking breakfast for the press in the 23rd inning and said if the game lasted any longer, they would start preparing lunch."[19]

At its conclusion, the Astros-Mets game was the longest game with a winner. (The 26-inning game between the Brooklyn Robins and Boston Braves played on May 1, 1920, ended in a 1–1 tie.) Since then, the St. Louis Cardinals beat the New York Mets in a 25-inning game on September 11, 1974, and the Chicago White Sox beat the Milwaukee Brewers in 25 innings on May 8, 1984. The Detroit Tigers and Philadelphia Athletics also played to a 1–1 tie in 24 innings on July 21, 1945.[20]

Arthur Daley of *The New York Times* outlined the poor regard in which the Mets were held following this loss, saying: "Maybe they're trying to tell us something. The message has to be that they can't hit worth a damn."[21]

At the same time, Daley emphasized the striking way that the game ended on an error, commenting: "Historians used to say that 'everything happens to the Dodgers.' It certainly appeared that way, too. Let there be one wayward happening or unlikely incident and it was a cinch that the Brooklyns were involved in it. Now it has to seem that the Mets have inherited that dubious distinction….The Mets fancy up everything in a reverse alchemy that turns gold to dross."[22] On the other hand, the Astros were in first place following the game.

Stellino noted that the Mets caught a plane right after the game for New York—it had originally been scheduled to arrive in New York at four AM, but the game ended only 83 minutes before that."[23] Both teams, fortunately, had a day off on April 16.[24] Stunningly, both catchers—Grote for the Mets and King for the Astros—caught every inning for their respective teams.

As Gil Hodges said following the game: "These long games can really be murder."[25] ∎

Acknowlegments

With thanks to the Baseball Hall of Fame for providing clippings of vintage articles cited in this piece.

Notes

1. Vito Stellino, "24 Innings, Six Hours, One Run," *The Sporting News*, April 27, 1968.
2. Play-by-play of this game may be found via Baseball-Reference.com at www.baseball-reference.com/boxes/HOU/HOU196804150.shtml.
3. "Astros Beat Mets, 1–0, in 24 Innings!: Longest Scoreless Game Ends on Error by Weis," *Chicago Tribune*, April 16, 1968.
4. "Mets Lose in 24th, Longest Night Game," *The New York Times*, April 16, 1968.
5. Stellino, "24 Innings, Six Hours, One Run."
6. "After 24-Inning Encounter, Astros, Mets Glad for Rest," *Washington Post*, April 17, 1968.
7. Stellino, "24 Innings, Six Hours, One Run."
8. Joseph Durso, "Mets Will Oppose Giants in Home Opener at Shea Stadium Today," *The New York Times*, April 17, 1968.
9. Ibid.
10. Ibid.
11. "Astros Beat Mets, 1–0, in 24 Innings!: Longest Scoreless Game Ends on Error by Weis," *Chicago Tribune*.
12. Durso, "Mets Will Oppose Giants in Home Opener at Shea Stadium Today."
13. Ibid.
14. "Astros Beat Mets 1–0 in 24 Innings!" *Chicago Tribune*.
15. "After 24-Inning Encounter, Astros, Mets Glad for Rest," *Washington Post*.
16. Stellino, "24 Innings, Six Hours, One Run."
17. Ibid.
18. See Stellino and also "After 24-Inning Encounter, Astros, Mets Glad for Rest," *Washington Post*.
19. "Astros Beat Mets 1–0 in 24 Innings!" *Chicago Tribune*.
20. "The 10 Longest MLB Games of All Time," Yahoo Sports. Available at http://sports.yahoo.com/news/10-longest-mlb-games-time-204400545--mlb.html
21. Arthur Daley, "The Marathoners," *The New York Times*, April 17, 1968.
22. Ibid.
23. Stellino, "24 Innings, Six Hours, One Run," *The Sporting News*.
24. Ibid.
25. "After 24-Inning Encounter, Astros, Mets Glad for Rest," *Washington Post*.

The 1968 All-Star Game

Brendan Bingham

In the early 1960s, each of the recent expansion cities played host to the MLB All-Star Game, New York in 1964, Anaheim in 1967, Houston in 1968, and Washington DC in 1969.

The 1968 baseball season took place against a backdrop of racial violence. The late 1960s trembled with social and political turbulence, with the summer of 1968 at its epicenter. The season's Opening Day games were postponed due to Dr. Martin Luther King Jr.'s funeral.[1] Throughout the year, rioting took place in many American cities, including Detroit, Baltimore, Louisville, and Miami.[2] The All-Star Game in Houston on Tuesday July 9 was a mere five weeks after the assassination of Robert Kennedy in Los Angeles and seven weeks before the violent demonstrations at the Democratic National Convention in Chicago.

Houston experienced some unrest, but less than many American cities. The Texas Southern University riot of 1967 and the 1970 shooting death of militant activist Carl Hampton stand as Houston's two most noteworthy cases of racial violence during that era.[3,4] Reflective of the city's place in the political landscape of the time, in 1966 Houston had elected Barbara Jordan to the Texas State Senate. Jordan was the first African American since 1883 to serve in that capacity, and in 1973 she would become her state's first woman and first African American since 1883 to serve in the U.S. House of Representatives.[5]

On the professional sports scene, Houston had been the solution to a racial problem a few years earlier. In January 1965 the American Football League All-Star Game was scheduled to take place in New Orleans, but a player boycott in response to racial discrimination in the city threatened cancellation of the game. The game was instead played in Houston.[6] Given the tenor of the times, Houston was a good place for Major League Baseball to showcase its talent in the 1968 mid-summer classic.

Starting position players were elected to the All-Star team by the leagues' players in 1968. Fan voting had last taken place in 1957, the year of the Cincinnati ballot box stuffing incident, and would not be re-instituted until 1970.[7] The AL player vote produced this starting roster:

Bill Freehan (C, Det)
Harmon Killebrew (1B, Min)
Rod Carew (2B, Min)
Brooks Robinson (3B, Bal)
Jim Fregosi (SS, Cal)
Frank Howard (OF, Was)
Carl Yastrzemski (OF, Bos)
Willie Horton (OF, Det)

Regular-season left fielders Yastrzemski and Horton started in center and right field, respectively. Robinson was the AL starter who was most experienced in All-Star competition, making the team for a twelfth time, while Howard, who led the AL in home runs at mid-season, was in his first All-Star contest.[8]

The NL voting resulted in this roster of starters:
Jerry Grote (C, NY)
Willie McCovey (1B, SF)
Tommy Helms (2B, Cin)
Ron Santo (3B, Chi)
Don Kessinger (SS, Chi)
Pete Rose (OF, Cin)
Curt Flood (OF, StL)
Henry Aaron (OF, Atl)[9]

Aaron, having narrowly edged Willie Mays (SF) for the third starting outfield position, was the only surprising selection.[10] Aaron had struggled through May and June, batting only .195 for the two-month period, but he would return to form after the All-Star break, ending the season with 29 home runs and a .287 batting average.[11] Rose suffered a broken thumb only days before the All-Star break and would be replaced in the starting lineup by Mays.[12]

AL manager Dick Williams of Boston assembled a pitching staff of Luis Tiant (Cle), Sam McDowell (Cle), Tommy John (Chi), Denny McLain (Det), John "Blue Moon" Odom (Oak), Mel Stottlemyre (NY), and Jose Santiago (Bos),[13] with the injured Santiago later being replaced by his teammate, pitcher Gary Bell.[14] Tiant

The Astrodome hosted the 1968 midsummer classic, the first All-Star Game to be played at night.

and McLain were the league's most dominant pitchers at mid-season, en route to their post-season honors, the AL ERA title for Tiant and the MVP and Cy Young awards for 31-game winner McLain. Although it would later become customary to rest All-Star pitchers on the weekend prior to the break, in 1968 this practice was not yet in place, limiting how Williams could deploy his pitchers for the game. McLain and Stottlemyre had each pitched complete games on the Sunday before the All-Star Game, and Tiant had gone 6⅓ innings.

To complete the AL roster, Williams chose catchers Joe Azcue (Cle) and Duane Josephson (Chi), first basemen Mickey Mantle (NY) and Boog Powell (Bal), second baseman Davey Johnson (Bal), third baseman Don Wert (Det), shortstop Bert Campaneris (Oak), and outfielders Rick Monday (Oak), Ken Harrelson (Bos), and Tony Oliva (Min).[15] All but Mantle and Oliva were first-time All-Stars.

NL manager Red Schoendienst selected a pitching staff of Don Drysdale (LA), Steve Carlton (StL), Bob Gibson (StL), Woody Fryman (Phi), Juan Marichal (SF), Ron Reed (Atl), Tom Seaver (NY), and Jerry Koosman (NY).[16] Ninth-time honoree Drysdale and eighth-timer Marichal brought the most All-Star experience to the staff, while Carlton, Fryman, Koosman, and Reed were first-time All-Stars. Koosman and Seaver were the only NL hurlers who had pitched on the Sunday before the break, but they had not been taxed, combining for one relief inning to close out a

Mets victory. Of greater consequence, a day earlier Gibson and Marichal had faced off against each other in a game at Candlestick Park in which both went the full nine innings. At season's end, Gibson would be the NL's MVP and Cy Young Award winner, with Marichal finishing fifth in the MVP voting.

The NL roster was filled out with catchers Johnny Bench (Cin) and Tom Haller (LA), first baseman Rusty Staub (Hou), second baseman Julian Javier (StL), third baseman Tony Perez (Cin), shortstop Gene Alley (Pit)—later replaced by Leo Cardenas (Cin)[17]—and outfielders Felipe Alou (Atl), Matty Alou (Pit), and Billy Williams (Chi).[18] Williams was the roster replacement for the injured Rose.[19] In contrast to their AL counterparts, the NL reserves were mostly an experienced lot, with only Bench and Matty Alou as first-time All-Stars.

The game was the first mid-summer classic to be played indoors. Calling attention to it also being one of the first All-Star Games broadcast in prime time, *The New York Times* writer Leonard Koppett referred to the venue as "the world's largest television studio and only indoor ballpark."[20] The Astrodome was in only its fourth year of existence, and the game would be the first chance that most of the AL All-Stars would have to play there. Schoendienst, the St. Louis skipper, denied that there would be a home field advantage for his squad of All-Stars. "Our club comes in here three times a year," he noted, "and it takes us a couple of games to get used to it each time."[21]

COURTESY OF THE HOUSTON ASTROS

Houston's lone All-Star in 1968 was first baseman Rusty Staub, who pinch hit in the sixth inning.

Play began auspiciously enough for the AL team. Fregosi led off the game with a double, but he would get no farther than third base, as Drysdale, starting his fifth All-Star Game, set down Carew, Yastrzemski, and Howard to quell the threat.[22] The AL would not produce another baserunner until late in the game, as Drysdale, Marichal, and Carlton handcuffed the AL hitters through the sixth inning.

For the NL the opportunities came early and often. Mays led off the bottom of the first with a single. A series of missteps followed. Before offering another pitch, starter Tiant made two pick off throws to first base, the second of which caught Mays off base. He would have been out, except that the throw got past Killebrew. Mays advanced to second, and Tiant was charged with an error. Flood then walked. Two on, no out would have been bad enough, but to make matters worse, ball four was a wild pitch, advancing Mays to third. McCovey then grounded into a double play, scoring Mays. Tiant allowed another walk, to Aaron, but then ended the inning by inducing Santo to ground out. Mays's run was unearned, and no RBI was awarded, but the damage was done. The NL led, 1–0.

As the game proceeded, the NL team threatened, but failed to build on their lead. Facing Tiant, Helms led off the second inning with a double to right field, but two strike outs and a fly ball ended the inning. Odom offered up walks to Santo and Helms in the fourth, but allowed no hits and no runs. McLain walked Flood in the bottom of the fifth, but allowed no further damage. A sixth-inning Aaron single and stolen base followed by a Santo base on balls made for the beginnings of another rally, but McLain worked out of

the jam, retiring Helms, Staub, and Williams. The NL's last base runners came in the bottom of the seventh, when Matty Alou beat out an infield single, and Santo singled in the eighth.

Meanwhile, it was the top of the seventh before the AL threatened to snap the shutout. Oliva touched Seaver for a double to left-center field. The ball struck high off the outfield wall, just shy of becoming a game-tying home run, but the rally ended as the next batter, Azcue, struck out. The AL managed another two-out double in the eighth, this one by Wert, but Seaver struck out Monday to end the threat.

To face the AL in the top of the ninth, Schoendienst chose Reed, who did not disappoint. The tall right hander retired Campaneris on a grounder to third and Johnson on a strike out. Koosman closed the game with a strike out of Yastrzemski to seal the 1–0 NL victory.

In the heat of battle, it is best to remember that the All-Star Game is an exhibition, the outcome of little consequence no matter how seriously the players might take it. The bottom of the third inning offered such a reminder. Fregosi's throw to first on a Flood ground ball headed wide of the mark. Killebrew made an all-out stretch and successfully fielded the throw for the put out, but his maneuver left him with a torn hamstring, an injury that would keep him out of the Twins' lineup until September.[23] A less serious incident took place in the top of the seventh. Earlier in the plate appearance that produced his opposite field hit, Oliva let go of his bat on a wild swing, launching the lumber into the NL dugout. Fortunately, no damage resulted, just minor bumps to Schoendienst and Felipe Alou.[24]

From the historical perspective of a veteran sportswriter, Koppett saw an absence of star power on the 1968 squads.

It's all a far cry from the first All-Star Game in 1933, whose cast included Babe Ruth, Al Simmons, Charlie Gehringer, Lou Gehrig, Bill Dickey, Lefty Grove, Jimmy Foxx, Joe Cronin, Gabby Hartnett, Carl Hubbell, Bill Terry, Pie Traynor, Paul Waner and Frank Frisch–all subsequently elected to baseball's Hall of Fame.

It's unlikely that 14 of this game's participants will attain that honor.[25]

Time and the baseball writers have proved this prediction wrong, as the Hall of Fame has enshrined 17 players from the 1968 game. In Koppett's defense, could anyone in 1968 have anticipated that first-time All-Stars Bench and Carlton would in time be considered among the game's elites? Moreover, the notion that the 1933 game was populated with the greater number of all-time greats continues to hold true, as four more 1933 All-Stars have since been inducted as Veterans Committee picks, bringing those squads' tally to 18. (17 who played: Bill Dickey did not get into the game.) Then again, Cooperstown might not be finished summoning 1968 All-Stars, as John, Staub, Tiant, and perhaps others continue to be candidates for enshrinement.[26]

The 1968 season has been tagged the Year of the Pitcher, and the All-Star Game in Houston was 1968 in microcosm. Precise and overpowering, the NL pitchers allowed only three base runners—all on doubles—while also striking out 11. The AL pitchers, giving up only five hits, replied with nine strikeouts of their own, but the Mays first-inning unearned run proved decisive. ∎

Notes

1. Leonard Koppett, "Baseball Season Opens Today With All 20 Clubs Listed for Action," *The New York Times*, April 10, 1968.
2. "List of incidents of civil unrest in the United States," Wikipedia, http://en.wikipedia.org/wiki/List_of_incidents_of_civil_unrest_in_the_United_States, accessed February 22, 2014.
3. Brian D. Behnken, "Texas Southern University riot of 1967," in *Encyclopedia of American Race Riots*, vol. 2, ed. Walter C. Rucker and James N. Upton, 635-636. (Greenwood Publishing Group, 2007).
4. Martin Waldron, "Black militant slain by Houston police; gun fight injures 4," *The New York Times*, July 28, 1970.
5. Francis X. Clines, "Barbara Jordan dies at 59; Her Voice Stirred the Nation," *The New York Times*, January 18, 1996.
6. William N. Wallace, "Race Issue Shifts All-Star Game From New Orleans to Houston," *The New York Times*, January 12, 1965.
7. "3 Dodgers Named to All-Star Team," *The New York Times*, July 4, 1957.
8. "Howard Is Named to All-Star Team," *The New York Times*, June 27, 1968.
9. "Aaron, at .236, Grote on All-Star Team," *The New York Times*, June 25, 1968.
10. "Voting by Players," *The New York Times*, June 25, 1968.
11. "Hank Aaron 1968 Batting Splits," Baseball-reference.com, www.baseball-reference.com/players/split.cgi?id=aaronha01&year=1968&t=b, accessed February 24, 2014.
12. "Mays to Replace Rose in All-Star Line-Up," *The New York Times*, July 8, 1968.
13. "McLain, Stottlemyre Named American League All-Stars," *The New York Times*, June 28, 1968.
14. "Visitors Study Grass and Roof," *The New York Times*, July 9, 1968.
15. "Mantle Named to All-Star Team 16th Year by American League," *The New York Times*, July 2, 1968.
16. "Mays an All-Star for 19th Time As Schoendienst Fills Out Squad," *The New York Times*, July 4, 1968.
17. "Reds' Cardenas Replaces Alley in All-Star Contest," *The New York Times*, July 7, 1968.
18. "Mays an All-Star for 19th Time As Schoendienst Fills Out Squad," *The New York Times*, July 4, 1968.
19. "Visitors Study Grass and Roof," *The New York Times*, July 9, 1968.
20. Leonard Koppett, "Drysdale and Tiant Chosen to Start in All-Star Game at Houston Tonight," *The New York Times*, July 9, 1968. Two previous All-Star Games had broadcasts that overlapped prime time viewing hours in the East: Both the second game in 1959 and the 1967 contest started at 4:00 PM Pacific, so were "day games."
21. "Visitors Study Grass and Roof," *The New York Times*, July 9, 1968.
22. Accounts of the game action are from three main sources: "July 9, 1968 All-Star Game Play-By-Play and Box Score," Baseball-reference.com, www.baseball-reference.com/boxes/NLS/NLS196807090.shtml, accessed January 3, 2014; "All-Star Game Played on Tuesday, July 9, 1968 (N) at Astrodome," Retrosheet.org, www.retrosheet.org/boxesetc/1968/B07090NLS1968.htm, accessed January 3, 2014; and David Vincent, Lyle Spatz, and David W. Smith, *The Midsummer Classic: The complete history of baseball's All-Star game* (University of Nebraska Press, 2001).
23. Joseph Durso, "Baseball in Grip of a Power Failure," *The New York Times*, July 11, 1968.
24. Ibid.
25. Leonard Koppett, "Drysdale and Tiant Chosen to Start in All-Star Game at Houston Tonight," *The New York Times*, July 9, 1968.
26. John was listed on the Expansion Era ballot in 2010 and 2013 and Staub in 2010 ("Twelve Finalists Comprise Expansion Era Ballot For Hall of Fame Consideration in 2014," National Baseball Hall of Fame and Museum, http://baseballhall.org/news/press-releases/twelve-finalists-comprise-expansion-era-ballot-hall-fame-consideration-2014, accessed February 24, 2014); Tiant ranks among the top five pitchers not in the Hall of Fame, according to one player ranking algorithm ("Hall of Stats," www.hallofstats.com, accessed February 24, 2014).

The Saga of J.R. Richard's Debut

Blowing Away 15 Sticks at Candlestick

Dan VanDeMortel

When Houston Astros right-handed flamethrower James Rodney Richard, the number two pick in the June 1969 draft, debuted against the San Francisco Giants at Candlestick Park on September 5, 1971, he did so in relative anonymity. He received no television coverage, and no radio broadcast beyond the clubs' local markets. Fans were unaware of his 100-mph fastball or 94-mph slider.[1] And Willie Mays and baseball's fourth-best offense awaited him. Think of it as the polar opposite of Stephen Strasburg's uber-hyped 2010 debut against the Pittsburgh Pirates (then MLB's second-worst offense). Richard accomplished what Strasburg did not: striking out 15 batters to tie the 1954 debut record set by Brooklyn Dodger Karl Spooner—also against Mays's Giants. Unfortunately, scant media attention, future pitching heroics, and well-chronicled personal tribulations shadowed Richard's debut, obscuring an intriguing tale with its own Strasburg-like dominance.[2]

Richard's path to Candlestick began in 1950, when he was born in rural Vienna, Louisiana. About growing up in a self-described middle-class black family, Richard reflected, "My father and I had a long talk one day and he said, 'Have more for your family than I have for you.' And somehow it came to me that I wanted to be the best at everything I did and never take nothing for granted."[3]

Cemented with determination and athleticism housed inside a gangly frame—he graduated at 6' 8", 222 pounds—Richard took nearby Ruston's basketball, football, and baseball teams by storm, earning multiple scholarship offers. Once drafted, Richard chose baseball, primarily due to receiving $100,000 bonus money. Astros player personnel director Tal Smith opined that Richard had an arm "a scout might see once about every 500,000 miles."[4]

Richard progressed quickly through the minors, advancing to the Astros' Triple-A Oklahoma City 89ers in 1971, where he led the league in strikeouts and ERA. Control issues occasionally plagued him, but with an impressive arsenal of fastballs, sliders, and curves, "J.R." or "The Big Fellow," as hailed by teammates, was promoted to the Astros on September 1. He later remembered it felt good to be in the majors, but "I didn't feel a jolt or surge.... It wasn't a big change because of my attitude. I just wanted to be the best."[5]

He joined a team 16 games out of first, fighting for fourth place in the NL's Western Division. Despite a league second-best 3.13 ERA, Houston was doomed to mediocrity by anemic offense, key injuries, and players' contretemps with manager Harry "The Hat" Walker. Richard was informed the following day that he would start Sunday's second game of a doubleheader against the Giants. Departing Houston that evening for a four-game series, the team arrived sleepily in San Francisco early Friday morning.

The club they encountered was formidable, spearheaded by four future Cooperstown inductees: 40-years-young center fielder Mays, first baseman Willie McCovey, and pitchers Juan Marichal and Gaylord Perry. Right behind were five-tool star Bobby Bonds and rookie masher Dave Kingman. Although the team had cooled after a blistering 37–14 start, San Francisco maintained a large first-place lead en route to winning its division and compiling a second best 51–30 home record. The Giants were patient, too, as evidenced by leading the NL in walks. Spoiler alert: The Giants also led the major leagues in strikeouts.

The first match that Sunday set the table for the second. In the first inning, McCovey suffered a split left hand while attempting to field a vicious bouncer. With backup first baseman Kingman absent with appendicitis, the versatile Mays moved to first. Having few other options on short notice, manager Charlie Fox would be forced to play Mays there for both games. The Astros took advantage, squeaking out a 1–0 victory, emphatically stamped by starter Jack Billingham, who struck out a season-high 11. Keep that number in mind.

Around 3:00 PM, Richard warmed up in the Astros bullpen along the left-field line. He would have been hard-pressed to envision a more alien landscape for his debut. Candlestick had bid adieu to the open outfield expanse of the 1960s, when Mays's cap seemingly always fell to the grass as he snagged every fly ball.

Instead, the football 49ers had recently abandoned cramped Kezar Stadium in favor of this automobile-friendly location on the city's edge. The result? Goodbye baseball-only park, hello ongoing conversion to a multi-use stadium. Candlestick's renovations included rock-hard AstroTurf, an enclosing outfield area negating visibility of the outside world, and unfinished construction along the upper deck resembling "a construction job deserted by the hardhats after a hot labor-management dispute."[6]

The weather, too, contributed an otherworldly vibe. The previous day's yearly high of 85 had fallen 19 degrees, as coalescing marine fog hovered along the Pacific, waiting to steamroll inland. With the fog came "The Hawk," the nickname for gusts that frequently buffeted day games, the talons of which arrived habitually around three, turning the bullpen into a breezy swirl of food wrappers, plastics, and anything else lighter than a small dog.

Blessedly, the fog lingered somewhere beyond the upper deck overhang, permitting sunshine. Damningly, The Hawk was in flight, swirling at 10–20 mph, perhaps harder in unlucky microclimates. As the *San Francisco Chronicle*'s Bob Stevens acutely described, it was a "sometimes chill-blasted day."[7]

Whether due to the Hawk, nervousness, or innate wildness, Richard captured Fox's attention: "I watched him warm up in the bullpen. He threw at least a dozen balls that the catcher couldn't reach."[8] After finishing, Richard returned to the dugout, then watched as Jim Willoughby, also making his debut, shut Houston down in the top of the first.

Switch-hitter Ken Henderson led off for the Giants. How did one of the tallest pitchers in history appear to him, catcher Larry Howard, and home plate umpire Billy Williams? Stevens observed Richard came off the mound "like a huge crane."[9] As Dave Parker would later describe: "When he...let the ball go, he look[ed] like he [was] 10 feet away from you instead of 60 [, which caused] you to lean a little bit and [made] you think you [had] to swing the bat quicker."[10] Perhaps the Pirates' Richie Hebner summed it up best: "He [was] so close to the plate when he finish[ed] his windup that I [was] thankful he didn't eat onions before the game."[11]

Somehow, Henderson stroked a single to center. Switch-hitting Tito Fuentes was not so fortunate, grounding out to advance Henderson to second. Next up, Mays: a god compared to the Astros neophyte. Lacking the bat speed of years past, Mays nonetheless entered the game at .294/.436/.521, eventually compiling the eighth-best wins above replacement (WAR)

All six feet, eight inches of J.R. Richard, at an early-70's spring training workout

and best on-base percentage in the league.[12] A storybook battle of youth vs. experience.

Youth won. Mays struck out swinging. Richard had little time to savor his first "K," though. The strikeout-prone Bonds beat out an infield bouncer, then scored with Henderson on an RBI double by hot-hitting "Dirty" Al Gallagher for a 2–0 Giants lead.[13]

What ensued is a classic baseball legend in three acts. In act one, Astros first base coach Hub Kittle recalled, "The first time Mays came to bat, J.R. just threw that fastball by him." As Mays returned to first for the second inning, he asked Kittle in a high-pitched voice, "Hubert! My Lord! Who was that? He nearly scared me half to death! Where'd you get him?"[14]

Leaving act one, after the Astros failed to score, Richard answered, issuing a walk but nailing Willoughby for his second swinging strikeout. In the third, the Astros discovered their bats. After Richard grounded out in his inaugural at bat, Houston tied the score on RBI singles by Cesar Geronimo and Cesar Cedeño. The Giants failed to respond in kind. Translation: Richard struck out the side of Fuentes, Mays, and Bonds, with Mays looking at a called strike three. At this point, turning to act two, Kittle recalled Mays shaking his head while returning to first.[15]

The Astros added another run in the fourth for a 3–2 lead on an RBI single by Howard, Richard's former Oklahoma City batterymate. With that, Fox summoned rookie Jim Barr to successfully shut the door. Richard responded in the bottom frame by again allowing no runs. San Francisco achieved a moral victory, however: No Giant struck out.

COURTESY OF THE HOUSTON ASTROS

Richard at the peak of his career, holding eight baseballs with his enormous pitching hand.

on a Bonds foul fly to first baseman John Mayberry—incredibly shrewd baserunning by the still-speedy veteran.[18] Richard seized momentum by striking out Gallagher looking. Mays grabbed it right back, however, scoring when third baseman Denis Menke booted a Chris Speier grounder. After an infield single advanced Speier to second, Fox called catcher Fran Healy from the bullpen to pinch hit. Richard quickly fell behind 3–0 on two curves, "then went back to his hummer and simply blew the next three casts past [him]," the last strike looking.[19] As an awestruck Healy recalled: "...I [came] back to the dugout and [Fox] said, 'We have his pitches.' (Richard was tipping off his pitches.) And I said, 'So do I.' Jeez, he was throwing a hundred miles an hour."[20]

In the bottom of the ninth, pitching in shadows covering the infield, Richard stood on the cusp of history with 12 strikeouts. Mays was due up fourth.

First batter? Dietz, again. Result: same as it ever was, strikeout 13, swinging.

Second batter? Henderson. A contact hitter who would whiff only 76 times in 598 plate appearances, he hadn't yet struck out that day. Result: strikeout 14, swinging.

Next potential victim? Subbing for Fuentes in the eighth, Hal Lanier was the quintessential 1970s punchless-hitting infielder, but entering the game with 24 strikeouts in 205 plate appearances, he was hardly a swing-and-miss machine. Plus, he was assisted by the distracting influence of Mays on deck. Or, had Mays quit?

No. Baseball writer Rob Neyer correctly observed in 2008 that with the Giants contesting a close game in a pennant race, the notion of Mays removing himself seemed "preposterous, at the very least."[21] Hindsight in 2014 conclusively reveals Kittle's tale as a great fishing story, but a story nonetheless. First of all, Mays had struck out four times on April 24 and June 18, something he would easily remember. Second, no reporters mentioned another Giant waiting on deck, certainly a noticeable development given how Mays's movements were analyzed like the Zapruder film. Lastly, if Mays departed and the game became tied, who would play first? McCovey and Kingman were unavailable. When asked afterward who would play first going forward, Fox answered Mays, griping "Who else is there who can play it?"[22] Thus, a matchup for the ages waited in the wings.

Houston widened its margin in the fifth with its last two runs of the day on RBIs again by Geronimo and Cedeño. Armed with a 5–2 cushion, Richard took charge. Catcher Dick Dietz, inserted on a double-switch in the top of the inning, joined the strikeout club, going down swinging. After a Henderson out, Fuentes initiated a rally with a single to left-center, bringing up Mays. We will never know how vociferously Giants' fans cheered for home run number 646 off his bat, but surely a collective groan escaped when Richard strangled hope, striking out Mays swinging.

Now comes act three. After striking out, Mays slowly walked to first, exclaiming, "Hubert! You know what! Nobody's ever struck out Mays four times, have they? Well, I tell you what. That guy ain't going to strike me out again, because I ain't playing anymore."[16] According to Kittle, Mays then took himself out of the game at some unspecified point.[17] Was Mays serious? More to be revealed.

San Francisco's bats disappeared once more in the sixth as Richard navigated around his second walk by striking out Bonds again and light-hitting Jimmy Rosario, both on swinging third strikes. With no Astros runs or rendition of "Take Me Out to the Ballgame" or "God Bless America" to delay him in the seventh, Richard returned to the bump, sitting on nine strikeouts. Make that 10, as Dietz looked at a called third strike.

Rookie pitcher Steve Stone overcame a Mays error to escape damage in the eighth, bringing up the heart of the Giants order. Whether from newfound confidence or lacking an exit strategy, Mays grabbed his bat and opened proceedings with a walk. He advanced to second on a passed ball, and later scampered to third

Alas, Lanier failed to comply. Strikeout 15! Richard tied the record at the two-hour, 39-minute mark on his 155th pitch, a swinging third strike, "seemingly still throwing with the same power as in the early innings."[23,24] As Lanier retreated to the dugout, the Astros "rushed out to congratulate their new, instant hero."[25] Billingham and Richard embraced, for their combined 26 strikeouts still ties the record for the most strikeouts thrown by a team's starters in a twin bill: a safe standard given the modern disappearance of doubleheaders.

In the clubhouse, reporters flocked to Richard like a new Hollywood star. Stevens observed, "...very few Giants...dared dig in on him, and you certainly can't fault them for that."[26] The *San Jose Mercury News* and *Houston Chronicle* both marveled how Giants batters took many called strikes while stepping away from the plate.[27] The *Houston Post* even compared him to fellow Louisianan Vida Blue, the 1971 American League Most Valuable Player and Cy Young Award winner.[28]

Mays chimed in less enthusiastically. Concurring with Bonds's postgame assessment that Richard was not quite as fast as anticipated, he dryly credited Richard with always being around the plate.[29] His subdued remarks remain incongruous with his three-strikeout workday and whatever joke or threat he may have offered to encourage Kittle's storytelling abilities.

Postgame sabermetric insights were non-existent at the time. Current tools rate Richard a 75 game score, which tied Strasburg's effort, primarily since The Big Fellow pitched a complete game, while Strasburg's was a pitch count-limited seven-innings, with 94 pitches and no walks.[30] Both trailed Spooner's 93 game score for a three-hit shutout on 143 pitches. Spooner's 1954 performance, while impressive and historic, slightly trails Richard's accomplishment in two key respects. First, he pitched at home in Brooklyn before a spring training-like 3,256 crowd. Second, the Giants had clinched the NL pennant on September 20, just two days earlier. As 1971 Giants pitching coach Larry Jansen recalled after watching Richard's performance, "We had quite a party the night before Spooner pitched. There weren't too many regulars in the lineup that day."[31]

As for Richard's reaction, he was as cool as the proverbial other side of the pillow: "I wasn't keeping track of the strikeouts. I didn't think a lot about facing Mays, Bobby Bonds and other good hitters. I just felt if something was going to happen, it was going to happen[32]

"There wasn't anything to get nervous about. They gave me the ball. After that there was nothing to do about it but to pitch.... I wasn't thinking strikeout

Richard and newly acquired teammate Nolan Ryan—a strikeout-hurling tandem for only half the 1980 season due to Richard's career ending-stroke.

today. Actually, I just tried to get the ball over the plate," he politely added, agreeing with Howard that he did not have the elite fastball he had that day in Oklahoma City when he struck out 17—with 16 in the first six innings before developing a finger blister.[33] As for comparisons to Blue, he refused to take the bait: "Others have done that, not me."[34]

Richard explained laconically that he threw fastballs and sliders to Mays, and offered no clichés then or now about tying the record of, to him, an unknown ballplayer from a time when baseball was in black and white, literally and figuratively.[35] Yet the memory of stifling Mays, the connective tissue between the two events, still remains.[36] As Richard observed years later, "My biggest game was my major league debut.... I didn't realize what was going on until it was over.... All I could remember was Willie Mays going down swinging. My slider moved this much (holding his hands about five feet apart)."[37]

The promise Richard demonstrated that day slowly flowered. Overcoming wildness, inconsistency, and injuries, he finally secured a rotation spot in 1975, won 20 games in 1976 and struck out over 300 batters in 1978 and 1979. In 1980 he started the All-Star Game for the NL. On the mound, he "went out there with the mentality if you beat me I'm gonna die trying. I was willing to give my life for it."[38]

He very nearly did. Days after the All-Star Game, Richard suffered a stroke. His reputation was smeared in a miasma of medical complications and media-fueled accusations of malingering: at best inaccurate, at worst racist. After failed comeback attempts, he was cut by the Astros in 1984. A downward personal spiral ultimately left him homeless at times under a bridge in Houston. Then, at his nadir, came redemption. With help from friends and religious inspiration, he recovered, and he began counseling in Houston-area churches and mentoring youths on baseball and life. In 2012, he was inducted into the Astros' Walk of Fame. At peace, he is now "peacock proud and honeymoon happy" enough to say with levity and Southern sass, "I'm the only man in the world who [could] throw a ball through a car wash and never get it wet."[39] ∎

SOURCES
All statistics are cited from or calculated from Baseball-Reference.com (http://www.baseball-reference.com) unless otherwise noted. *The Sporting News Official Baseball Guide* (1972) also provided helpful background.

NOTES

1. Pitch speeds are the consensus from various referenced speeds spanning Richard's career.
2. *The New York Times* recorded "Jim" Richard's accomplishment in one paragraph sans headline: *The New York Times*, September 6, 1971. The *Washington Post* and *Los Angeles Times* ran brief wire service accounts sans quotes from participants: "Astros' Pitchers Stop Giants Twice," *Washington Post*, September 6, 1971; "Astros Sweep Giants; Rookie Strikes Out 15," *Los Angeles Times*, September 6, 1971.
3. Blake Jackson, "The Collected Wisdom of James Rodney Richard," NewsOK, June 18, 2006, http://newsok.com/the-collected-wisdom-of-james-rodney-richard/article/1875003.
4. Wil A. Linkugel and Edward J. Pappas, *They Tasted Glory: Among the Missing at the Baseball Hall of Fame* (Jefferson, NC: McFarland & Company, Inc., 1998), 145.
5. Jackson, op. cit.; Dave Hollander, "J.R. Richard: The Human Condition," *Houston Press*, September 2, 2004, www.houstonpress.com/2004-09-02/news/j-r-richard-the-human-condition/.
6. Charles McCabe, "The New Candlestick," *San Francisco Chronicle*, April 13, 1971.
7. Bob Stevens, "Giants Lose 2; McCovey Hurt," *San Francisco Chronicle*, September 6, 1971.
8. Bucky Walter, "15 Strikeouts in Astro's 1st Start," *San Francisco Examiner*, September 6, 1971.
9. Stevens, op. cit.
10. Ron Reid, "Sweet Whiff of Success," *Sports Illustrated*, September 4, 1978, http://sportsillustrated.cnn.com/vault/article/magazine/MAG1135814/index.htm.
11. Harry Shattuck, "King Richard a Real Highness in Houston," *The Sporting News*, May 26, 1979.
12. Mays struck out a career-high 123 times in 1971.
13. Bonds set a then major league record with 187 strikeouts in 1969 and broke it with 189 in 1970. He was on pace for an improved total of 137 in 1971.
14. All Kittle quotes are from SABR's BioProject: Hubert Kittle, http://sabr.org/bioproj/person/4d152362 (see fn 129). Phil Pepe, *Talkin' Baseball, An Oral History of Baseball in the 1970s* (New York: Ballantine Books, 1998), 53–4 contains a similar version. This article opts for SABR's version over most, but not all, of Pepe's, being that it is an earlier version with more detail, taken from a 1992 television interview.
15. SABR BioProject: Hubert Kittle, op cit.
16. Ibid.
17. Pepe, op. cit., 53-54.
18. Baseball-Reference.com indicates Howard was responsible for two passed balls in this game. However, all newspaper box scores indicate only one; no game account mentions a second.
19. Stevens, op. cit.; Pepe, op. cit., 53.
20. Pepe, op. cit., 53.
21. Rob Neyer, *Rob Neyer's Big Book of Baseball Legends* (New York: Simon & Schuster, 2008), 141–2.
22. Dick Friendlich, "Mays Back to First," *San Francisco Chronicle*, September 6, 1971. Fox alluded to the possible future deployment of backup catcher Russ Gibson or Lanier to first: Dick O'Connor, "Giants, Dodgers Clash Tonight," *Palo Alto Times*, September 6, 1971. But, Gibson had already been replaced by Dietz and Fox's options for replacing Lanier at second were limited. Recent triple-A callups infielder Chris Arnold and outfielder Bernie Williams were the only available position players. Using either in some convoluted switch to honor a Mays request to leave the game would have weakened the lineup offensively and defensively, and given Fox even fewer bench options in the event of extra innings or injuries.
23. An exact pitch count is not available. This approximation was derived via Tom Tango's Basic Pitch Count Estimator, http://en.wikipedia.org/wiki/Basic_pitch_count_estimator.
24. John Wilson, "Richard Fans 15 in Sweep," *Houston Chronicle*, September 6, 1971, www.astrosdaily.com/history.
25. Joe Heiling, "Richard Fans 15, Ties Rookie Mark for First MLB Start," September 6, 1971, www.astrosdaily.com/history.
26. Stevens, op. cit.
27. Jack Hanley, "Twin Loss for Giants," *San Jose Mercury News*, September 6, 1971; Wilson, op. cit., "Richard Fans 15 in Sweep."
28. Heiling, op. cit.
29. O'Connor, op. cit.
30. Game score is a metric devised by sabermetrican Bill James to numerically evaluate the strength of a starting pitcher's performance. The higher the score, the more successful the performance. See http://en.wikipedia.org/wiki/Game_score.
31. O'Connor, op. cit. Left fielder Monte Irvin was the only Giants starter to play the entire game; all others rested or were confined to two or fewer at bats. Jansen's recollection on timing of the Giants celebration(s) could be slightly off, but even *The Sporting News* cautioned that Spooner benefited from facing a weak lineup and a Giants team "bound to be more or less indifferent" after clinching the pennant, with some batters possibly "swinging at the first pitch to get [the game] over with." Bill Roeder, "$600 Dollar Spooner Looks Like Million in Fall Debut," *The Sporting News*, Oct. 6, 1954. Sadly, Spooner's career abruptly ended the following season due to a throwing-shoulder injury.
32. Pat Frizzell, "Giants Lose Mac for One Week," *Oakland Tribune*, September 6, 1971.
33. Walter, op. cit.; John Wilson, "J.R. Gives Astros Happy Expectations," *The Sporting News*, November 27, 1971.
34. Heiling, op. cit.
35. Walter, op. cit.
36. Mays singled in two at bats versus Spooner with no strikeouts.
37. Jackson, op. cit.
38. Wesley Wright, Past Meets Present Interview of J.R. Richard, MLB.com, August 6, 2012, http://m.mlb.com/video/topic/0/v23666167/past-meets-present-jr-richard-and-wesley-wright.
39. Zachary Levine, "J.R. Richard Appreciates Astros Honor But Wants More," Ultimate Astros, May 31, 2012, http://blog.chron.com/ultimateastros/2012/05/31/j-r-richard-appreciates-astros-honor-but-wants-more; Darryl Hamilton, Joe Magrane, and Paul Severino Interview of J.R. Richard at 2013 Urban Invitational, MLB.com, February 23, 2013, http://m.mlb.com/video/topic/15886078/v25615153/jr-richard-on-importance-of-having-a-good-mindset.

From the Gashouse to the Glasshouse

Leo Durocher and the 1972–73 Houston Astros

Jimmy Keenan

On July 23,1972, Leo Durocher stepped down as manager of the Chicago Cubs. Durocher had taken over an underachieving Cubs team in 1966 and in two years, turned them into a contender, but Durocher's abrasive style of managing alienated many of his players. There were also run-ins with umpires, health problems, and several unexcused absences that led to a "Dump Durocher" movement by the Chicago fans.

After his 1972 ouster, Leo and his wife Lynne began making arrangements for a USO junket to the Far East. The Durochers received their travel vaccines, updated their passports, and were planning their itinerary. Around midnight on the evening of August 25–26 their plans changed when Durocher received an unexpected telephone call from Spec Richardson, a longtime friend and the general manager of the Houston Astros. Richardson had just fired manager Harry Walker and was calling to see if Durocher was interested in the job. Leo politely declined and hung up. Richardson called back five times that night before Durocher finally said yes.

When asked about hiring the 67-year-old Durocher, Richardson told the United Press International, "Leo's age didn't bother me, I thought our club ought to be doing better, and Leo might fire 'em up."[1]

The Astros' new skipper was a light-hitting infielder who played for the Yankees, Reds, Cardinals, and Dodgers. As a player, he won a World Series with the New York Yankees in 1928 and another with the St. Louis Cardinals Gashouse Gang in 1934. Durocher took over as player-manager of the Brooklyn Dodgers in 1939. He remained at the helm until July 1948 when he left to manage the New York Giants. In 1947, he was suspended for the entire season by baseball commissioner "Happy" Chandler for several reasons including allegedly consorting with known gamblers. Durocher managed the Giants 1948–55, winning two National League pennants and a World Series. He was named *The Sporting News* manager of the year three times. He later coached the Los Angeles Dodgers.

Astros GM Harold B. "Spec" Richardson began his career in baseball in 1946 as the concessions manager for the Columbus Cardinals in the Class A South Atlantic League. He became the team's business manager in 1949. In 1953, Richardson was hired as the general manager of the Jacksonville Braves, the Milwaukee Braves affiliate in the South Atlantic League. Jacksonville finished in first place three times under Richardson's guidance. In December 1959, Richardson was named GM of the minor-league Houston Buffaloes. In October 1961, he became the business manager of Houston's fledgling National League franchise, the Colt 45s. In 1967, Richardson was promoted to GM of the renamed Astros. The press occasionally referred to the Astros as the "Glasshouse Gang," alluding to the skylights in the Astrodome roof.

With Durocher at the helm, Houston reeled off five straight victories. The club's new skipper predicted that his Astros would catch the first-place Cincinnati Reds, who were 8 games up in the standings when he took over. It didn't happen, and on September 22 the Reds defeated the Astros, 4–3, to clinch the National League West Division. That same night, Durocher pulled pitcher Larry Dierker in the first inning after he gave up two earned runs. Dierker was visibly upset over his removal, which angered Durocher. After the game Durocher told *The Sporting News*, "I told my players that I will not show them up on the field or in the dugout and that I expect the same of them."[2]

Durocher benched Dierker for the remainder of the season but insisted there would be no future repercussions over the incident.

Houston finished the 1972 campaign 16–15 under Durocher. When the season ended, Durocher fired coaches Salty Parker and Buddy Hancken. They were replaced by Preston Gomez and Grady Hatton. Gomez, an infielder with the Washington Nationals in 1944, had been let go by the San Diego Padres after managing the team 1969–72. Hatton, another former major league infielder (1946–60), had worked for the Houston organization in a number of high profile positions, including manager, since 1961. Gomez was Durocher's choice but Hatton was Richardson's man, placed to monitor the unpredictable Durocher.

Things got off to a bad start in January when Dierker underwent surgery to remove a calcium deposit at the base of the index finger on his pitching hand. His recovery was delayed when the sutures used in the procedure grew back into his hand, requiring a second surgery.

The Astros held their spring training at Cocoa, Florida. The 52-acre site had four practice fields and a 5,000 seat stadium. The complex was located in the backwoods, five miles inland from the town of Cocoa. Most of the baseball writers who covered spring training normally by-passed the facility, but now that Durocher was managing the Astros, the place was a hotbed of activity.

In early March, Marvin Miller, the Executive Director of the Major League Baseball Players Association, began visiting spring training sites to brief the players on the new three-year deal with the owners. According to Miller these meetings were legally necessary in order to ratify the agreement. Spec Richardson was livid when he learned that Miller scheduled the Astros meeting on March 12 before a game with the Texas Rangers at Pompano, 165 miles away.

On March 11, the Astros played the Minnesota Twins at Orlando in a game that was televised in Houston. Durocher wanted the Astros fans to get a good look at his team so he played his starters all nine innings. When Durocher posted the list for the traveling squad that was going to Pompano the next morning it was made up of nearly all non-starters. He put up a second list for any of his regulars who wanted to take another bus that would leave an hour earlier (6:30 AM) in order to make Miller's 10:30 AM meeting. A couple of players volunteered to take the early bus then changed their mind when none of the other regulars signed up.[3] It would've been a seven-hour round-trip bus ride. Richardson felt that Miller could've come to the Astros spring training facility or met the club a few days earlier at Daytona Beach, only sixty miles away.

The Astros arrived in Pompano around 10:45 AM and joined the Rangers who were meeting with Miller in center field. The players had listened to Miller for about 30 minutes when Durocher came out and broke up the gathering, saying, "Come on, let's go, it's 11:30. We hit in ten minutes."[4] Miller and his attorney Dick Moss were furious, saying the Astros violated the agreement, which specified that each team be available for a 90-minute meeting.

This wasn't the first time that Durocher ran afoul of organized labor. In 1936, the Central Trades and Labor Union threatened to boycott St. Louis Cardinals games after Durocher sided with his wife when she crossed the picket line during a garment workers strike. He later apologized and the boycott was lifted. In the spring of 1946, Durocher and Branch Rickey banned union organizer Robert Murphy, founder of the ill-fated American Baseball Guild, from Dodgers camp.

Durocher's actions that day in Pompano drew the ire of National League president "Chub" Feeney, who fined him $250. Durocher said he would retire before he'd pay the fine. Richardson backed his manager, telling *The Sporting News*, "Leo was right. Thirty-eight ballplayers, every man on our under-control-roster, have said that they didn't want to meet with Marvin Miller—not in Pompano. That's a heckuva blow to him. I think his pride is hurt. I think Durocher is the only man in baseball with the guts to do this and I think he is right."[5]

In order to keep the peace, a check was sent to Feeney, but in his autobiography, *Nice Guys Finish Last*, Durocher asserts it was never cashed.

Excitement was growing in Houston over the upcoming season thanks in part to the slogan "1973—The Year of The Astros" that was posted on billboards all over the city. Durocher felt that his infield of Lee May (1B), Tommy Helms (2B), Roger Metzger (SS), and Doug Rader (3B) was the best in the National League. The outfield was set with Cesar Cedeño and Jim Wynn. Newly acquired Tommie Agee would fill the final outfield spot if Bob Watson was able to make the transition to catcher. If not, Watson would play the outfield and Agee would come off the bench. The other catching candidates were John Edwards, Larry Howard, Cliff Johnson, and Skip Jutze. There were a number of reserves who would see action including Bob Gallagher, Hector Torres, Jimmy Stewart, and Jesus Alou.

Durocher was a proponent of the four-man rotation. With Dierker sidelined, he went with Dave Roberts, Ken Forsch, Don Wilson, and Jerry Reuss. The rest of the Astros staff consisted of Fred Gladding, Tom Griffin, Jim Ray, Jim Crawford, Jim York, Mike Cosgrove, and Doug Konieczny. Juan Pizarro and Cecil Upshaw were acquired during the season and rookie J.R. Richard was called up later in the year.

Durocher told the Associated Press, "We have one of the best balanced ballclubs I have ever seen. We are set at seven positions and there aren't any players in the National League who can beat out our players at their positions even if they played for us. I've got power, I've got speed and I have a good defense. What I'm looking for is pitching. That's what we're looking for more than anything this spring is pitching. I know the arms are there it's just the question of finding the right ones. I know our pitching wasn't what it is was

Leo Durocher was 67 years old when he took his last managing stint in the big leagues with Houston. His health kept him from taking a 1976 position with the Taiheiyo Club Lions. He passed away in 1991.

supposed to have been last year but I know these pitchers and I'm confident that they are much better than what they showed."[6]

In a move that caught many of the Astros by surprise, Durocher fired pitching coach Jim Owens the day before the season opener. He filled the vacancy on the staff with former Astro Bob Lillis. Richardson spoke to the Associated Press about the move, "Durocher said he wasn't completely happy with the pitching staff and thought a change was in order."[7]

Houston started out the 1973 season playing good ball, posting a 14–10 record in April and 15–12 in May. Unfortunately, it was all downhill from there. The same problems that plagued Durocher in Chicago arose again in Houston. Durocher wrote in his book *Nice Guys Finish Last* that he tried a new approach with the Astros: The dictator would become one of the boys. He'd play cards with the guys and share stories in an attempt to gain their friendship. This new tactic failed miserably. He felt that it undermined his authority in the clubhouse, causing him to lose the respect of the team. Durocher lamented that the modern players' high salaries gave them too much leverage with management. He also noted that Richardson was too close to the players, who complained to him whenever they felt slighted.

Dierker and Durocher were never on the same page. Dierker developed shoulder problems when he returned to the team and was used sparingly. He would later tell the Associated Press what is was like playing for Durocher. "I did not say anything to the press or make any complaint about it. But frankly I was afraid of what that guy in there would do. You couldn't tell what he'd do. He might have given me

the ball and told me to pitch and left me in there until my arm fell off. I know myself well enough to know that if he kept giving me the ball I'd take it. My arm had been hurt seriously a couple of times and I did not want to jeopardize my whole future in the hands of Durocher. I figured it would be better to sit and wait and hope he was fired or that I was traded."[8]

Durocher had a well-publicized argument with pitcher Don Wilson on the team bus. Wilson was fined $300 and later apologized. When comparing Durocher to his eventual successor Preston Gomez, Wilson told *The Sporting News*, "I like what I've seen of [Gomez]. He doesn't do things on impulse or superstition, like the last guy. Every move he makes is on sound judgment. Preston thinks about winning. He's not like Leo who just thinks about getting his name in the paper."[9]

Pitcher Jerry Reuss, who called Durocher "the dummy we had (in the dugout)" got into a heated argument with his manager after he was removed in the fourth inning while leading 7–3 with two outs and two men on base.[10] Durocher explained to Reuss why he took him out, saying, "I didn't want the married men in the infield killed. They were hitting bullets off you."[11] Later in the season, Reuss was getting hit hard again. This time Durocher gave him a chance to work out of the jam. Unable to stop the rally, he was finally taken out. When Reuss sat down in the dugout he looked at Durocher and asked, "What the hell took you so long?"[12]

Durocher also had problems with catchers Larry Howard and Skip Jutze. Howard was traded to the Braves after incurring Durocher's wrath for lackadaisical play. Jutze briefly quit the Houston organization after refusing a minor-league assignment. He would eventually report and was called up in May 1973.

When Durocher joined the Astros he compared Cesar Cedeño to a young Willie Mays. Cedeño put together a fine statistical season in 1973 (.320 BA, 25 HR, 70 RBIs). However, his inability to play through injuries coupled with his unwillingness to take coaching advice was a source of consternation for both Durocher and Richardson.

The experiment of using Bob Watson behind the plate didn't pan out, which relegated Tommie Agee to a back-up role. An ankle injury affected Agee's overall play and he never got on track. He was traded to the Cardinals in August. Watson (.312 BA, 16 HR, 94 RBIs) went on to have an excellent year.

No season would be complete without Durocher battling with umpires. On May 15 the Astros played the Braves at the Astrodome. The fireworks started when umpire Bruce Froemming ruled that Hector

Torres didn't touch second base while turning a double play. The second part of the controversy occurred when first baseman Lee May, thinking the inning was over, flipped the ball to umpire Paul Pryor. With the Braves Dusty Baker running around the bases, Pryor dropped the ball on the ground. Durocher accused Pryor of throwing the ball away from May, allowing Baker to score. Because of Froemming's call and Pryor's actions, Durocher informed the umpires that he was playing the game under protest. Richardson, still upset over a disputed home run call by Augie Donatelli two days earlier, instructed the Astrodome scoreboard operator to post the following message, "Manager Leo Durocher has announced the game will be played under protest. Umpires Froemming and Donatelli have blown two decisions in the last three days." Richardson was fined $300 by the league office but remained unrepentant. On June 26, Durocher was ejected and fined $150 after he kicked a batting helmet into the shins of umpire John Kibler while arguing a call.

Durocher also fell ill twice during the year with diverticulitis of the colon. He was hospitalized in late April through early May and again in August. The team went 16–5 under interim manager Preston Gomez during his absence.

The Astros finished the 1973 season in fourth place with a record of 82–80. Richardson summed up the year in an interview with *The Sporting News*: "This team is a lot better than it has shown in the standings. They've not lived up to their potential. They've been a big disappointment to me. The bullpen has been here a long time... the whole pitching staff practically for that matter. Wilson, Dierker, Ray and Griffin... and pitching has been a problem. The staff has a good year one year and is lousy the next. I expect to make changes. You can take every position on the field except shortstop (Roger Metzger) and second base (Tommy Helms) and have something critical to say about it. Wynn started good and went into a long slump and has never gotten out of it. Cedeño got hurt and stayed hurt the rest of the year. He can't play with any pain. Despite his statistics its been a disappointing year for Cedeño in my book. He hasn't done all we expected of him. Lee May? He'll end up with around 30 home runs and 100 RBIs but that doesn't give a true picture. He started out slow—just like Rader—and didn't do much early in the year. Watson dropped off late. Metzger is probably the best player I've had all year. As far as consistency is concerned, if I was voting for the most valuable player on our team, I'd vote for Metzger."[13]

Richardson remained with the Astros through the 1975 season. From there he moved on to the San Francisco Giants where he was named executive of the year in 1978. In 1994, he was inducted into the South Atlantic League Hall of Fame.

Late in the year, Durocher informed some of the veterans on the club that he was retiring at the end of the season. He wrote in *Nice Guys Finish Last*, "It isn't the game I used to know. In the first place there are the players. They're a different breed. They've got a union, headed by Marvin Miller, and they're carting their money off in bushel baskets. You can't tell them what to do. They have to be consulted; they want to know why. Not how but why. The battle cry of today's player is: I don't have to."[14]

Some Astros never respected Durocher or his past accomplishments and felt he was a relic from an era that was no longer relevant. On October 1, 1973, Durocher resigned, telling the United Press International, "Baseball has been 45 years of a wonderful life. But I have a lot of things to do now. I'm going out to Palm Springs and I'm going to tee it up and play a lot of golf."[15]

In 1976, the Taiheiyo Club Lions of the Japanese Pacific League offered him a reported $150,000 to manage the team for one season.[16] A slow recovery from heart surgery along with a recent bout of pneumonia precluded him from taking the job. Leo Durocher never managed again, passing away in 1991. He was elected to the Baseball Hall of Fame three years later. ∎

Sources

Online

Baseball-almanac.com, www.baseball-Almanac.com/players/ awards.php?p=durocle01, accessed December 12, 2013.

Baseball-reference.com, www.baseball-reference.com/managers/ durocle01.shtml, accessed January 10, 2014.

The Official Site of the Class A South Atlantic League www.milb.com/ content/page.jsp?sid=l116&ymd=20080228&content_ id=352571&vkey=league3, accessed December 23, 2013.

Books

Eskenazi, Gerald. *The Lip: A Biography of Leo Durocher* (New York: William Morrow, 1993.

Durocher, Leo with Ed Linn. *Nice Guys Finish Last* (New York: Simon & Schuster), 1975.

Wynn, Jimmy and Bill McCurdy. *Toy Cannon: The Autobiography of Jimmy Wynn* (Jefferson, North Carolina, McFarland and Company 2010).

Lowenfish, Lee. *Branch Rickey: Baseball's Ferocious Gentleman* (Lincoln, University of Nebraska Press, 2007).

Newspapers

Bend (Oregon) *Bulletin*
Lewiston (Maine) *Daily News*
Miami News
Montreal Gazette
(Connecticut) *Morning Record*

Nashua (New York) *Telegraph*
Sumter (South Carolina) *Daily Item*
The Sporting News
(North Carolina) *Times-News*
Tuscaloosa News
(Texas) *Victoria-Advocate*

Notes

1. Edwin Shrake,"I Talk Real Polite And Nice," *Sports Illustrated*, August 13, 1973 volume 39, issue number 7.
2. John Wilson,"A Durocher-Dierker Feud?" *The Sporting News*, October 14, 1972, 13.
3. *The Sporting News* gives two different accounts of which players volunteered to take the early bus to Pompano. One account listed Larry Dierker, Jerry Reuss and Cliff Johnson. The other lists Dierker and Cesar Cedeño. Dierker reportedly wanted to speak with Marvin Miller about resigning as the team's union representative. Cedeño wanted to visit his friend Rico Carty who was playing for the Rangers. There were no reasons given as to why Johnson and Reuss wanted to make the trip. (Joe Heiling,"Here Comes Leo- Quick Astros Exit," *The Sporting News*, March 31,1973, 30.)
4. Ibid.
5. Ibid.
6. "Durocher Picks Excellent Year for Well-Balanced Astros," Associated Press. Quote excerpted from the (Connecticut) Morning Record, March 13, 1973, 9.
7. Hersche L. Nissenson,"Durocher Shuffles Staff, Fires Owens," *Nashua* (New York) *Telegraph*, April 14, 1973, 14.
8. Joe Heiling, "Dierker Ready to Go, Jubilant Astros Claim," *The Sporting News*, February 23 1973, 27.
9. Joe Heiling,"Low Key Gomez Strikes High Note with Wilson," *The Sporting News*, January 5, 1974, 27.
10. "Reuss Criticizes Trade–Durocher," Associated Press, Quote excerpted from the *Victoria* (Texas) *Advocate* November 3, 1973, 3.
11. Leo Durocher and Ed Linn."The Old Way is Dead," *Sports Illustrated* April 28, 1975 volume 42, issue 17.
12. Ibid.
13. Joe Heiling,"Faded Astros Face Pruning by Fed-Up GM Richardson," *The Sporting News*, September 22, 1973, 17.
14. Leo Durocher with Ed Linn. *Nice Guys Finish Last* (New York: Simon & Schuster), 1975. 410.
15. "Durocher Resigns, Astros Hire Gomez", United Press International, Quote excerpted from the *Montreal Gazette*, October 2,1973, 25.
16. *The Sporting News* of January 3, 1976 (7) listed Durocher's salary offer from the Taiheiyo Club Lions as $150,000. *The Sporting News* of April 3, 1976 (47) noted the salary offer had risen to $220,000. This article notes that Durocher signed the contract but it was later voided due to his health issues.

There Used to Be a Big Dome

Francis Kinlaw

There used to be a big dome right here
Where the field was carpeted green
And where fans watched lots of wild games
And plays we'd never seen.
The air was set to a desired temp,
There were hot dogs and beer…
Yes, there used to be a big dome, right here.

And we used to sip big sodas
On Texas-sized Fourths of July,
With electronic fireworks exploding on a scoreboard
Over which homers would sometimes fly.
People looked around in wonder,
In comfort they'd laugh and cheer…
There used to be a big dome, right here.

Upon becoming the home of Houston's team
In the Spring of '65,
This "Eighth Wonder of the World" was where
Bouncing balls were quite alive!
No insects could invade the place,
Big mosquitos caused no fear…
Back when there used to be a big dome, right here.
Now the children try to find it
But they are a bit intrigued,
'Cause the old place is no longer there
And the current team has switched leagues.
Skyward views in the new park are often blocked
By a roof above the upper tier
As outside it's hot and humid, this and every year.

Yes, there used to be a big dome, right here.

AUTHOR'S NOTE: The words of this poem are patterned upon the lyrics of Frank Sinatra's popular recording of "There Used to be a Ballpark," which was released in 1973. The lyrics of the Sinatra recording, written by Joe Raposo, may be accessed on the Internet.

Houston's Fallen Star

Don Wilson

Matthew M. Clifford

Wow! Look at all those bright colors. The baseball field at the Astrodome suddenly resembled a Tequila Sunrise. Yellow, red, and orange floated over jade green Astroturf as the players took their positions. Perplexed fanatics couldn't take their eyes off the gaudy new 1975 uniforms on the backs of their Houston Astros. Thankfully, the back of the shirts accurately identified the players. But the numbers on the front of the jerseys slipped off the fabric and landed on the right hip of the players' pants?

While the fans digested the new Astros garb, they noticed another change. Each Houston jersey had a circular black patch on the left shoulder with "40" in white. The pointing and giggles at the new costumes abruptly stopped as fanatics recognized what it signified. The number "40" had belonged to fireballing righthander Don Wilson. Houston's new uniforms were created to commemorate the tenth anniversary of the Astrodome— a ceremony Don Wilson was unable to attend.

Born in Monroe, Louisiana, on February 12, 1945, Donald Edward Wilson grew up a baseball fan. He idolized Ernie Banks, Hank Aaron, and Willie Mays. Don and his family migrated to California and settled in the busy city of Compton. He enjoyed playing in the local Little Leagues and for his high school team, the Centennial High Apaches. He played shortstop and third base while his older brother Willy handled pitching duties for the Apaches. On one occasion Willy called his little brother in for relief. Don recalled his exciting assignment in a 1967 interview. "[Willy] was getting mighty tired, so he asked me to pitch a few games to spell him. I did and I've been hooked on pitching ever since."[1]

During his freshman year at Compton Community College in 1964, the scouts took note of Don's fiery right arm. Houston's baseball talent birddog, Karl Kuehl, reviewed Wilson's performance and appeared interested—and then he disappeared. Disappointed by Kuehl's apathy, the young pitcher threw a lightning bolt at the screen fence behind the batter's box. "I got mad at what I thought was a brush-off and fired one with all my might. It took off and hit the screen."[2]

To Wilson's surprise, Kuehl witnessed Don's angry fastball, spying from a distance. The Astros' ivory hunter approached the frustrated player after the game and told him, "The only pitch you threw hard was the one that hit the screen."[3]

Kuehl signed Wilson and sent his recruit to play for the Cocoa Colts of Florida's Cocoa Rookie League. Wilson spent his time with the Colts working as a reliever and adding speed to his fastball.

Don graduated to the Florida State League in 1965, playing Class A ball for the Cocoa Astros. Manager Billy Goodman put Wilson to the test as a starting pitcher. Don handled 181 innings with a 10–8 record. Before the season ended, Wilson and his wife Bernice celebrated the birth of their first child, Denise. In 1966 Don was sent to play for the Amarillo Sonics of the Class AA Texas League. Sonics skipper Buddy Hancken also used the 21-year-old as a starting pitcher. Don dished out 197 strikeouts in 187 innings before the Astros interrupted the TL schedule. The Houston Astros plucked him from the Sonics' roster a few days before the minor league season closed. On September 29, 1966, Don Wilson made his debut at Crosley Field against the Cincinnati Reds, notching his first major league win after striking out seven Reds and leaving Pete Rose hitless.

In 1967 Wilson made the Astros roster for good. Before the season started, he bought a new baseball to secretly carry with him. He confessed the reason for the private purchase in a 1968 interview: "I bought that baseball to get the autographs of all my boyhood heroes—Willie Mays, Henry Aaron, Ernie Banks and all the others."[4]

Astros Manager Grady Hatton immediately put Wilson in the pitching rotation. As one of the youngsters on the hurling squad, Wilson learned tricks and tips while practicing with Houston's seasoned pitchers, Miguel "Mike" Cuellar and Bobby "Bo" Belinsky. Don was excited to enjoy his first full season in the majors and the chance to pitch in the famous Astrodome. Wilson would make history on the Astrodome's artificial grass that June.

Wilson came to Houston for good in 1967 and pitched a no-hitter on June 18.

The Atlanta Braves came to Houston on June 18 with their heavy hitter, Henry "Hammerin' Hank" Aaron. Hatton put Wilson in to start the game. Nine innings later, Don found himself drenched in champagne with his Houston contract torn to shreds. After facing 30 Atlanta batters and doling out 15 strikeouts, Wilson had pitched the first no-hit game at the Astrodome. Prior to the game, he had racked up 62 strikeouts. With 77 big Ks on the year and a no-hit game on his record, Wilson couldn't stop smiling.

Wilson worried during his final inning against the Braves. The screams from the Houston crowd filled the dome when Atlanta's final batter came to the plate: Don's longtime hero, Hank Aaron. With all the precision he could muster, Don delivered three slingshot fireballs past Aaron's bat. The crowd went wild. Striking out "Hammerin' Hank" was the cherry on top of Wilson's "no-hit sundae." Immediately after the game, Aaron told the press, "It's young guys like this that make me want to retire."[5]

While Hank spoke of retirement, Don Wilson was getting showered with champagne in the Houston locker room. Wilson mentioned his worries facing Aaron in an interview that immediately followed the game: "I didn't want to face Aaron, but after I walked [Denis] Menke in the eighth, I knew I'd have to. I consider him one of the best clutchers in the game."[6]

Astros' manager Hatton remarked, "I was amazed that he was able to pitch that long and hard with so much stuff after such a hard game. But that last pitch he threw to Aaron was as hard as any pitch he threw all day."[7]

Owner Roy Hofheinz tore up Wilson's contract and had it rewritten to include a $1,000 raise. Wilson stayed on fire as he delivered a sweltering streak of 29 scoreless innings from July 9 to 26. When the season closed, Wilson had 159 strikeouts, a 2.79 ERA, and a 10–9 record. With help from his summer raise, Don and Bernice purchased a home in South Houston. The pitcher spent his offseason working at a sporting goods store. In one of his many interviews, the pitcher mentioned his only complaint about playing in the majors. He preferred the hot temperatures of California rather than the chill of Philadelphia, Chicago, or the air conditioned Astrodome. He suffered muscle strains from pitching in the cold and wore two jackets between innings trying to keep warm. "I'm a warm weather pitcher. I like it when it's hot. It keeps me loose. Sure I get tired in the heat. But it keeps my arm from tightening up."[8]

Three months into the 1968 season, Astros General Manager H.B. "Spec" Richardson fired Hatton and replaced him with the team's batting instructor Harry Walker, but the Astros still crawled last across the NL finish line. One highlight of the season happened on July 14 when Wilson struck out 18 Reds in the second game of a doubleheader at Crosley Field. But medical troubles found him on August 4 during a game against Philadelphia. After pitching seven innings, he complained of chest pains and was taken to Methodist Hospital in Houston. Don admitted to doctors that he had been suffering the pain for some time but had kept his complaints to himself so he could finish the season. Doctors cleared him to resume play days later. Wilson racked up 175 strikeouts in 1968, but his ERA increased almost half a run.

In 1969, Don notched another distinctive mark in the baseball record books. On April 30 the Astros arrived at Crosley Field to play the Reds in a match that would leave every Houston player seeing red—including Wilson. The bad blood between the Reds and Astros had started eight days earlier when the Cincinnati team clobbered the Astros, 14–0. Tensions increased when the peppered twirls of right-handed Cincy pitcher Jim Maloney kept the Astros bats cold on April 30. Despite a painful groin muscle strain handicapping his talent, Maloney no-hit Houston. Hoots and teasing from the Reds added insult to injury. Wilson went to bed angry, vowing revenge. The next day, Don took the mound and threw the hardest pitches he could. He kept the Reds hitless in the first inning. The scoreless scene suddenly seemed all too familiar. Eight hitless innings followed and Don added another no-hitter to his resume. It was the second time in major league history that two teams exchanged no-hitters on successive days.[9]

Moments after Wilson achieved victory, the press swarmed him. "There were a couple of times my legs were shaking so much I had to step off the mound," said Wilson. "I never wanted anything so bad in all my life as to pitch that no hitter."[10]

Wilson told the press that Reds manager Dave Bristol added fuel to his personal flame by taunting him from the dugout with the word "gutless." He also said that all the excitement of the no-hitter may have upset his wife (who was pregnant with their second child and weeks away from delivery) as she watched on TV. Don jokingly told the press to give Bernice his personal message, "Don't get excited and have that baby now."[11]

When asked for his remarks on Wilson's performance, Houston pilot Harry Walker said, "There's not a lot to say. What was said was made from the pitching mound. One man just over-powered nine men."[12]

The familiar scene of a shredded contract and well-deserved raise followed the performance. Wilson's reliable backstop Don Bryant also received a raise from Astros GM Spec Richardson. Wilson personally gave Bryant an engraved wristwatch days after the game.

Wilson and teammate Curt Blefary made newspaper ink in June after the two were ridiculed by several major league players and fans because they shared hotel rooms on the road. Blefary, Houston's Italian-Caucasian first baseman, was not bashful to those who objected to his African-American roomie: "They said they couldn't believe I was rooming with a colored guy. I told them to go to hell."[13]

Don admitted that he received an anonymous hate letter about rooming with a white player. "It's just hard for them to get it through their heads that we are just two human beings trying to make a living in the same game."[14]

As the tension and hoopla of no-hit games and broken color barriers calmed, Don and Bernice celebrated the birth of their son, Donald Alexander. Wilson notched a 4.00 ERA in 1969, the highest of his playing career.

The start of the 1970 season was difficult as Wilson developed an acute case of tendonitis in his right elbow, hitting the 21-day disabled list in early April. Wilson returned in late April and immediately went back to work throwing fastballs. He closed the season with an 11–6 pitching record and 3.91 ERA.

The 1971 season would be Wilson's best, with a 16–10 record and the lowest ERA (2.45) of his career. Wilson was selected to play in the 1971 All-Star Game at Tiger Stadium in Detroit and was recognized as the Most Valuable Player of the 1971 Houston Astros. The following offseason Harry Walker boasted to the press:

"Last year, I thought [Wilson] was one of the best pitchers in the league. The next five or six years will be his best in baseball."[15]

On August 20, 1972, Don confirmed Walker's confidence in him as he fanned 14 Phillies at Veterans Stadium. A week later, the Astros fired Harry Walker and installed Leo "The Lip" Durocher as the new manager. On July 27, 1973, Wilson's lip earned a $300 fine from Durocher after he called his manager a name on the team bus at Houston International Airport. Three months after the argument, Durocher resigned from his management position. Spec Richardson replaced Leo with Houston's third base coach, Preston Gomez. Wilson wound up with a 1973 record of 11–16 and a 3.20 ERA.

Gomez kept the helm in 1974. On September 4 at the Astrodome, Don Wilson reached for his third no-hit game against his favorite competitors—the Cincinnati Reds. The Reds' George Foster and Cesar Geronimo got free passes from Wilson and the two were tediously shifted to score two runs but the Reds were no-hit through eight innings. With the score 2–1 in Cincinnati's favor, Gomez needed a run on the board. Wilson was benched for pinch hitter Tommy Helms. Helms grounded out. Shortstop Roger Metzger hit a single, but Cedeño struck out and Metzger was caught trying to steal. The attempt had failed and Gomez was assailed by boos when he sent left-hander Mike Cosgrove to the Astrodome mound in the ninth.

Cincinnati didn't produce any runs against Cosgrove, though they did get a hit and the end tally remained in favor of the Reds, 2–1.

Wilson, initially upset with his manager's decision, disappeared into the clubhouse after the game. The pitcher emerged hours later to speak with the press. "I respect Preston Gomez as a manager and I respect him more than ever. He wants to win and I want to win as much as he does. When people start putting personal goals ahead of the team, you'll never have a winner. I understand how Preston feels."[16]

Don ended the season with a record of 11–13 and a 3.08 ERA. ABC TV contacted Wilson during his winter break and asked if he would act as a judge on the televised sports show *The Superstars*. The show involved female athletes from every sport competing in "Olympic-type" events. The production was filmed at the Astrodome on December 21, 1974. Tennis star Billie Jean King was in attendance, as was pro golfer Sandy Palmer and Olympic swimmer Debbie Meyer. The event was plagued by poor attendance and the 4,000 spectators in the Astrodome stands preferred to mock the women's sport competition rather than cheer. Marilyn Preston, a television critic for the *Chicago Tribune*, summarized her opinions of the show: "I just figured this out. ABC only gets its kicks when the girls look like fools. This is the worst exploitation of women yet."[17]

During a time of the controversial '70's feminist movement, it appeared that the original intentions of ABC's *Superstars* had taken a very wrong turn. Don Wilson experienced some feminine fire during the softball throw competition. One competitor crossed the throw line and Wilson failed to call the violation. After a short review, Don agreed with the violation and the competitor was disqualified. Billie Jean King protested Wilson's judgment. "The judges were told to be lenient about this stuff. Now you're getting technical?"[18]

ABC reporter Donna de Varona attacked Wilson's stalled decision. A meet official noticed that Wilson was getting frustrated with de Varona's interrogation. The official warned de Varona to stick to her report and refrain from arguing. De Varona exclaimed, "I'm not arguing, I'm investigating. I'm an investigative reporter." Wilson, who was clearly annoyed by the situation, replied to Donna de Varona with sarcasm, "I need THIS?"[19]

Don and Bernice celebrated Christmas with their children, Denise and Alex. But shortly after, a terrible calamity took place at the Wilsons'. On Sunday, January 5, at one o'clock in the afternoon, Bernice Wilson called a friend and asked her to come to the house because something was "wrong."

Bernice explained that Don was sleeping in his car parked in the garage and her children were still sleeping. The acquaintance was puzzled at the thought of Don and the kids sleeping into the afternoon hours. She advised Bernice to set down the phone and physically check Don. Bernice returned to the phone and gave her friend the results. She told Bernice to call an ambulance then hung up and called the Houston Police Department herself. When the ambulance arrived, Bernice answered the door wearing a green velvet robe. The house was still dressed with Christmas decorations, including braided silver garland that zigzagged the banister of the winding staircase in the center of the house. The paramedics immediately noticed the left side of Bernice's face was swollen and bruised. Bernice stayed in the living room while the paramedics went upstairs. Another paramedic went into the garage. Moments later, they told Bernice they were taking Denise to the hospital, but that her 29-year-old husband Don and her five-year-old son Alex were deceased. The Houston Police arrived on scene and found the Wilsons' brown 1972 Ford Thunderbird on the left side of the two-car garage, their Datsun 240Z on the right, and a black stain on the concrete floor below the tailpipe of the Thunderbird.

The same black stain was found on the bottom edge of the overhead electric garage door. Don was reclined in the passenger seat of the Thunderbird, his ankles crossed in front of him and his hands on his lap, an open pack of cigarettes on the dashboard. The ignition keys were in the "start" position and the gas gauge read "E." Alex had been found in the bed of the master bedroom on the second floor above the garage. Denise had been found unconscious—in critical condition—in bed in her bedroom on the second floor. Ambulance services took Denise to Texas Children's Hospital, while Bernice was taken to Southwest Memorial.

Six hours later, the police questioned her. She told them that she did not know how her jaw was injured and that she and Don had been with Don's teammate, Cesar Cedeño, on Saturday evening. She remembered waking up in the middle of the night after she heard a car running in the garage and her children crying in their sleep. Bernice explained that she went to check the children. She felt Denise's face and noted that her daughter was "hot and sweaty." She retrieved a wet cloth and

Wilson spent his entire major league career with the Astros.

wiped Denise's face. When she felt Alex, his skin felt cold. Bernice took Alex out of Denise's bed and put him in the bed of the master bedroom where she stayed with him.

Investigators asked Bernice when she found her husband. Mrs. Wilson explained that when she found her husband, she called her friend for help. When she went to the garage initially, the vehicle was running and its doors were locked. One newspaper mentioned that the car's radio was on when Don was found. Bernice retrieved her set of Thunderbird keys and unlocked the passenger door to get to Don, who appeared to be sleeping.

Bernice also said that she and Don were not having any domestic problems. Mrs. Wilson remained at the hospital for treatment of her jaw pending additional X-rays. Her daughter Denise had drifted into a coma. The Harris County Medical Examiner, Dr. Joseph Jachimczyk, completed autopsies on both Don and Alex Wilson. Upon review of Don's blood analysis, the medical examiner found a level of 68 percent carbon monoxide and a blood alcohol content of .167. Alex's blood test noted a 62 percent level of carbon monoxide. (A 40 percent level of carbon monoxide in the bloodstream is lethal.) Several neighbors were interviewed by the Houston Police Department and none of them mentioned any domestic troubles occurring at the Wilson address. Police interviewed Cesar Cedeño twice during their investigation and the Houston player explained that he and Don were out together on the evening hours of Friday, January 3, not Saturday, January 4. Police also interviewed Houston first baseman Bob Watson since he lived close to the Wilson address. Watson explained that he did not know of any domestic problems between Don and Bernice.

Details of Don and Alex Wilson's deaths made instant headlines in the newspaper. Several of the reports mentioned the possibility of Don attempting suicide. Those who knew Don staunchly disagreed with the notion. If a man were going to commit suicide, why would he do it on the passenger side of a vehicle? Wilson was 6-foot-3 inches and weighed approximately 230 pounds at the time of his death. The Ford was parked two feet from the driver's side of the Datsun. The length of the passenger door on the Thunderbird measured six feet. How did Don squeeze his way into the passenger side with only two feet of clearance to open a six-foot door? Some believed that the vehicle was pulled into the garage by someone while Don was seated on the passenger side. A blood test proved that Wilson was intoxicated. Was he passed out drunk when his driver left the vehicle running? Two burning question haunted

Houston police detectives: was it a homicide or a suicide? and why did Bernice Wilson have a jaw injury she could not explain? During one interrogation, Bernice stated that she vaguely recalled falling into a wall two days before she found her husband dead.

Peggy Nedruft, a spokesperson for Southwest Memorial Hospital, explained new details involving Bernice's injury. Mrs. Wilson's jaw was not fractured but was "swollen, bruised, and quite painful." The heartbreaking story took a light turn when Denise Wilson came out of coma and was in stable condition on January 7. She suffered some brain damage from carbon monoxide and would not be able to attend the funerals of her father and little brother. Memorial services for Donald Edward Wilson and his son Donald Alexander Wilson took place in Houston on February 9. The following day, they were laid to rest at the Forest Lawn Memorial Park mausoleum in Covina, California.

It was clear that Don, Alex, and Denise were poisoned by carbon monoxide. But if Bernice was in the house with Don, the kids, and the Thunderbird's fumes, why didn't she suffer from the effects of poisoning? Detective Larry Ott was quoted, "We're not pointing the finger at anyone. We just want to tie up loose ends, clear up some unanswered questions and inconsistencies."[ ]

Houston pitcher Dave Roberts disagreed with talk of Don committing suicide. He told the press: "Don had everything going for him. He had it all together."[21]

Dave and Don had been working together in the Astros' speakers bureau, a business that arranged speaking engagements for Houston baseball players. Mention of suicide also disturbed another member of Houston's pitching squad, Tom Griffin. Evidence showed that Wilson had plans to meet and work with Griffin on Sunday, January 5, at an Astros pitching school. Don had agreed to attend the workshop as a substitute instructor for Ken Forsch, who was unable to participate. Griffin mentioned this fact to the press and added, "I really enjoyed being around him. He was a great person. I want people to know what kind of guy he was. He was a good human being."[22]

Astros teammate Doug Rader bet his life on Don's personal stability. "I've heard all kinds of crazy things, rumors, about how Don Wilson died. I don't care what anyone says. I'll never believe he killed himself. He loved life too much. His death simply had to be an accident. I'd stake my life on that."[23]

When detectives attempted to interview Bernice on January 14, she informed them that she had retained an attorney and she would not answer any questions without her counsel present. On January 19, Denise

Wilson was told that her father and brother had died. On February 5, seven days before what would have been Don's thirtieth birthday, Harris County Medical Examiner Dr. Joseph Jachimczyk ruled the deaths of Don and Alex Wilson "accidental." The case was officially closed. The Houston Astros retired Don Wilson's jersey number "40" on April 14, 1975. A special plaque displaying a photo of Don Wilson and his retired number is currently displayed on the Astros' "Wall of Honor" at Houston's Minute Maid Park. ■

Notes

1. "No-Hit Pitcher Got Start When Brother Got Tired," *The Washington Afro-American*, June 20, 1967, Volume 97, 14.
2. Arthur Daley, "Wilson Ball Big-Time." *St. Petersburg Times*, March 20, 1968, Volume 84, No. 240, 40.
3. Ibid.
4. Ibid.
5. John Wilson, "Wilson's No-Hit Smoke Blinds Braves," *The Sporting News*, July 1, 1967, Volume 163, No. 24, 7.
6. "Astro Rookie Don Wilson Hurls No-Hitter At Braves," *Sarasota Herald Tribune*, June 19, 1967, Volume 42, No. 239, 18.
7. Wilson, op. cit.
8. "Astro Pitcher Doesn't Like Image," *Ellensburg Daily Record* (Ellensburg, WA), July 3, 1974, Volume 73, Number 156, 14.
9. The identical coincidence took place in 1968 when Gaylord Perry of the Giants and the Cardinals' Ray Washburn completed the odd feat of two consecutive "Cadillacs" on September 17 and 18.
10. Earl Lawson, "Wilson Was Boiling Mad During His No-Hitter," *The Sporting News*, May 17, 1969, Volume 167, Number 18, 8.
11. "Angry Wilson Scalds Reds With No-Hitter, Remarks." *Eugene Register-Guard*, May 2, 1969, Volume 102, Number 191, 11.
12. Ibid.
13. Sam Lacy, "It Happened In Texas Of All Places." *Baltimore Afro-American*, June 3, 1969, Volume 77, Number 93, 5.
14. "It's No Big Thing, Says Don Wilson," *The Free Lance-Star* (Fredericksburg, VA), May 27, 1969, Volume 85, Number 125, 5.
15. "Walker Expects Good Astro Club," *Spartanburg Herald-Journal*, January 23, 1972, Volume 100, Number 6, 5.
16. "Gomez Right Says Astros' Don Wilson," *The Victoria (TX) Advocate*, September 6, 1974, Volume 129., Number122, 5B.
17. Curry Kirkpatrick, "There Is Nothing Like A Dame," *Sports Illustrated*, January 6, 1975, 22.
18. Ibid.
19. Ibid.
20. "Wilson Death Probe 'Open' For 'Unanswered Questions,'" *The Gazette* (Montreal, Canada), January 8, 1975. Volume 197. 28.
21. "Don Wilson, Son Dead," *The Ledger* (Lakeland, FL), January 6, 1975, Volume 68. Number 82, 10.
22. Ibid.
23. Milton Richman, "Competitive Described Don Wilson," *The Beaver County Times*, January 6, 1975, 11.

Rainout in the Astrodome

Rick Schabowski

A rainout in the Astrodome? How is that possible? It's domed, protected from the elements. The Astros don't even have the traditional rain check printed on their tickets! Yet on Tuesday, June 15, 1976, the supposed impossible happened. A game between the Astros and the Pittsburgh Pirates was postponed because of rain.

A powerful thunderstorm developed over the Houston area when very humid, unstable atmospheric conditions along the Gulf Coast were followed by a cold front, extending all the way through central Texas. The storm hit Houston shortly before noon. Seven hours later, downtown Houston had received 7.48 inches of rain. The worst flooding occurred around Market Street, the East Loop, Denver Harbor, and Reveille. The heaviest recorded rainfall was 13.06 inches at the Houston Ship Channel near 75th Street, and 10.47 inches was unofficially recorded at the Texas Medical Center, located just north of the Astrodome, where the most flooding occurred.

Houston Astros authentication manager Mike Acosta recalled, "It was like a tropical storm. It was raining hard, and it just kept coming down. It got to the point where the streets around the Astrodome were flooded and impassable. Fans couldn't get to the stadium. Neither could Astrodome workers. Remember, the Astrodome floor was 45 feet below ground level. So the lower ramps and entries were flooded also."[1]

Astros general manager Tal Smith recalled, "It was an absolute downpour. There was flooding all over, and people were just marooned. Houston has a low water table, we're not that far above ground, a marshy area, and when we get torrential downpours, we have flooding."[2]

What would happen to the game scheduled for the evening as a result of this deluge? Tal Smith said, "At the time, it was quite a story. Obviously we could have played, but we would have done so without any umpires, without any fans. The players were there, and our offices were in the Dome, but nobody else could get there. The umpires stayed at the Shamrock Hotel which was not that far from the Dome, maybe two miles at the most. The umpire chief called me about four o'clock that afternoon and said they tried to get there and just couldn't get out, and by that time we had reports from all around the stadium, about the roads being impassable and so on."[3] Later it was reported that the umpires had made a determined effort to arrive for the game, but their cars had stalled in high water and they had to wade back to their hotel.

How did the players manage to arrive for the game without major issues? Acosta answered, "Both teams were here. Players started arriving around 1:00, when it was still possible to get to the stadium. They had to be dressed by 3:00 or 3:30. The Pirates team bus made it through, as did the Astros coming by themselves."[4]

Indeed, the players were there, but the trip there, even before the storm reached its worst stage, was not easy.

Astros pitcher Paul Siebert thought the game would be played, but recalled, "My girlfriend dropped me off. She came back, drove through water over the hood. My 1975 Grand Prix was in the shop for a week drying out."[5]

It was a special day for George (Doc) Medich. "June 16, 1976, was our seventh wedding anniversary. I was supposed to pitch. I spent the afternoon reading a Robert Ludlum book in my hotel room and remember watching it rain, and rain, and rain. It rained hard for a long time. I recall the rain lasting at least seven hours. I mean a very hard steady rain. About 2:00, I was beginning to wonder if the game might even be called even though it was played inside. Houston is very flat, and the water doesn't run off very fast. Around 3:00, I took a cab over to the Dome, it might have been with Tommy Helms. When we got there, there were a few of our players and coaches already there."[6]

Pirates pitcher Jerry Reuss remembered, "The Pirates stayed at the Shamrock Hotel that year and the bus ride to the Dome was normally 10 or 15 minutes. On the bus ride to the park, I noticed the canals that collect the run-off from the frequent Houston rainstorms were unusually high and in some cases, were spilling over their banks and into the adjacent streets.

Although the playing field of the Astrodome was protected from the weather, severe flooding made roads impassable, preventing the umpires from arriving, and the lower ramps inside the dome filled with water, too.

I lived in Houston for two years and never saw that happen. The trip from the hotel to the Dome that day was around a half hour and the storm was the topic of conversation in the clubhouse. Still, we dressed and it was business as usual during our time on the field."[7]

Astros manager Bill Virdon's wife Shirley, commenting about the ride in, recalled, "I remember it well! My daughter and I were stranded in our car on top of the Interstate at the Kirby exit to the Dome. I sat in the car 5½ hours waiting for the rain to subside, and the water to go away so I could get off the freeway. Our daughter waded over to the Dome."[8]

The players inside the Astrodome didn't have knowledge of what was going on outside, or if the game would be played or postponed. When Astros manager Bill Virdon arrived he thought, "When we first got on the field we thought we would play."[9] Larry Dierker, "Didn't know," but Astros infielder Rob Andrews mentioned, "We did have our doubts when water began to cascade over the outfield scoreboard."[10]

The Astros' Mike Cosgrove "couldn't believe the water outside, cars were under water!"[11]

A decision had to be made. Tal Smith, assessing the situation, made the logical decision to postpone the game. The main reason was concern for not putting fans and employees in harm's way. The decision was announced around 5:00 PM, while rains were still heavy and showing no signs of subsiding. The announcement of the postponement was the lead story on both the five o'clock and six o'clock local TV news broadcasts.

Smith thought it wasn't a difficult decision. "Nobody could get there, and I just thought the intelligent thing

to do was to call the game. There was some concern by some of our other people, some of my management associates, particularly in the non-baseball side that this would make us look bad. I said to the contrary, I think it's a major news story, it's nothing we've done, that it's a question of the elements, the weather and so on. It was the responsible, prudent thing to do. On that day, June 15, it was the trading deadline, and Joe Brown was the general manager of the Pittsburgh club at the time. I conferred with him, told him what I was going to do, which was fine."[12]

An Astros spokesman told the press, "It wasn't exactly a rain-out. It was a rain-in."[13]

About 20 fans did make it to the game, and they became dinner guests of the Astros in one of the stadium cafeterias. The players were also treated to a meal, but rather than a cafeteria setting, they ate on the field. Doc Medich recalled, "The Astros brought food down onto the field and served it on tables out by second base."[14] Bill Virdon said that the players from both teams, "were happy to be fed at that time."[15] Mike Cosgrove thought it was, "Great—a great gesture by whoever put it on."[16]

None of the players can recall what was on the menu that evening. The *Houston Post* reported they were catered steak dinners, and Paul Siebert remarked, "I don't remember, more drinks than food."[17] Mike Acosta's recollection was, "Concession workers set up a buffet and tables behind second base, and both teams ate dinner on the field together. The players were in uniforms, but some of them were wearing shower flip-flops on their feet. The Astrodome staff ate with the players as well."[18]

Rob Andrews stayed the night in a dome luxury suite and described the drive home the next day on the roads littered with abandoned cars like "some kind of world-ending disaster flick."

Jerry Reuss noted, "Since the Astros players and office personnel were in the same predicament, a decision was made to make everyone as comfortable as possible. A makeshift kitchen was set up just beyond the infield, picnic tables were placed nearby as personnel from both clubs were invited to the impromptu meal."[19]

After the meal, a few of the Astros including Larry Dierker decided to climb to the top of the Dome and crawl on the catwalk.

Tal Smith's intelligent decision saved many fans from being put in harm's way attempting to get to the game, but there was one last hurdle to conquer. How would the people at the Astrodome get safely home?

Paul Siebert recalled, "We left late. My car didn't start. We got a ride with Ed Herrmann."[20]

Doc Medich's trip home began "around 8:00 PM, I guess the rain slacked off enough for us to get a bus back to the hotel. The streets were still flooded and the bus had to go very slow through the streets."[21] Bill Virdon was able to get home in his car, but his wife Shirley had to leave her car sitting on a bridge near the stadium. As the evening grew later, the danger decreased. Larry Dierker recalled leaving at around 10:00, and Roger Metzger around midnight. Rob Andrews and Mike Cosgrove chose to ride home in the morning, after spending the night in an Astrodome luxury suite, sleeping while the waters subsided.

The next morning things were still far from normal. Rob Andrews remembered, "The drive home was surreal. No one was on the roads. As I got on the Interstate by the Dome I had to weave through abandoned cars left right where they stalled the night before. I couldn't shake the feeling I was in some kind of world-ending disaster flick."[22]

Tal Smith recalled another rain adventure that happened to him in 2004. "Driving home during one of these torrential downpours, I flooded my car out. Sometimes you just have no chance. You're able to drive, and all of a sudden you run into a situation where there's massive water that's risen so rapidly, there's no place to go."[23] ∎

Sources

Houston Post
Houston Chronicle

Personal interview

Tal Smith, telephone interview, February 3, 2014

Notes

1. Hoffmann, Ken, "Astros made history with a rainout," *Houston Chronicle*, June 17, 2009.
2. Smith, Tal, Personal interview, February 3, 2014.
3. Ibid.
4. Ibid.
5. Paul Siebert, written correspondence, February 15, 2014.
6. Doc Medich, written correspondence, February 16, 2014.
7. Jerry Reuss, written correspondence, February 17, 2014.
8. Bill Virdon, written correspondence, February 19, 2014.
9. Ibid.
10. Rob Andrews, written correspondence, February 15, 2014.
11. Mike Cosgrove, written correspondence, February 19, 2014.
12. Smith.
13. Hoffmann.
14. Medich.
15. Virdon.
16. Cosgrove.
17. Siebert.
18. Hoffmann.
19. Reuss.
20. Siebert.
21. Medich.
22. Andrews.
23. Smith.

Catching Rainbows and Calling Stars

Alan Ashby and the Houston Astros

Maxwell Kates

Few individuals saw more Astros history that Alan Ashby. An Astro for 20 of their first 50 seasons, he spent eleven on the Astrodome carpet, coordinating one of the more challenging pitching staffs of his time. After one year as their bullpen coach Ashby moved to the broadcast booth for another eight, culminating with Houston's first trip to the World Series. Ashby, a Mormon, channeled his strong work ethic into a 17-year playing career, becoming a fan favorite in Cleveland, Toronto, and Houston.

Alan Dean Ashby was born July 8, 1951, in Long Beach, California. When he was six years old, developments in Brooklyn would shape his professional career as the Dodgers announced they were moving to California. Ashby spent his childhood listening to Vin Scully and Jerry Doggett call radio play-by-play. The Dodgers moved into Chavez Ravine before two World Championships and the emergence of a pitching superstar:

"I was just a skinny kid who idolized Sandy Koufax. When I grew up in Los Angeles, I saw two of Koufax's no-hitters."[1] Indeed, he was eyewitness to Koufax's perfect game against the Chicago Cubs at Dodger Stadium on September 9, 1965.[2]

The natural left-handed hitter graduated from San Pedro High School in 1969, two years behind Garry Maddox.[3] As he told *Toronto Star* columnist Neil Mac-Carl, a quirk in the Dodgers' batting order influenced the way he played: "[The Dodgers] had an infield of four switch hitters—Wes Parker, Jim Lefebvre, Maury Wills, and Junior Gilliam. I thought that's what you had to do, so I would throw a ball against the garage door and take 10 swings right and then 10 swings left."[4]

The Cleveland Indians selected the 6'2" catcher in the third round of the June 1969 draft.[5] During his minor league offseasons, he attended classes at Harbor Junior College. Batting .226 with three home runs and 13 RBIs for Evansville and Oklahoma City of the American Association in 1973, he was recalled on July 3 to replace the injured Dave Duncan.[6] Ashby admitted that he was unfazed until he arrived at Municipal Stadium and "saw Al Kaline sitting across the room."[7] Tabbed to

start the following day, he touched Detroit pitcher Mike Strahler for an RBI single on his first pitch.[8]

The Indians won 5–2 and Ashby earned the praise of manager Ken Aspromonte. "I was especially impressed with his receiving," Aspromonte said. "Maybe the biggest thing is that he showed confidence in [Milt] Wilcox by making him throw certain pitches at certain times, which made Milt better."[9]

After splitting 1974 between Cleveland and Oklahoma City, Ashby returned to the Indians in 1975. He batted below .200 until switching to a shorter, lighter bat in July. Immediately he went 25-for-83 and ultimately became the regular. As Ashby told Russ Schneider of the *Cleveland Plain Dealer*, "I get special satisfaction proving the team can win with me behind the plate. I've felt that all along."[10]

Among the toughest judges in baseball, manager Frank Robinson described Ashby as "one of the nicest surprises of this season. You can see so much improvement in his [ability] since he has been playing."[11] For his team-oriented positive attitude, the Indians awarded Ashby the 1976 Gordon Cobbledick Golden Tomahawk Award.[12]

Though batting .224 with five home runs and 32 RBIs in 1975, Ashby's average improved to .239 in 1976 as he shared catching duties with Ray Fosse. The expansion Toronto Blue Jays arranged to trade for Ashby in a three-player deal for pitcher Al Fitzmorris on November 5, 1976.[13]

As the regular season broke, the Blue Jays boasted three areas of surplus: snow, losses, and catchers. The morning of the opener on April 7, Exhibition Stadium was blanketed with a blizzard. After beating the Chicago White Sox 9–5, they recorded only 53 more wins against 107 losses. Ashby's former Cleveland teammate Rick Cerone was named starting catcher in 1977. With Phil Roof as Cerone's backup and Ernie Whitt in the minors, where did Ashby fit?

"All spring...there were rumors that I was going to be traded to the Angels for Ron Jackson. The Blue Jays kind of went about that entire spring that I wasn't going to be a part of the team."[14] Would Ashby commute to Anaheim Stadium from his Mission Viejo home? Trade talks never materialized; one week after catching Bill Singer in the opener, Cerone broke his thumb. Sidelined until August, his 1977 season was limited to 100 at-bats.[15]

Ashby emerged as the regular, becoming the first Blue Jay to play 100 games.[16] Though an injury to his right hand in June limited his offense to a disappointing .210 with 2 home runs and 29 RBIs, he developed a reputation among "the most accurate throwing catchers in the league."[17] He threw out 48 percent of would-be baserunners in 1977.[18] Platooning with Cerone in 1978, Ashby batted .261 with nine home runs.[19] After two years of conjecture, the Blue Jays decided to trade one of their catchers. On November 27, 1978, Ashby was dealt to the Houston Astros for pitcher Mark Lemongello, outfielder Joe Cannon, and infielder Pedro Hernandez.[20]

At the time, the Astros' successes were modest. Attendance exceeded two million only in 1965 with fans more interested in the Astrodome than the product on the field. Star players Rusty Staub, Jerry Grote, John Mayberry, and especially Joe Morgan were traded be-

PHOTO BY J. McCARTHY, COURTESY OF DWAYNE LABAKAS

Alan Ashby spent two seasons with the Blue Jays before going to Houston, where he would spend the next 11 years, to the end of his major league career.

fore their prime. Others like Larry Dierker and Jimmy Wynn remained. However, in a division dominated by the Reds and the Dodgers, only in 1972 did the Astros finish higher than third. They were more famous for plastic grass, exploding scoreboards, and *Ball Four*. Their rainbow uniforms were a "pupil gouging horror" which "smacked of chain motel bedspread or 747 jumbo jet upholstery."[21] To Red Smith, the Astros were "a turkey ever since the novelty wore off the Astrodome."[22] By the mid-1970s, the Astros had no owner to speak of; trustees assigned the club to Ford and General Electric, creditors of Roy Hofheinz when he filed for bankruptcy. In the midst of a 64–97 deluge in 1975 following the death of pitcher Don Wilson, the Astros lured general manager Tal Smith away from the Yankees.

"I had been with [Houston] from Day One and I had been involved...with the construction of the Astrodome," remembers Smith, who left the Astros in 1973 to join his mentor Gabe Paul in New York. "The only place I would have left the Yankees was to return to Houston. Here was a unique opportunity to run a franchise completely."[23] Despite finishing last, the Astros featured a talented lineup with Enos Cabell, Ken Forsch, and J.R. Richard. Cesar Cedeño was winning Gold Gloves in center field while in left, Jose Cruz was emerging as "one of the top players in the league."[24] The Astros claimed pitcher Joe Niekro whose knuckleball made him a superstar. Promoting Joe Sambito from the minors in 1976 and Terry Puhl in 1977, the Astros augmented their roster with deals for Joaquin Andujar, Denny Walling, and Jeffrey Leonard. After two years of modest progress, the Astros regressed in 1978.

"Over that time frame," recalled Tal Smith, "I traded Bob Watson, Cliff Johnson, Doug Rader, and Roger Metzger. We had to rebuild the club. We had two weaknesses, one at short and one behind the plate."[25] Houston hurlers in 1978 faced six different catchers for a 3.63 ERA, fifth worst in the league. For his catcher, Smith looked to Pat Gillick, his erstwhile farm director now working as the Blue Jays' general manager. With Ashby and Houston native Craig Reynolds added to the starting lineup, the Astros in 1979 enjoyed one of their best starts in franchise history.

On April 7, one night after catching J.R. Richard's Opening Day victory over Atlanta, Ashby called a no-hitter by Ken Forsch.[26] By July 1, the Astros and their 50–31 record sat atop the National League West, a commanding 8.5 game lead over Cincinnati.[27] Bill Brown was a broadcaster for the Reds at that time:

"The Reds had retooled after winning consecutive World Series crowns in 1975 and 1976. They traded

Tony Perez after 1976, but they still retained some of the key components of the Big Red Machine era." Brown described the emerging rivalry as "intense" with "solid fundamentals based on strong pitching and supportive defensive play."[28]

The Astros led the league in complete games and shutouts while their ERA of 3.20 was second only to the Montreal Expos.[29] Many pitchers credited their newfound success to their rapport with Alan Ashby. To quote Virdon, "After last season, we had to find a catcher if we were to make any headway, and Alan has done an outstanding job."[30] Ashby also won the endorsement of their broadcaster who spent 13 years harnessing Houston catchers from the mound:

"Alan Ashby brought stability to the catcher position during his years with the Astros," recalled Larry Dierker. "Although he was not a great hitter, he was better than any other catcher the Astros ever had. He was also adept at calling the game, which gave the young pitchers a lot of confidence."[31]

Ashby did not have the easiest catching assignment. Unfamiliar with the National League, every fourth day he faced the flaming 98 mile an hour fastball and suicide slider of 6'8" James Rodney Richard:

"J.R. Richard might have been the most fear-provoking guy I ever caught. When he was on the mound, hitters were scared to death. [Righthanders] wanted no part of the action. He was wild enough that you had no idea where it was going to go and hard enough that even if he threw right over [the plate], you expected to have a tough time."[32] Richard in 1979 won 18 with a 2.71 ERA while fanning 313 hitters. Within the twentieth century, only Sandy Koufax had previously eclipsed 300 strikes in two consecutive National League seasons.[33]

Then Ashby had to face Joe Niekro's knuckleball every fourth day:

"To me, there was nothing quite like catching Joe Niekro. My broken fingers come from the knuckleball and it practically ruined my catching ability. For some reason, I lost the ability to handle him with one hand. I became very two-handed and it infiltrated the rest of my game defensively for years to follow and that knuckleball just destroyed me."[34] Niekro tied his brother Phil with 21 wins and earned the title of Astros' MVP.[35] Ashby, meanwhile, was virtually flawless defensively. As for his batting average—.202 in 1979—he deflected criticism with humor, "I'm convinced there is a lot more hitting ability inside me. Maybe it's hiding."[36]

True to Tom Seaver's midseason prediction, inexperience caused the Astros to "fall like a lead balloon" as the Reds surpassed them in September for the division

After hitting .202 in 1979, Ashby remarked, "I'm convinced there is a lot more hitting ability inside me. Maybe it's hiding."

title.[37] Despite missing most of September after breaking a finger catching Niekro, Ashby was rewarded with a three-year contract extension.[38]

Ashby credited the manager for overseeing the rapid development of the team: "Bill Virdon might have been my favorite manager...Frankly I enjoyed playing for those kinds of guys because I felt I was always going to try my best. There's no place for [horseplay] in Major League Baseball and a manager shouldn't tolerate it. Bill Virdon would take guys...if you weren't going in his estimation 100 percent, he would take you out right then. You're done. He'd take you out and bring in another guy. I found that very respect-worthy and I like a manager who demands everything at all times because I think everybody on your ballclub ought to be playing that way."[39]

Off the field, shipping tycoon John McMullen and others purchased the Astros from Roy Hofheinz's creditors. After a near-miss in 1979, McMullen granted Tal Smith authority to build a champion in 1980. Smith signed J.R. Richard to a lucrative extension before enticing Joe Morgan to return to Houston as a free agent.

McMullen also signed the plum of the market, a 32-year-old Texan after a disappointing 16–14 campaign with the Angels. As described by biographer Kenny Hand, "McMullen didn't know an RBI from a UFO when he bought the Astros in 1979, but he knew enough to know he wanted Nolan Ryan. At any price."[40] The price commanded was the wealthiest baseball contract to that time. At $4.5 million over four years, it was slightly below half the Astros' gross revenues in

1979.[41] Ashby was familiar with Ryan's fastball; he quoted Cleveland teammate Oscar Gamble that "a good night is 0-for-4 and don't get hit in the head."[42] When he considered additional bruises from catching Richard, Niekro, and now Ryan, Ashby quipped that "maybe I should've brought that up before I signed my contract."[43] True to his work ethic, Ashby was already catching Ryan in Astrodome practices before spring training began.

Ashby coordinated starting pitchers to a 67–53 record as he batted .256 with 19 doubles.[44] In the bullpen, Sambito and rookie Dave Smith combined for 27 saves. Even in football-mad Houston, "Luv Ya, Orange" had supplanted the "blue" slogan of the NFL Oilers.[45] A season-ending sweep by the Dodgers forced a one-game playoff, which the Astros won, 7–1. After leading the league with 93 wins, 929 strikeouts, and an ERA of 3.10, the Astros were finally playoff bound. Meanwhile, the Astros shattered their attendance record set in 1965. As Larry Dierker remembered, "Season ticket sales skyrocketed [and] daily walk-up attendance also flourished because the team was once again in the race and this time they won it."[46]

"We believed all year that we could win it all this year," recalled Ashby. "The first words out of Bill Virdon's mouth were 'We've got the best team in the National League. Now let's go get it.'"[47] The Astros faced the Philadelphia Phillies in one of the most evenly matched National League Championship Series ever played. Four games required extra innings and after three, the Astros led two games to one. Despite leading after seven innings in both the fourth and fifth games, the Astros lost both matches and the series to the Phillies. Del Unser's statement that "we shined...because the Astros pushed us harder than anyone" was hardly comforting to the Astros and their fans.[48]

In some respects, the Astros were defeated by their own disabled list. After posting a 10–4 record with a 1.90 ERA and starting the All-Star Game in Los Angeles, J.R. Richard was crippled by a stroke in July, never to pitch in the majors again. Meanwhile, Cesar Cedeño suffered a gruesome ankle injury rounding first base in game three, ending his season and shortening his career. To Ashby, Cedeño's reputation as baseball's heir apparent to Willie Mays had been justified. "Cesar Cedeño was initially the most talented player I had been around...You talk about five tool guys—and five tool can get really overtalked—but he had all the tools. He had them all and he was truly amazing."[49]

Ashby, meanwhile, missed several postseason games while nursing a broken rib. He remarked that although "both teams deserved to play in the World Series...only one can make it and that's the Phillies."[50] Ashby added that "our team's character is like the character of our fans. We showed America something about Houston...that's sincerely how I feel tonight."[51] To paraphrase a Larry Dierker lyric, it made a fellow proud to be an Astro.[52]

The Astros revamped their roster for 1981, replacing Richard and Forsch in the starting rotation with Don Sutton and Bob Knepper, and eventually substituting Phil Garner for Joe Morgan at second base. The season, punctuated by a midseason strike, provided an opportunity for eight teams to reach the playoffs in a split-season format. With the Dodgers already clinching a playoff spot, the chase for the second-half title provided the highlight of Ashby's season when Nolan Ryan faced Los Angeles at home. Having called 135 of Ryan's starts and witnessing 874 strikeouts, both records for Big Tex catchers, Ashby felt history was possible with each passing start by the Express.[53] "He had great stuff every time he went out there. What I remember a lot about catching Nolan is coming back to the bench after the innings and my teammates would always ask 'Is he going to throw one today?'"[54]

On September 26, Ryan threw one, fanning 11 Dodgers as the contest was broadcast on NBC's Game of the Week. "I caught [Ryan's] fifth no-hitter, the record breaker," said Ashby. "At the time, it was phenomenal to me...to have caught Nolan Ryan's record breaking fifth no-hitter over [Sandy Koufax], my hero, was too much to believe."[55] Ashby contributed to the cause by driving in two of the Astros' five runs.[56] He recalls Dusty Baker ending the game by rolling a hanging curveball for a ground ball to Art Howe at 3rd base: "...I thought he was going to crush it."[57]

The score was deadlocked at one in the ninth inning of the Division Series opener. As Craig Reynolds walked to the plate, Ashby remembers saying, "Get on base and I'll drive you home."[58] His prediction was nothing short of accurate. With two out and a runner on, Ashby provided the fireworks with a walkoff home run against Dave Stewart.[59] "I'm not a home run hitter, but from about the time I swung and saw it in the air, I knew it was going to creep out. I was jumping for joy in the batter's box before the crowd even realized what had happened."[60]

Awestruck by the blast, Dave Smith observed that "if this...was not a Dome, it would have wound up in Galveston."[61] The Astros won the second game, but the Dodgers swept the next three in a best-of-five series on their way to a World Series championship.

Ashby adjusted to hitting in the National League. He improved to .256 with three home runs in 1980 and

Ashby, pictured here with Tony Scott, was the first Astro to homer from both sides of the plate in a single game.

.271 with four home runs in 1981. Then in 1982, as he hit .257 with 12 home runs and 49 RBIs, Ashby accomplished an unprecedented feat. He became the first Astro to homer from both sides of the plate in one game, touching John Montefusco and Chris Welsh in a 7–3 victory over the Padres on September 27.[62] As Expos manager Jim Fanning once remarked, however, players often exceeded their statistical mean in their free agent season.[63]

Emerging as a National League dynasty was no longer within the Astros' budget. As recently as 1979, the Astros had the lowest payroll in the senior circuit.[64] Three years later, it was the second highest.[65] To show for it were two failed World Series attempts followed by a disappointing fifth-place finish (77–85). Neither Tal Smith nor Bill Virdon remained in the organization by 1982; under general manager Al Rosen, the Astros became more conservative in contract negotiations. The first free agent to test their newfound austerity was Alan Ashby.

"We want to sign him," remarked John McMullen. "He's a fine person and player [and] we'll make every effort to keep him in the organization."[66] Where Ashby and McMullen disagreed, however, were the length and terms of the proposed contract. Catchers throughout baseball paid careful attention to the eight-year, $16 million contract Gary Carter signed with the Expos in 1982. While Ashby was not asking for parity with Carter, his request for a five-year $3.5 million contract was double the Astros' budgeted amount. Furthermore, McMullen was averse to approving any deals exceeding three years. When trade negotiations with the Pirates for Tony Pena failed, the Astros compromised on job security, signing Ashby to a four-year, $1.7 million contract.[67]

Ashby was catching in Queens on May 2, 1983, when Mets infielder Hubie Brooks became Nolan Ryan's 3,510th strikeout victim, breaking Walter Johnson's lifetime record. Two years later, on October 5, 1985, he was the catalyst in a 9–3 victory over San Diego as he victimized Ed Wojna with his first National League grand slam.[68]

"You're always striving for something," surmised Ashby.[69] Years of catching a difficult staff took a toll on Ashby's fielding. Having sustained multiple finger fractures catching Niekro's "butterfly on steroids," Ashby began to rely increasingly on young Mark Bailey to assist behind the plate.

In 1986, the Astros hired Hal Lanier as their new manager. A disciple of Whitey Herzog, Lanier led the Astros to 13 wins in their first 19 games and didn't relinquish the divisional lead after July 19. They were led by young players Glenn Davis, Billy Hatcher, and Kevin Bass, but the Astros' key to their division was Mike Scott and his split finger fastball:

"For a small window," Ashby told David Laurila, "Mike was really, really good...he was low-to-mid 90s and he learned how to create some movement."[70] Ashby caught Scott's September 25 no-hitter against the Giants for the third of his career. Better yet, it clinched the division for the Astros:

"I had bigger days offensively...but the no-hitters from Nolan and Scott were big."[71] Late in the game, a conference on the mound demonstrated Ashby's ability to coach and motivate pitchers in pressure situations. Approaching Scott, he assured him that "we're gonna win this and we're gonna win the pennant. But let's not get crazy and throw a 2–0 fastball right down the middle."[72]

Larry Dierker remembers 1986 as the best Astros team Ashby played on: "The 1980 and '81 teams were based on pitching speed and defense (sic), the perfect combination for the Astrodome. The '86 team was even better because [of] balance between hitting and pitching and...between left- and right-handed hitters and pitchers."[73]

Ashby was integral to Scott's two playoff victories over the New York Mets. Scott fanned 14 Mets in the first game while Ashby's two-run homer won game four at Shea Stadium.[74] Ashby caught all 16 innings of the infamous game six, a 7–6 Mets victory which ended the Astros' season.

"We played our hearts out," Ashby told the Associated Press. "We played the best we could and got the support we needed [but] the Mets still beat us. They beat us in their last at-bat and that's something we've been doing all season."[75] Two decades later, Ashby took pride that "if you look at the teams that beat us— the Phillies, the Dodgers, the Mets—all of them went on to win the World Series. We got beaten by the best every time."[76]

After signing a two-year contract extension, Ashby reached his offensive zenith in 1987. He hit .317 with 19 RBIs through May 26.[77] At 36, he set career marks, hitting .288 with 14 home runs and 63 RBIs in 125 games. Meanwhile, he led National League catchers with a .993 fielding percentage.[78] His acumen at the plate earned the admiration of new Astros broadcaster Bill Brown: "Ashby, frequently batting seventh, provided an all-important bottom-of-the-order complement to [Glenn] Davis and was able to drive in key runners from the middle of the lineup who were on base when he batted."[79]

Meanwhile Ashby attributed his offensive zenith to "playing every day," adding that "I enjoy getting another chance to show I can still play."[80] Ashby played exceptionally again in early 1988 but was sidelined for two months with a dislocated vertebra on June 25.[81] The Astros recalled catching prospect Craig Biggio from Tuscon while Ashby's extended contract was about to expire.

Said Ashby, "I thought a lot about my future when I was injured and I don't want anyone to get the idea that my career is finished."[82] The Pirates proposed a trade for outfielder Glenn Wilson in May 1989. As the father of six young children and a 10-and-5 man, Ashby rejected the deal.[83] Preparing to board a flight to Chicago on May 10, Ashby learned that he was placed on irrevocable waivers.[84] He was batting only .164 with no home runs and three RBIs.

"It was very devastating to me," he told Neal Hohlfeld at the time. "Frankly, I don't know if I want to play for another team."[85] Ashby realized that rejecting the Pittsburgh trade had been a bad career move but stated that "family is my primary concern."[86] He retired with 183 doubles, 13 triples, 90 home runs and 513 RBIs in 1,370 games over 17 seasons, hitting .245.

As Astros' rebuilding phase continued early into the 1990s, Ashby began his second career with a television studio in Houston.[87] He returned to professional baseball in 1994 to manage the Rio Grande Valley Whitewings of the independent Texas-Louisiana League. Based in nearby Harlingen, the Whitewings finished in third place (40–48) in the West Division in 1994 and third place (53–46) in 1995.[88] He managed again in 1996, piloting the Astros' Florida State League affiliate at Kissimmee to a fifth place (60–75) finish in the East Division.[89]

The Astros had completed their rebuilding process under new owner Drayton McLane. After Tal Smith returned to the front office, "Houston's Brand of Baseball" reached into its history to harness its present. With Vern Ruhle, Jose Cruz, and Bill Virdon hired as coaches in 1997, manager Larry Dierker named Ashby as his bullpen coach. One year later, he joined Milo Hamilton in the broadcast booth.

Hamilton wrote in his autobiography that he "...tried to get Ashby in the booth even before that," adding that he "thought he had all the tools it took to be a great broadcaster."[90] The Astros' modest 84 wins were sufficient to capture the Central Division title in 1997. Winning 102 games in 1998, they were poised to challenge the Atlanta Braves as the flagship team in the National League.

Ashby considered the 1998 club to be "the best...in Astros history. It featured the original Killer B's—Bagwell, Biggio, and Derek Bell—plus Moises Alou and a pitching staff anchored by Randy Johnson, Jose Lima, and Billy Wagner."[91] Johnson and his 10–1 record were especially dominant after he was acquired from Seattle on July 31 to bolster a rotation anchored by Shane Reynolds and Mike Hampton. Ashby achieved personal milestones in 1999 as he was named the Astros' All-Time Catcher in 1999 and elected to the Texas Baseball Hall of Fame. Having abandoned the Astrodome for Minute Maid Park, the Astros in 2001 clinched their fourth title in five years. However, after failing to advance past the Divisional Series, Dierker was relieved of his managerial duties.

"The reason we got eliminated in the first round every time is that we got out-pitched," said Dierker of his postseason opponents, adding that "Maddux and Glavine didn't get in the Hall of Fame by accident."[92]

Houston returned to the playoffs in 2004 under Phil Garner. Keeping their late 1990s lineup virtually intact, the Astros, in Ashby's estimation, credited the midseason acquisition of Carlos Beltrán from Kansas City as the difference in the playoffs: "With the Astros in the postseason I have never seen a talent just take over and dominate the game. He can fly, he can do everything defensively, he can hit home runs, he can hit for average, although he hasn't hit for average as much in his career as he should have, but the guy is a phenomenal talent."[93] The Astros finally defeated the Braves in the Division Series but lost to the St. Louis Cardinals in the National League Championship Series.

The 2005 Astros overcame Beltrán's free agent departure and an abysmal 15–30 start to win the Wild Card with a record of 89–73. After beating the Braves and Cardinals in the postseason, the Astros were going to their first World Series.

The "October Classic" proved anticlimactic. "I called four World Series losers with the Astros to the White Sox. Those ended up being the last games I called for the Astros."[94] Praised throughout baseball for his non-partisan constructive criticism, Ashby's on-air candor was more than owner McLane could tolerate; his contract was not renewed for 2006.[95] Ashby later remarked that "apparently, I took the blame for the Astros losing the World Series."[96]

Ashby returned to the broadcast booth in 2007 with the Blue Jays. Sportswriter Bruce Dowbiggin praised his style for "[getting] his points across without turning it into a battle of personalities."[97] Ashby could also "[work] his way through the minutiae of play-by-play and commercial breaks" and was equally effective on television as on radio.[98]

Alan Ashby and his wife Kathryn live in Cypress, Texas, a suburb of Houston. Although he never played in a World Series or an All-Star Game, Ashby participated in many key events in the Astros' first half-century. He coordinated a challenging pitching staff featuring J.R. Richard, Joe Niekro, Nolan Ryan, and Mike Scott. As a broadcaster, he earned his reputation as an analytic baseball mind. The 2005 World Series games were, in fact, not the last four Ashby called for the Astros. Early in 2013, he resigned from the Blue Jays to return to Houston, working for new owner Jim Crane.

Lifelong Astros fan Mark Wernick lauded the broadcasting move: "I'm delighted to learn he is returning to work again for the new ownership of the Astros. This constitutes the new ownership's first significant move that people here will likely support."[99] After the 2013 season, broadcast partner Bill Brown assessed Ashby's style of commentary as "insightful...from the perspective of a former catcher who is involved in the selection of pitches and all other aspects, adding analysis on defensive positioning, offensive strategy and all other elements of the game."[100]

With the team's transfer to the American League, history will determine which key moments Ashby shall witness in the second half century of the Houston Astros. ∎

Acknowledgments

Alan Ashby, Kathryn Ashby, Jim Bouton, Matt Brejak, Bruce Brenner, Kevin Briand, Bill Brown, Wanda Chirnside, Francine Cole, Rick Cole, Lloyd Davis, Larry Dierker, Bob Dorrill, Harry Einbinder, Dan Epstein, Jim Fanning, Bill Gibson, Gwyneth Gibson, Bob Hulsey, Nanda Lwin, Jason Magder, Clay Marston, Jeffrey Miller, Ted Nelkin, Michael Pascoe, Darlene Petrescue, Ephraim Petrescue, Phil Petrescue, William Petrescue, John Robertson, Brendan Rodgers, Marianne Rodgers, Susan Ross, David Sahker, Harvey Sahker, Joe Sambito, Dan Schlossberg, Hartley Sigal, Tal Smith, Mike Suddick, Allen Tait, Chris Tait, Andy Topolie, Fred Toulch, Julius Toulch (1918-2009), Richard Voldimer, Jim Vykol, Perry Waisglass, Norm Watt, Mark Wernick, Don Wouters, David York, Eric Zweig.

Notes

1. Interview with Alan Ashby, September 29, 2007.
2. Brian McTaggart, "Game to Remember: Alan Ashby" on The Official Site of the Houston Astros (July 5, 2012): par 5 [journal online]; available from http://houston.astros.mlb.com; accessed December 26, 2012.
3. *Astros 1979 Photo Album* (Houston: Home Savings Association, 1979), 14.
4. Neil MacCarl, "In the Beginning..." in *Toronto Blue Jays Official 25th Anniversary Commemorative Book*, Eric Zweig, ed. (Toronto: Dan Diamond and Associates Inc., 2001), 11.
5. *Astros 1979 Photo Album*, 14.
6. Russell Schneider, "Ashby Comes on Indians Like Cavalry Charge" (*The Sporting News*: August 4, 1973), 18.
7. Schneider (August 4, 1973), 18.
8. Schneider (August 4, 1973), 18.
9. Schneider (August 4, 1973), 18.
10. Russell Schneider, "Ashby Eases Tribe's Catching Woes" (*The Sporting News*: September 27, 1975), 10.
11. Schneider (September 27, 1975), 10.
12. Russell Schneider, "Ashby Swings Indians' Tomahawk" (*The Sporting News*: May 8, 1976), 8.
13. Louis Cauz, *Baseball's Back in Town: From the Don to the Blue Jays, A History of Baseball in Toronto* (Toronto: Controlled Media Corporation, 1977), 191.
14. Ashby Interview, September 29, 2007.
15. Neil MacCarl, "Ashby Remains with Jays Despite Trade Talk" (*The Sporting News*: December 31, 1977), 55.
16. MacCarl (December 31, 1977), 55.
17. MacCarl (December 31, 1977), 55.
18. *Astros 1979 Photo Album*, 14.
19. Neil MacCarl, "Jays Swap Ashby, Obtain Lemongello" (*The Sporting News*: December 9, 1978), 41.
20. MacCarl, (December 9, 1978), 41.
21. Dan Epstein, *Big Hair and Plastic Grass: A Funky Ride Through Baseball and America in the Swinging '70s* (New York: St. Martin's Press, 2010), 112.
22. Bob Elliott, *Canada's World Champions: Blue Jays Trivia Quiz Book* (Toronto: McClelland & Stewart Inc., 1993), 137–9.
23. Interview with Tal Smith, January 8, 2014.
24. Correspondence with Bill Brown, January 5, 2014.
25. Smith Interview, January 8, 2014.
26. Mike Ryan and Bill Shannon, eds, *1982 Official Astros Yearbook* (New York: Harry M. Stevens Inc., 1982), 15.
27. www.retrosheet.org
28. Correspondence with Bill Brown, January 5, 2014.
29. www.baseball-reference.com
30. Harry Shattuck, "Reynolds and Ashby Fuel Orbiting Astros," (*The Sporting News*: August 11, 1979), 30.
31. Dierker Interview, January 8, 2014.
32. Ashby Interview, September 29, 2007.
33. Two nineteenth century pitchers managed the feat: Amos Rusie in 1890–92 and Hoss Radbourn 1883-84. Jim "Mudcat" Grant and Tom Sabellico. *The Black Aces: Baseball's Only African-American Twenty-Game Winners*, (Farmingdale, NY: Black Aces LLC, 2006), 381.

34. Ashby Interview, September 29, 2007.
35. Andrew Goodman, publisher, *Houston Astros 1980 National League Championship Series Program* (New York: Professional Sports Publications Inc., 1980), 64.
36. Shattuck (August 11, 1979), 30.
37. Sean Mooney, prod, *A Silver Odyssey: 25 Years of Houston Astros Baseball* [VHS], (East Rutherford, NJ: Phoenix Communication Group Inc., 1986).
38. Harry Shattuck, "Big Challenge for Ashby" (*The Sporting News*: February 23, 1980), 34; and Goodman, 43.
39. Ashby Interview, September 29, 2007.
40. Kenny Hand, Bill Shaikin, et al, *Nolan Ryan: The Authorized Pictorial History* (Ft. Worth: The Summit Group, 1991), 87.
41. Hand (Nolan Ryan), 87.
42. Shaikin, 64.
43. Shattuck, (February 23, 1980), 34.
44. www.retrosheet.org
45. Harry Shattuck, "Astros Proud of an 'Almost' Year" (*The Sporting News*: October 25, 1980), 27.
46. Dierker Interview, January 8, 2014.
47. Shattuck, (October 25, 1980), 27.
48. Shattuck (October 25, 1980), 27.
49. Ashby Interview, September 29, 2007.
50. Shattuck (October 25, 1980), 27.
51. Shattuck (October 25, 1980), 27.
52. Jim Bouton, *Ball Four: The Final Pitch* (North Egremont, MA: Bulldog Press, 2000), 338.
53. McTaggart par 11.
54. McTaggart par 12.
55. Ashby Interview, September 29, 2007.
56. McTaggart par 7.
57. McTaggart par 10.
58. Bill Brown and Mike Acosta, *Houston Astros Deep in the Heart: Blazing a Trail from Expansion to the World Series* (Houston: Bright Sky Press, 2013), 94.
59. Ryan, 63.
60. "Game 1 Notes: 1981 National League Divisional Series," *Dallas Morning News* (October 7, 1981):par 2 [journal online]; available from www.astrosdaily.com; accessed December 28, 2012.
61. Kenny Hand, "Playoffs Past" in *Houston Astros 1986 National League Championship Series Official Souvenir Scorebook*, Rob Matwick, exec. ed, (Houston: Houston Sports Association Inc., 1986), 27.
62. www.retrosheet.org
63. Interview with Jim Fanning, April 14, 2002.
64. Trey Wilkinson, "Back Where He Belongs" in *Celebrating Thirty Years of Astrodome History: Houston Astros Official 1995 Scorebook Magazine*, Rob Matwick, Tyler Barnes, and Trey Wilkinson, eds., (Houston: Houston Astros Baseball Club, 1995), 23.
65. Harry Shattuck, "Astros' Ashby Pitch is $1 Million Short"(*The Sporting News*: November 1, 1982), 47.
66. Shattuck (November 1, 1982), 47.
67. www.retrosheet.org

68. Chris Ello, "Ashby Pulls Astros to Within One Game of Padres," *Los Angeles Times* (October 6, 1985): par 1; [journal online]; available from articles.latimes.com; accessed January 1, 2013.
69. Ello par 12.
70. David Laurila, "Q&A: Alan Ashby, Catching the Best of an Era" on Fangraphs (December 3, 2012); par 34; [journal online]; available from www.fangraphs.com; accessed December 26, 2012.
71. McTaggart par 8.
72. Brown, 106–7.
73. Dierker Interview, January 8, 2014.
74. Mooney, *A Silver Odyssey: 25 Years of Houston Astros Baseball*.
75. "NL Championship Series: New York vs. Houston-Astros Disappointed at Outcome but Have Some Sweet Memories," *Los Angeles Times* (October 16, 1986): par 14; available from articles.latimes.com; accessed January 1, 2013.
76. Ashby Interview, September 29, 2007.
77. Neal Hohlfeld, "Ashby is a Regular Guy" (*The Sporting News*: June 8, 1987), 22.
78. Lee Pfeifer, ed, *A Season to Remember: Astros 99 Yearbook* (Santa Monica, CA: CWC Sports, 1999), 64.
79. Hohlfeld (June 8, 1987), 22.
80. Neal Hohlfeld, "September Opening Day" (*The Sporting News*: September 12, 1988), 16.
81. Correspondence with Bill Brown, January 5, 2014.
82. Hohlfeld (September 12, 1988), 16.
83. "Astros' Ashby Turns Down Deal to Pittsburgh," *Los Angeles Times* (May 8, 1989): par 3; [journal online]; available from articles.latimes.com; accessed January 1, 2013.
84. Neal Hohlfeld, "Waivers Surprise Ashby" (*The Sporting News*: May 22, 1989), 14.
85. Hohlfeld (May 22, 1989), 14.
86. Hohlfeld (May 22, 1989), 14.
87. Milo Hamilton, Dan Schlossberg, and Bob Ibach. *Making Airwaves: 60 Years at Milo's Microphone* (Champaign, IL: Sports Publishing LLC, 2006), 119.
88. Lloyd Johnson, Lloyd and Miles Wolff. *The Encyclopedia of Minor League Baseball, 2nd ed* (Durham, NC: Baseball America Inc., 1997) 624, 633.
89. Johnson, 633.
90. Hamilton, 120.
91. Hamilton, 126.
92. Dierker Interview, January 8, 2014.
93. Ashby Interview, September 29, 2007.
94. Ashby Interview, September 29, 2007.
95. Bruce Dowbiggin, "Alan Ashby Delivers on Radio and TV," *Globe and Mail* (May 18, 2011): par 4; [journal online]. available from www.theglobeandmail.com; accessed December 12, 2012.
96. Ashby Interview, September 29, 2007.
97. Dowbiggin par 3.
98. Dowbiggin par 4.
99. Correspondence with Mark Wernick, January 7, 2013.
100. Correspondence with Bill Brown, January 5, 2014.

The Greatest Game Ever Played?

October 15, 1986

Ron Briley

Fans of the Houston Astros are a long-suffering lot. While the Chicago Cubs have gone over a century without winning a World Series, the "Cubbies" maintain a loyal fan base and a national following. The Houston franchise, however, does not elicit the same national passion as the Cubs. In 2013 the Houston club, after fifty years of frustration in the National League, was "realigned" by Major League Baseball into the American League West. Supposedly the Astros' natural rivalry with the Texas Rangers would increase interest in baseball in the Lone Star state. Unfortunately, the Astros lost 17 of 19 to the Rangers, on the way to a disastrous 111 losses, including the last 15 games of the year, the third consecutive season in which Houston lost over 100 games. But for longtime Houston fans, these recent failures may be somewhat less painful than the agonizing times the club came close to attaining a championship, only to fall short. During its National League tenure, the Houston franchise won six division titles and made two playoff appearances as a wild card entry. In 2005, Houston won its only pennant but was swept in four games by the Chicago White Sox despite being outscored by only six runs.

Two of the most exasperating losses in Houston history were the National League Championship Series of 1980 and 1986. The 1980 best-of-five was lost despite the Astros entering the eighth in game five with a three-run lead and Nolan Ryan on the mound. But an even more discouraging defeat awaited the Astros and their fans on October 15, 1986, in a seven-game NLCS with the New York Mets. The Mets led Houston three games to two after an extra-inning victory in game five at Shea Stadium. Game six was scheduled for Houston, and most in baseball, including many of the Mets players, assumed that the Astros would roll on to win game seven if they could somehow manage a victory in game six at home. Waiting in the wings to start game seven for Houston was their ace Mike Scott, whose split-fingered fastball baffled the Mets in games one and four, both won by the Astros. But they would have to win game six first. New York sportswriter Jerry Izenberg would call the contest The Greatest Game Ever Played.[1]

Perhaps it was appropriate that the Mets were the nemesis for Houston in 1986. The clubs both entered the National League in 1962. Although the Houston franchise initially performed better on the field than their New York City counterparts, the Texans could not compete for attention with the Mets in the center of America's media empire. By 1986 the Mets had performed a baseball miracle in 1969 by defeating the Baltimore Orioles in the World Series and after some lean years in the late 1970s and early 1980s, the Mets were a National League powerhouse in the mid-1980s. The Mets finished second in both 1984 and 1985 before winning the National League Eastern Division with 108 victories in 1986.

The '86 Mets were led by first baseman Keith Hernandez (.310 batting average); outfielders Darryl Strawberry (27 home runs and 93 runs batted in), Lenny Dykstra (.295), and Mookie Wilson (.289); catcher Gary Carter (24 home runs and 105 runs batted in); and second baseman Wally Backman (.320). The starting pitching staff included five hurlers with double digit victory totals, including Dwight Gooden at 17–6 and Bob Ojeda at 18–5. The bullpen was anchored by right-hander Roger McDowell, who saved 22 games while winning 14, and left-hander Jesse Orosco, who saved 21 games while posting eight victories. The team was managed by Davey Johnson, a former All-Star second baseman for the Baltimore Orioles, who was noted for employing percentages and computer models. The Mets expected to win, and many considered the team arrogant.

The same could hardly be said for the Astros who were led in 1986 by rookie manager Hal Lanier, an infielder who had played for the San Francisco Giants and New York Yankees and was the son of former major league pitcher Max Lanier. In 1985, under the leadership of former club shortstop Bob Lillis, the Astros had gone 83–79, finishing third in the National League West. Expectations were relatively low for the 1986 season, but the club flourished and finished 30 games above

.500, winning 96 games. The Division champion Astros were a light-hitting team with the exception of first baseman Glenn Davis, a legitimate power threat who slammed 31 home runs and drove in 101 runs. Probably the most consistent batter on the club was Kevin Bass who compiled a .311 batting average while hitting 20 home runs and driving home 79. The strength of the Astros, however, was the pitching staff, which included starters Bob Knepper (17–12, 3.14 ERA), Jim Deshaies (12–5, 3.25), and veteran Nolan Ryan (12–8, 3.34). In the bullpen, the Astros relied upon Dave Smith (4–7, 2.73, and 33 saves) and Charlie Kerfeld (11–2, 2.59, 7 saves). The ace of the Houston staff was right-hander Mike Scott (18–10, 2.22) who struck fear in the hearts of the Mets hitters.

Scott was born April 26, 1955, in Santa Monica, California and pitched for Pepperdine University before being drafted by the Mets in 1976. Primarily a fastball pitcher, Scott performed reasonably well in the Mets minor league chain, earning promotion to the parent club in 1979. Over the next four years, Scott won 14 games for the New York club, while losing 27. On December 10, 1982, the Mets lost patience and traded Scott to the Astros for outfielder Danny Heep—and ironically the two would face one another in the 1986 championship series. The trade to Houston initially did little to alter Scott's career. In 1983, Scott went 10–6, but the following season his record fell to 5–11, while his earned run average inflated from 3.72 to 4.68.

With his career in jeopardy, Scott followed the advice of teammate Enos Cabell. Cabell, while with Detroit, had seen pitching coach Roger Craig (a member of the 1962 Mets) teach Jack Morris the split-fingered fastball. Morris subsequently emerged as one of the dominant pitchers in the American League. Craig was temporarily out of baseball in the winter of 1985, and Scott went to work with the former pitching coach at his San Diego home. According to Scott, "I went down there without having picked up a ball for probably two months. I just kind of got the basics and threw for about a week, enough to where I was good enough to know whether I could throw the pitch or not. And it was easy, real easy."[2]

With his new confidence in the split-finger, Scott abandoned his slider and change-up and became a two-pitch hurler. He continued to throw his fastball, complemented by a splitter that sometimes broke straight down and at other times moved sideways to both right- and left-handed hitters. Scott's career was resurrected, and in 1985, he went 18–8 with an ERA of 3.29. Scott continued his renaissance in 1986. Although he got off to somewhat of a slow start, Scott ended up

Dickie Thon, coming back from a 1984 beaning, platooned at shortstop with Craig Reynolds.

overwhelming National League hitters with a 2.22 earned run average and leading the National League in strikeouts with 306. On September 25, Scott clinched the West for Houston with a no-hitter as the Astros defeated the San Francisco Giants, 2–0. Ironically, Roger Craig, the man who had taught Scott the split-finger, was the Giants' manager. Earlier in the season, Craig suggested that the movement on Scott's pitches was due to scuffing the ball—a charge that the Mets would parrot during the League Championship Series. After the no-hitter, however, Craig seemed to back away from his previous accusation, asserting, "If he's doing anything illegal, he'd make a hell of a thief. I watched him pretty closely. If he does, there's no way the umpire can catch him. He was throwing the split-finger harder than I've ever seen. I told one of my coaches in the fourth or fifth inning, 'We're not going to get a hit off him.'"[3]

As Houston entered the postseason, Scott sustained his mastery. In game one of the championship series against the Mets in Houston, Scott faced off against Dwight Gooden, a 17-game winner. Gooden was sharp, but there was no margin for error when pitching against the Astros ace. In the second inning, first baseman Glenn Davis touched Gooden for a home run. That was all the run support that Scott needed, winning 1–0 and striking out 14—including Keith Hernandez and Gary Carter three times each, and Ray Knight and Darryl Strawberry twice. After Hernandez struck out in the first inning, Carter took a strike and demanded that umpire Doug Harvey examine the baseball. Finding no evidence that Scott had tampered with the ball, Harvey tossed it back to the pitcher, who proceeded to strike out Carter. The Astrodome crowd screamed with delight. Writing in *The Sporting News*, Paul Attner observed that Scott had so befuddled Carter "he reduced the swing of the Mets' star to something akin to the hack used to chop wood."[4]

On the other hand, columnist Mike Downey injected a note of humor into the controversy by suggesting that perhaps Scott was not of this world. Drawing upon the comments of teammate Kevin Bass that Scott's stuff made one wonder if the opposition would ever again score on the pitcher, Downey speculated, "Does he know something the rest of us don't? Does he know that Mike Scott is not of this world? That he wasn't born in Santa Monica, California, but transported there by capsule? That he is secretly Ace Astro right-hander from another planet?"[5]

The next day, however, the Astros were brought back to Earth. The game began with aging veteran Nolan Ryan retiring the first 10 Mets in order, striking out five, but in the fifth, the Mets drove Ryan from the mound. Meanwhile Bob Ojeda scattered 10 hits and pitched the Mets to a 5–1 victory. With the series even at one game each, the teams headed to New York. With left-hander Bob Knepper on the mound in game three, the Astros jumped out to a four-run lead, but in the sixth inning the Mets tallied four runs capped by Darryl Strawberry's three-run home run to tie the score. The resilient Astros were able to retake the lead in the seventh following a throwing error by Mets third baseman Ray Knight, a former Astro. With dependable Dave Smith relieving, the Astros appeared headed to a victory at Shea Stadium. The Mets, however, had a little magic of their own. Outfielder Lenny Dykstra, with only eight home runs for the season, struck a two-run home run to provide the Mets with a 6–5 victory.

With three days' rest, Scott faced the Mets again in game four of the series. Whether one believed that Scott enjoyed super powers, employed an emery board to doctor the ball, or simply possessed two superior pitches, Scott dominated the Mets with a 3–1 victory. Although he only struck out five, Scott induced 13 ground ball outs and issued no walks. The series was

tied at two games, and with a rain-out following the Scott victory in game four, the almost unhittable pitcher would be available for a game seven.

The Mets seemed to be losing their swagger as the specter of facing Scott one more time crept into their psyche. In what he called the "Dread Scott Decision," reporter Jerry Izenberg noted that the Mets continued to push their case that Scott was guilty of doctoring the baseball. During game four, the Mets ordered the bat boy to collect foul balls and any baseballs Scott discarded. After gathering seventeen baseballs, Mets general manager Frank Cashen appealed to National League President Chub Feeney for a hearing. Feeney scheduled a meeting for the Mets to present their evidence, but the Feeny concluded that he could find no evidence of tampering, observing, "As far as we know Mr. Scott is not guilty of any infraction. A man is innocent until proven guilty. However, we will be watching closely the next time he pitches and will take appropriate action if necessary."[6]

Paul Attner noted that "the Astros hardly were intimidated by the big city or the Mets for that matter." Astros reliever Charlie Kerfeld kept the club loose with an outlandish sense of humor, weird hats, and Jetson T-shirts. Meanwhile, Attner believed that outside of New York, the rest of the country was rooting for the Astros. Attner concluded that the Mets had "won too much and tossed up a few too many high-fives to allow themselves to court love—unless it's in the context of 'we love to see them lose.'"[7]

Themes of creeping doubt in New York's arrogance were acknowledged by Izenberg, as well. Speaking of New York City aggressive attitudes, Izenberg wrote, "From the cab drivers to the strap-hangers, it has its own peculiar meaning. It is the idea of outrageous boasts always backed up by the boasters." Yet, Mike Scott was challenging this attitude. Based upon his interviews, Izenberg concluded that the entire Mets team was convinced that they could not beat Scott.[8]

But before worries about a potential game seven, the Mets and Astros had to play game five which would be the final game of the series in New York City. With an extra day off due to rain, the Astros went with Nolan Ryan rather than rookie Jim Deshaies. Ryan would be opposed by the Mets ace Dwight Gooden, who had surrendered only one run in game one. Game five was scoreless in the top of the second when a controversial call by first base umpire Fred Brocklander may have altered the outcome of the series. With one out, Kevin Bass and Jose Cruz singled, placing Astros runners on first and third. At bat was shortstop Craig Reynolds who hit a ground ball to second baseman Wally Backman.

After cleanly fielding the ball, Backman flipped it to shortstop Rafael Santana for a force out at second. Santana then fired the ball to first baseman Keith Hernandez, and Brocklander declared Reynolds out on an exceedingly close play. The Astros protested to no avail, although television replays seemed to indicate that Reynolds was, indeed, safe.

The play was crucial as after nine innings the score was tied, 1–1, and Ryan was removed for a pinch hitter after throwing 134 pitches. If Reynolds had been declared safe, the Astros would have prevailed, 2–1. Instead, the game went to extra innings. Reliever Jesse Orosco retired all six Astros hitters he faced in the 11th and 12th innings, and in the bottom of the 12th, a struggling Gary Carter singled off Charlie Kerfeld to win game five for the Mets. Going back to Houston, down 3–2 in the series, the Astros would have to put Brocklander's call behind them. After all, as sportswriter Bill Conlin suggested, controversial calls were simply part of the game, and he asserted that baseball would never follow the example of the National Football League and rely upon instant replay. (Conlin did not prove to be a great prophet as MLB introduced challenges and video replays in the 2014 season.) Conlin concluded, "Baseball remains the most human of all games because errors are expected, catalogued in rich detail into the fabric of its traditions." According to Conlin, Brocklander was "proud, honest and certain he made the correct call based upon what he—not ABC—saw on the spur of the moment."[9]

Brocklander's decision gave a lift to the Mets. Gary Carter proclaimed that his game-winning hit proved that he was better than his .050 NLCS batting average. Carter gained a bit of revenge for game three in which Kerfeld snagged a sharply hit ball from the catcher and appeared to point the ball at Carter before making the throw to first base. Many New York fans perceived Kerfeld as taunting Carter, although the Mets catcher told reporters that he was uncertain as to the motives of Kerfeld, who had a reputation for being a bit crazy. Nevertheless, the Mets still had Mike Scott on their minds. Mets manager Davey Johnson insisted, "If we win the sixth game, we don't have to think about Scott in the seventh game." As the Mets prepared to face the Astros in the crucial game six, Dave Anderson of *The New York Times* seemed to sum up the hopes and fears of the Mets organization, proclaiming, "But if the Mets lose today, then the Astros' right hander who throws what the Mets suspect is a split-fingered sandpaper ball, will be out there on the mound in the Astrodome again tomorrow night. Never had it behooved the Mets quite so much to win."[10]

For both clubs, game six on October 15, 1986, was a must win, and Davey Johnson would manage accordingly despite being up one game in the series.

Game six was played in the Astrodome before a crowd of 45,000 who were on their feet cheering every pitch in anticipation of a victory that would assure Scott's appearance in game seven and place the Houston franchise in its first World Series. Izenberg expressed little respect for the Astrodome: "Aesthetically, it squats outside the sprawling Houston skyline looking for all the world like a concrete toad no princess would be caught dead kissing."[11]

Seeking to place the Astrodome within some historical and cultural perspective, Adam Chandler wrote in *The Atlantic*, "But to many in Texas and elsewhere, the Astrodome means to Houston what a 16th-century Spanish church means to Puerto Rico, what the first lighthouse means to Martha's Vineyard, and what the very first permanent English settlement in America, Jamestown means to Virginia." Chandler concludes, "The Astrodome was iconic not only because it was a landmark structure, but because it was also an unconventional, imaginative project created in an era of great ambition."[12] Despite lofty ambitions to move the image of Houston and its baseball franchise out of the Old West and into the space future, the Astrodome today is on the verge of being demolished after Houston voters rejected a renovation project to make the building over into a convention center.

Seventeen-game winner Bob Knepper shut out the Mets for the first eight innings.

COURTESY OF THE HOUSTON ASTROS

But on October 15, 1986, the Houston Astrodome was at the center of the baseball world. The ceremonial first pitch was assigned to Judge Jon Lindsay, a member of the Harris County Commission. Lindsay brandished aloft a piece of sandpaper with which he scraped the ball before his delivery of the ceremonial throw. The humorous tribute to the Scott controversy produced roars of approval from the crowd and even smiles from the Mets. There was no sense of humor displayed, however, when umpire Fred Brocklander, who in the eyes of Houston fans had cost them game five, took his place behind home plate. Izenberg quipped, "Hermann Goering probably got a better reception at the Nuremberg Trials."[13]

To build the bridge between games six and seven, the Astros gave the starting assignment to 17-game winner Bob Knepper. Throwing his usual collection of offspeed pitches, Knepper breezed through the first inning. Opposing Knepper was Bob Ojeda, who struggled in the bottom half of the inning. Billy Doran, the second baseman for the Astros, led off with a single, but he was forced out at second on center fielder Billy Hatcher's ground ball. Third baseman Phil Garner then followed with a double off the center field wall to score Hatcher. A single from Glenn Davis scored Garner from second, and Ojeda walked Kevin Bass, placing runners on first and second with only one out. Popular left fielder Jose Cruz, who at age 39 was perhaps being given his last opportunity to play in a World Series, looped a single to right, plating Davis for a 3–0 Houston lead and sending Bass to third. With catcher Alan Ashby at bat, Houston seemed on the verge of breaking the game open. Rookie manager Hal Lanier, however, took a more conservative approach. He signaled for Ashby to execute the suicide squeeze.

But Ashby missed Ojeda's fastball. Bass tried to retreat to third base, but he was thrown out by Carter to Knight, who applied the tag. Ashby then ended the inning with a soft liner to Mets shortstop Rafael Santana. Houston was up 3–0, but the botched squeeze play squelched what might have been a bigger inning, and the crowd was uneasy.

Knepper, however, was sharp, and it looked like three runs might be enough. On the other hand, Ojeda was settling into a groove as the game moved into the bottom of the fifth. After retiring shortstop Dickie Thon on a ground out, Ojeda committed the unpardonable baseball sin of walking the opposing pitcher. With Knepper at first, Doran forced the pitcher at second. Doran proceeded to steal second, and the next batter, Hatcher, hit a ground ball to Knight at third who flipped the ball to shortstop Santana covering third in an effort

to retire Doran. Initially safe at third, Doran's hard slide carried him off the base, and he was called out. Again the Astros had squandered an opportunity to add to their lead.

Meanwhile, Davey Johnson called on his stellar bullpen to keep the Astros in check. Rick Aguilera pitched three innings, surrendering one hit and no runs, but the Mets entered the top of the ninth inning still trailing by three. With the crowd chanting "Bob" for Knepper and "Mike" in anticipation of Scott's appearance for game seven—which was now only three outs away—Dykstra led off with a triple that barely eluded a diving Hatcher in center field. Mookie Wilson followed with a single to right, and the Mets were on the scoreboard. Outfielder Kevin Mitchell grounded out to third, as Wilson took second. Although retired by Knepper in three previous at bats, Keith Hernandez doubled to place the Mets within a run. Lanier then replaced a dejected Knepper with Dave Smith. Gary Carter worked the count to 3–2. Smith was frustrated when he assumed that he struck the catcher out on the next pitch, a slider which Brocklander called a ball. The Mets now had runners on first and second with only one out. Increasingly agitated with Brocklander, Smith walked Strawberry, and the Mets had the bases loaded. Ray Knight now stepped to the plate, and after two called strikes, the count was even at 2–2. Smith then delivered what he thought was a perfect pitch, and Brocklander called the pitch a ball. Smith and catcher Ashby voiced their dissent with the call, and Lanier charged onto the field to protect his players. As Lanier tried to calm Smith, Ashby and Knight began to exchange words, while Dickie Thon also walked in from shortstop to shout his displeasure with Knight.

After order was finally restored, Knight hit a sacrifice fly to right that scored Hernandez to tie the game, while Carter and Strawberry advanced to second and third on the throw home. Smith intentionally walked Wally Backman to load the bases. Davey Johnson responded by sending Danny Heep—as previously mentioned, the man who had been traded for Scott—to pinch hit for Rafael Santana. Heep, however, lacked a flair for the dramatic and was unable to demolish the bridge to Scott as he struck out on a full count pitch. The score was now tied, and Smith left the mound glowering at Brocklander. After the game, Smith complained, "I adjust to umpires, but how can two pitches be strikes, and a third one, which is even better, be a ball? I can't accept the fact that they're a better team. It all came down to just one call by the umpire on a single pitch."[14]

With the score tied, Johnson brought in his most consistent reliever, Roger McDowell, to slam the door on the Astros. McDowell shut down the deflated Astros in the bottom of the ninth, and the game went into extra innings. After Terry Puhl hit for Smith in the bottom of the 10th, Larry Andersen held the Mets scoreless in the 11th, 12th, and 13th innings. Meanwhile, the Astros could do little with McDowell, who pitched five scoreless innings in which the Astros could scratch only one hit. In using McDowell for such an extended stint, it was clear that Johnson was gambling on winning game six and avoiding Scott at all cost. McDowell would not be available for a possible game seven.

The score remained tied at three apiece going into the 14th when Lanier again surprised many Houston fans with his managing decision, bringing in veteran Aurelio Lopez rather than Charlie Kerfeld, who had a better year than Lopez in the Houston bullpen. Lopez immediately got into trouble. Carter led off the inning with a single to right, and Lopez walked Strawberry. Playing for one run, Johnson had Knight sacrifice, but Lopez was able to force Carter at third base. A sense of relief for the Houston fans was quickly crushed as Backman singled to put the Mets ahead and took second on the throw home. The Mets seemed poised to add to their 4–3 lead, but pinch hitter Howard Johnson fouled out to Ashby. The dangerous Dykstra was intentionally passed to load the bases, and Lopez responded by striking out Mookie Wilson.

The Astros were down to their final three outs. After McDowell was lifted for a pinch hitter, Johnson called upon his left-handed relief ace, Jesse Orosco, to save the game for the Mets. Orosco struck out Doran to start the inning, but the next batter, Billy Hatcher, who hit only six home runs during the regular season, worked Orosco to a three-two count before hitting a home run off the left-field foul pole screen. The score was again tied, and hope that Houston could get the game ball for game seven to Scott was revived. Orosco, however, settled down and retired Denny Walling (who had replaced Garner at third) and Glenn Davis to send the game to the 15th.

Both Orosco and Lopez were effective in the 15th, but in the 16th inning the game added a new note of high drama. Strawberry led off the top of the inning with a bloop double to shallow center field that fell between Doran and Hatcher. Although Strawberry struck out 12 times in 22 at bats in the series with a .227 batting average, he had started what proved to be the winning rally. At age 24, Strawberry had learned to handle pressure beginning with expectations as a first round draft pick, asserting, "It's nothing to hide from, or feel bad about. I really haven't had a great series. I'm just thankful that I've had a chance to come up

with some big hits that kept us in the ballgame, and let somebody else win it."[15]

Following Strawberry's double, Johnson decided to have Knight hit away, and the third baseman drove a single to right, scoring Strawberry and taking second on the throw home. With Lopez obviously tiring and a switch-hitter followed by two left-handed hitters due for the Mets, Lanier elected to bring in the Astros only lefty reliever, Jim Calhoun. Kerfeld, despite his fine season, continued to collect rust in the Houston bullpen. Making his first appearance in the series, Calhoun was nervous, and a wild pitch moved Knight to third, followed by a walk to Backman. With Orosco at the plate, Calhoun let loose with another wild pitch, scoring Knight and sending Backman to second. The Astros now trailed by two runs, and the partisan crowd was growing quiet. The specter of Mike Scott seemed to be fading. The Mets played solid conventional baseball, and Orosco bunted Backman to third. This brought Dykstra to the plate, hitting .273 for the series on a team that could muster only an anemic team average of .189. True to form, Dykstra slammed a single to right, and the Mets' run margin was three. Calhoun then induced Mookie Wilson to hit into a double play, but the damage was done. The Astros now entered the bottom of the 16th trailing 7–4.

The drama of this special game, however, was hardly over. With no one warming up in the Mets bullpen, Johnson was committed to Orosco, who responded to the faith placed in him by striking out Craig Reynolds to begin the bottom of the inning. Veteran Davey Lopes pinch hit for Calhoun and worked a walk. Doran followed with a single to center, bringing up Hatcher, whose home run in the 14th had again tied the game. Hatcher slammed a single to center scoring Lopes. Houston now trailed 7–5 with the tying runs on base, and the crowd was back into the game. Like the phoenix, the looming spirit of Mike Scott refused to be extinguished. The next hitter was Astros third baseman Denny Walling, who sent a grounder to the agile Hernandez at first base. The ball was hit too slowly for a double play, but Hernandez was able to force Hatcher at second.

The Astros were now down to their last out with the club's best power hitter, Glenn Davis, approaching the plate. Davis failed to hit the ball in his sweet spot, but he did loft a soft liner to center that moved Walling to second base and scored Doran, making the score 7–6.

Approaching the plate was Houston's most consistent hitter during the 1986 season, right fielder Kevin Bass. At a meeting on the mound, Hernandez berated Carter and Orosco for employing too many fastballs.

COURTESY OF THE HOUSTON ASTROS

The Great Scott who was selected as the Most Valuable Player of the 1986 NLCS.

The first baseman told Carter that if he called for another fastball there would be a fight. Carter assured Hernandez there would be no reason for fisticuffs. The Mets would deal with Bass through a steady diet of sliders. Bass expected the sliders and worked the count to 3–2, but he swung at the sixth slider and missed. The game was over, and the shadow of Mike Scott was vanquished. The Astrodome grew quiet. Orosco threw his glove into the air, and his teammates piled on top of him. Afterwards Orosco asserted, "I was satisfied. I could give up a run but we didn't let them tie it. That's all that matters."[16]

Orosco was credited with victories in three of the four Mets wins, but the Most Valuable Player Award went to Scott for his dominant pitching performances in games one and four.

The players from both teams were exhausted, but both the athletes and their partisans realized they had witnessed an instant classic. Dave Anderson of *The New York Times* proclaimed the Mets and Astros series as a 64-inning classic won by the Mets 21–17. Keith Hernandez echoed the sentiments of Anderson: "What a series—everybody out there was using that expression. Every time one of the Astros got to first base, Doran, Walling, Ashby, they'd turn to me and say, 'What a series.'"[17] Wally Backman agreed, insisting, "I

think it's the best series people have seen in America in a long time. I can't think of one that was better even when I was a kid."[18]

But perhaps the most common expression among the Mets was relief—they would not have to face Scott again. Carter said that he believed the Mets could beat him, but he did not want to have to prove it.[19]

Trying to preclude a game seven, Johnson emptied his bullpen and bench. Attner observed, "Johnson managed the sixth game as if he was facing sudden death that afternoon. When the game ended he was down to his last pinch hitter. He had used up the heart of his bullpen and would have been terribly shortsighted had a seventh game been necessary."[20]

After the game a relieved Johnson acknowledged concern about the looming prospect of confronting Scott one more time, observing, "I never get headaches, but I had a headache in the ninth inning, that's how tough this game was. Going into this series, some people were saying that we hadn't had to win a 'must' game all season. But we had four 'must' games in this series."[21]

As for the Astros, they were numb but cooperative with the press. Billy Hatcher summed up the pain many felt, explaining, "Any time you play a one-run game, a sixteen-inning game, it just eats you up. Sometimes you can't even sleep at night for thinking about the next game. I don't want to watch the World Series on television. I'm going to find somewhere to go where I can hide. I don't want to watch no more baseball." A reticent Mike Scott agreed that it was painful to watch and have no control over the game. As to what might have happened in a game seven, Scott made no idle boasts, but concluded that he would always wonder about what might have been. And a courageous Kevin Bass facing the national media presented the lament of defeat and frustration that has often characterized Houston baseball—a team that has been close so many times but has only one pennant and no World Series victory in over fifty years of disappointment. Bass quietly noted, "When you play as hard as we did . . . for as long as we did . . . and you still come up short . . . well, we just couldn't do it . . . I guess they were meant to win . . . It's just the way it is . . . We lost . . . They're going on and we're not . . . It's as simple as that."[22]

Yet for much of the series the Astros had outplayed the Mets. Sportswriter Bob Verdi noted that the Astros were tied or leading in 55 of the 64 innings played in the six-game series. Houston pitching dominated. The Mets struck out 57 times and had the lowest team batting average, .189, of any National League Championship Series winner. Yet, Verdi concluded that the Mets enjoyed the mystique of New York City. Indeed, going back to 1962 the fates of the two franchises appeared linked in a tale of two cities in which Houston always seemed to snatch defeat from the jaws of victory.[23]

Jerry Izenberg reflected this perspective in his comment that the Astros "were a team that shot to wound rather than kill. In other words, they sometimes gained the advantage only to kick it right back to you before you even realized you had it."[24]

This type of inferiority complex gripped Houston in the aftermath of the loss. Describing a despondent city in a piece for The New York Times, Peter Applebome wrote, "Amid anguish and soul searching over what might have been, the city did its best to resume normal life a day after the end of its baseball season. The playoff series became part baseball, part sociology and full-time civic obsession in a city that is quietly developing one of the nation's greatest records of sporting frustration." For example, Houston businessman Harrison Williams complained that God had deserted Houston, and even oil prices were dropping. In terms of sport, Houston was the fourth largest city in the country, but had no championships in the major team sports of basketball, football, or baseball—unless one counts the Houston Oiler American Football League championships in 1960 and 1961. The drought was finally shattered by the Houston Rockets of the National Basketball Association in 1994. Although some Houstonians were convinced that the city was jinxed, others expressed degrees of prejudice regarding Easterners from New York City and Boston who were playing in the 1986 World Series. Commercial photographer Mark Green displayed his contempt for New York City by asserting, "To tell you the truth, I went to a game at Shea Stadium this year, and the fans were animals. There were kids spitting on customers from a train. If that makes a great sports town, and animals tearing up the field when they win pennants, they can have it."[25]

In response, The New York Times editorialized that there was some pleasure in beating the team from Houston, "where bumper stickers once said, 'Let the Yankees freeze in the dark.'" Expressing a degree of humility, the paper concluded, "Deep down, New York has probably always been a National League city. It admired the Yankees, but loved the underdog like the old Dodgers. The 1986 Mets, their tenacity tested by the Astros, are no underdogs but they sure are easy to love."[26]

George Vecsey of The New York Times rejoiced that the Mets were finally victorious over Houston who had dominated them going back to that inaugural 1962 expansion season. Vecsey recalled that on the Mets' first road trip to Houston in May 1962, the team flight was delayed all night due to mechanical problems. When the aging Casey Stengel arrived at a Houston hotel in the early morning hours after a sleepless night and received his room key, he remarked, "If any of the writers come looking for me, tell them I'm being embalmed." The embalming story seemed to set the tone for the rivalry between the Mets and Houston franchise. After finishing ahead of the Mets in 1962, over the next twenty-four years Houston held an 111–59 bulge over the Mets in regular season games played in Texas, while the Mets home margin over Houston was a slender 86–81 advantage. Vecsey rejoiced that the Mets were finally able to "embalm the curse of Houston" with Jesse Orosco's slider.[27]

The Mets, however, had little time to celebrate as they faced the Boston Red Sox, who had narrowly defeated the California Angels in the American League Championship Series, in the 1986 World Series. This time the Mets staged a rally in game six, helped by Boston first baseman Billy Buckner's error, to force a game seven which the Mets won, 8–5. The Houston Astros could only dream of how close they had come and wait till next year.

In the spring of 1987, the Mets were still breathing a sigh of relief that they had not been forced to face Mike Scott a third time in the playoffs. Gary Carter proclaimed that Scott was the "main piece of unfinished business" for the Mets in 1987. But the catcher sounded less confident when he described Scott as, "Unbelievable. He went from 137 strikeouts to 306 strikeouts in one year. That's more than double. Phenomenal. You don't do that without doing something different." Expressing similar sentiments, Keith Hernandez insisted, "But Scott's not unbeatable" if he makes mistakes. The only problem according to Hernandez was that Scott "didn't make mistakes."[28]

The next season Scott remained one of the National League's best pitchers, but he was less overwhelming, striking out 233 batters with a 3.23 ERA and 16 wins against 13 losses. Meanwhile, Houston slumped in 1987, finishing 10 games under the .500 mark and 14 games behind the West Division champion San Francisco Giants. The Mets remained one of the best teams in the National League with a mark of 92–70, but three games behind the division-winning St. Louis Cardinals.

Since the memorable 1986 season, the Mets won the National League pennant in 2000 but were defeated by the Yankees in five games, while Houston gained the 2005 pennant before being swept by the Chicago White Sox in the World Series. With Mike Scott, Houston seemed on the verge of a pennant and World Series victory in 1986, but it slipped away. Scott remained a dominant pitcher into the 1990 season when he began to suffer from arm trouble. He retired after pitching two games in 1991 with a lifetime record of 124 wins against 108 defeats.[29]

But in 1986, he had seemed invincible, and Houston was tantalizingly close to a championship. Almost as close as Craig Biggio, who in 2014 gained 74.8 percent of the necessary 75 percentage of votes necessary to become the first player to enter the National Baseball Hall of Fame in Cooperstown wearing an Astros cap. Disappointment thy name is Houston. ■

Notes

1. Jerry Izenberg, *The Greatest Game Ever Played* (New York: Henry Holt and Company, 1987); and Jeff Pearlman, *The Bad Guys Won* (New York: Harper Perennial, 2005).
2. Rob Neyes, "Great Scott's Power Burned Brightest in '86," ESPN.COM, October 11, 2001, http://sports.espn.go.com/espn? (accessed January 19, 2014).
3. Neil Hohlfeld, " 'Great Scott' Clincher," *The Sporting News*, October 5, 1986, 12.
4. Paul Attner, "Scott Humiliates Mets," *The Sporting News*, October 20, 1986, 22.
5. Mike Downey, "Great Scott!: Ronco's Amazing Miracle Pitch," *The Sporting News*, October 20, 1986, 6.
6. Izenberg, *The Greatest Game Ever Played*, 23.
7. Paul Attner, "Scott Humiliates Mets," *The Sporting News*, October 20, 1986, 36.
8. Izenberg, *The Greatest Game Ever Played*, 17, 23.
9. Bill Colin, "Brocklander's Bad Call a Baseball Tradition," *The Sporting News*, October 27, 1986, 10.
10. Dave Anderson, "Sports of the Times: I'm Not an .050 Hitter," *The New York Times*, October 15, 1986.
11. Izenberg, *The Greatest Game Ever Played*, 31.
12. Adam Chandler, "The Sad Fate (but Historic Legacy) of the Houston Astrodome," *The Atlantic*, November 2013, www.theatlantic.com/entertainment/archive/2013/11/the-sad-fate-but-historic-legacy-of-the-houston-astrodome/281269 (accessed January 26, 2014).
13. Izenberg, *The Greatest Game Ever Played*, 74–5.
14. Paul Attner, "It Was in the Cards for the Mets," *The Sporting News*, October 27, 1986, 6.
15. Malcolm Moran, "Players; Strawberry Handles Pressure," *The New York Times*, October 16, 1986.
16. George Vecsey, "Sports of the Times; Jesse Finds the Way," *The New York Times*, October 16, 1986.
17. Dave Anderson, "Sports of the Times; 64-Inning Classic," *The New York Times*, October 16, 1986.
18. Joe Gergen, "N. L. Playoff Finale 'Was Like a Dream Game,'" *The Sporting News*, October 27, 1986, 10.
19. Ibid.
20. Paul Attner, "It Was in the Cards for the Mets," *The Sporting News*, October 27, 1986, 6.
21. Dave Anderson, "Sports of the Times; 64-Inning Classic," *The New York Times*, October 12, 1986.
22. Izenberg, *The Greatest Game Ever Played*, 152–4.
23. Bob Verdi, "Each Game Tasted Better—and More Thrilling," *The Sporting News*, October 27, 1986, 9.
24. Izenberg, *The Greatest Game Ever Played*, 91.
25. Peter Applebome, "Houston: A City of Agonizing Losses," *The New York Times*, October 17, 1986.
26. "New York, of the National League," *The New York Times*, October 17, 1986.
27. George Vecsey, "Sports of the Times; Jesse Finds the Way," *The New York Times*, October 16, 1986.
28. Joseph Durso, "Mets Preoccupied with Scott," *The New York Times*, March 5, 1987.
29. Roger Angell, "The Arms Talks," *New Yorker*, 63 (May 4, 1987), 103–23; and Dennis Tuttle, "The Split Decision: Does It End Careers or Resurrect Them?," *USA Today Baseball Weekly* (March 27, 1988), 12–7.

The Houston Astros Hall of Stats

Adam Darowski

The purpose of a Hall of Fame is to celebrate the greats and preserve history. But only 1.3 percent of major league players make it to Cooperstown[1]—and that percentage is considerably lower for recent generations. About half of Major League Baseball's clubs maintain team Halls of Fame, honoring players who may have fallen short of Cooperstown, but still made a lasting impact worthy of commemoration.[2] The Houston Astros, however, don't. The franchise is comparatively young, but half a century is certainly long enough to warrant a Hall of Fame. The Astros lag behind even newer teams like the San Diego Padres and Seattle Mariners in this regard.

If the Astros were to establish their own Hall of Fame, what would it look like? 809 players have appeared in at least one game for Houston through 2013, ranging from Chris Tremie (who caught a single inning but never batted) to Craig Biggio (who batted 12,504 times as an Astro). Of course, an Astros Hall of Fame would start with greats like Biggio, Jeff Bagwell, and Nolan Ryan. But where would it go from there? There are many different reasons a player could be considered a Hall of Famer, but I'm going to focus on one: value.

I run a website called the Hall of Stats. The Hall of Stats is an alternate Hall of Fame populated by a mathematical formula. I created the site as a reaction to the recent voting issues with the National Baseball Hall of Fame in Cooperstown—not just the effect of performance enhancing drugs, but also the BBWAA's inflated Hall of Fame standards and misconceptions of player value. My assessment of player value is not perfect, but when a pitcher with 254 wins, 186 losses, 1.78 strikeouts per walk, and a 105 ERA+ receives three times as many votes as a pitcher with 270 wins, 153 losses, 3.58 strikeouts per walk, and a 123 ERA+, there is clearly a disconnect between "value" and "fame."[3]

HALL RATING

I define "value" with Hall Rating, a metric that combines the value of a player's peak and his longevity. The National Baseball Hall of Fame includes 211 members who were elected for their major league player careers.[4] These inductees range from the best player of all time by Hall Rating (Babe Ruth) all the way down to the 1,729th-best player (Tommy McCarthy). The Hall of Stats populates itself with the top 211 eligible players by Hall Rating. The result is about a third of Cooperstown's inductees are removed and replaced with 69 new players.[5,6] This technique establishes what a Hall of Fame might look like if the road to induction was based solely on statistical merit rather than intangibles and narratives.

Here is the formula for Hall Rating:[7]

$$\text{Hall Rating} = \text{adjWAR} + (1.79 * \text{adjWAA})$$

adjWAR, or adjusted wins above replacement, is used to measure the value of a player's longevity. It begins with the Baseball-Reference version of wins above replacement (WAR) and makes the following adjustments:

Schedule length: Nineteenth century schedules were shorter than today's. Fewer games means fewer opportunities to accumulate WAR. adjWAR prorates the WAR total a player could have earned in a 162-game schedule and then splits the difference. For example, if a player earned 2.0 WAR while his team played an 81-game schedule (regardless of how many games the player actually appeared in), adjWAR gives him credit for 3.0 WAR rather than 4.0 WAR.

Catchers: While WAR awards catchers some extra credit through the positional adjustment, that only accounts for the games they actually play. Due to the rigors of the position, catchers play fewer games and therefore have a harder time accumulating WAR totals on par with other positions. If Hall Rating didn't make an additional catcher adjustment, the Hall of Stats would only include a handful of catchers. adjWAR gives a 20 percent bonus to catchers—but that bonus is given out based on how often a player caught. If a player caught all of his games, he would receive the full

20 percent bonus. If a player caught in half his games, he would receive a 10 percent bonus. Thurman Munson (who caught 90 percent of his games) takes advantage of this adjustment more than a player like Joe Torre, who appeared as a catcher more than any other position, but still only caught in 41 percent of his games.

Relief pitchers: Relief pitchers also have relatively low WAR totals, so adjWAR gives them the same adjustment as catchers (and applies it based on percentage of games in relief). Even with this adjustment, only two relief pitchers rank as Hall-worthy—Mariano Rivera and Hoyt Wilhelm. (Hall Rating considers Dennis Eckersley a starting pitcher since that's where he provided considerably more WAR.) This means either relief pitchers are very rarely Hall-worthy or the formula doesn't make enough of an adjustment.

Nineteenth century pitchers: Pitchers don't receive the schedule length adjustment above (except during strike years). In fact, pre-1893 pitchers are "given" an additional adjustment to suppress their WAR totals, as they threw such high percentages of their team's innings. Otherwise, we'd have an overwhelming number of nineteenth century pitchers in the Hall of Stats. (Some might argue that Hall Rating still doesn't suppress these scores enough).

adjWAA, or adjusted wins above average, is used to measure the value of a player's peak. It begins with the Baseball-Reference version of wins above average (WAA) and makes the following adjustments:

Negative seasons are ignored: Since adjWAA is a measure of peak, it ignores any seasons where the player performed below average. This has a big effect on a player like Pete Rose, who hung around for several years trying to break Ty Cobb's hit record. He was performing below average level, which cut into his WAA total. adjWAA doesn't penalize him for that.

Where average is replacement: In a couple situations (such as the Union Association in 1884 and hitting stats for pitchers), replacement level and league average are basically equal.[8] In those situations, no WAA is counted.

Catchers, relief pitchers, and nineteenth century pitchers: Same as above.

The 1.79 in the formula gives extra weight to adjWAA. Hall Rating values longevity (adjWAR) and peak (adjWAA) equally. But since adjWAA contains no replacement level runs, the totals are lower. The 1.79 simply boosts the adjWAA numbers so they are equally weighted.

The formula then sets the Hall of Stats borderline to a Hall Rating of 100. The 211th best eligible player by Hall Rating (the one who sits precisely on the Hall of Stats borderline) is given a Hall Rating of 100 and everyone else is adjusted accordingly. The 211th player is currently Billy Pierce. Babe Ruth has the highest Hall Rating of all time at 395, while Bill Bergen's is the lowest: –15. Tommy McCarthy's 28 is the lowest among Hall of Famers. The highest for an eligible player outside the Hall of Fame is Barry Bonds with 359. Among eligible former players not currently on the Hall of Fame ballot, Pete Rose leads the way with 148. The top eligible player outside the Hall who is not currently on the BBWAA Hall of Fame ballot is Bill Dahlen with 143. (Dahlen did appear on the most recent pre-integration committee ballot.)

It's worth noting that the Hall Rating formula doesn't account for Negro League stats, military service, or postseason performance.

Since Hall Rating gives us a simple but systematic way to rank all players in history, we can also rank all Astros in history. To create a Houston Astros Hall of Stats, all we need to do is decide on a cutoff.

THE CUTOFF

To determine an approximate size of the Astros Hall of Stats, I'll turn to the Red Sox and Reds for guidance, as they have two of the more established and inclusive team Halls of Fame. The Cincinnati Reds Hall of Fame covers an incredible 145 years, even including Harry Wright for his role with the famous 1869 Cincinnati Red Stockings. The Reds Hall of Fame has inducted a total of 74 members primarily as players.[9] That gives them 0.51 Hall of Famers per year.

Meanwhile, the Red Sox have been in existence for 113 years and have enshrined 63 men primarily for their playing careers.[10] That is a ratio of 0.56 Hall of Famers per year. If we keep a similar ratio of Hall of Famers for the Astros, in their 52 years of history they should honor somewhere between 27 and 29 players. There are 27 Astros players with Hall Rating of 30 or more, so we'll make that our cutoff.[11]

THE INDUCTEES

Following are the 27 members of the Astros Hall of Stats (Hall Rating with the Astros in parentheses).

Jeff Bagwell, 1B (162): Hall Rating ranks Bagwell as the best player in Astros history as well as one of the best eligible players not yet in Cooperstown. Bagwell may not have collected 3,000 hits like Craig Biggio and may trail Lance Berkman in OPS by a few points, but once all of his contributions are considered and context-adjusted, he towers over both.

Jeff Bagwell

The 1994 National League MVP, four-time All Star, and two-time 30/30 man ranks second among all Astros in hits, on-base percentage, slugging percentage, and OPS, but ranks first in home runs, runs batted in, batting average, and walks. He also ranks first in the context-adjusted OPS + because early in his career he played in the Astrodome, a notorious pitcher's park that suppressed his offensive numbers.[12] Bagwell's 591 WAR batting runs are the most in franchise history by over 200 runs.

What really makes Bagwell stand out is his all-around game. He won a Gold Glove and WAR's fielding runs suggest he could have won more. His 54 fielding runs above average rank fifth all-time among Astros (across all positions, but not factoring in the positional adjustment). He also stole the sixth-most bases in franchise history at a high success rate, placing his 31 WAR base-running runs third in club history. Add it all up and Bagwell was a unique and well-rounded player—and the best first baseman between Jimmie Foxx and Albert Pujols.[13]

Craig Biggio, 2B (125): Biggio, a seven-time All Star and Astros lifer, leads the club in plate appearances and hits while ranking second in runs batted in and stolen bases and third in home runs. Among WAR components, Biggio ranks second in baserunning and third in hitting.

Craig Biggio

What separates Biggio from Bagwell is fielding. While WAR gives Biggio plenty of credit for playing high-value positions (catcher, second base, and center field), the numbers suggest he didn't play them particularly well. Despite four Gold Glove awards (all at second base), Biggio clocks in at 100 runs below average. Biggio was an astounding 79 runs below average from age 35 on during his (successful) quest for 3,000 hits. He was also worth −20 runs defensively in his four years as a catcher. Subtract those years and he was essentially an average defensive second baseman in his prime, which seems much more reasonable.

All that said, Biggio still deserves his reputation as one of Houston's Killer B's as well as a place in Cooperstown.

César Cedeño, CF (96): When the Astros traded Cedeño to the Cincinnati Reds after the 1981 season, he already had five Gold Gloves, four All Star selections, and a 96 Hall Rating. He would only reach 100 by the end of his career. Cedeño was on a Hall of Fame track, but with his prime too far removed from memory, voters ignored him. Still, he was an incredible mix of speed, fielding, and offense and was perhaps the greatest outfielder in Astros history. Cedeño ranks first among Astros in both stolen bases and WAR base-running runs. He also finished fifth in batting runs and fourth in hits during his dozen seasons in the Astrodome.

Roy Oswalt, P (94): Oswalt spent 10 seasons with Houston, was named an All Star three times, and ranks second in club history in victories and strikeouts. He ranks sixth in ERA (1,000 + innings), but adjusting for context (he pitched in a hitter's park during the steroid era) places him first in ERA+. Recent research by Bill James suggests that Oswalt may also be the best "Big Game" pitcher of all time.[14] That and a 104 Hall Rating should make him a viable Hall of Fame candidate.

José Cruz, LF (93): Cruz was a well-rounded and underrated star for Houston across 13 seasons. By WAR components, he was sixth in batting and second in fielding. He also ranked third in stolen bases (as well as third in hits and fourth in RBIs).

José Cruz

Lance Berkman, LF (91): Berkman retired after the 2013 season with a 98 Hall Rating and almost all of it came as an Astro. He ranks behind only Bagwell offensively, placing second in WAR batting runs, home runs, and OPS +. He is first in on-base percentage, slugging, and OPS while finishing third in RBIs and fifth in hits. In his 12 seasons in Houston, he was an All Star five times.

Jim Wynn, CF (80): Wynn, according to WAR, is the best position player to never receive a single Hall of Fame vote. (Among pitchers, it is Frank Tanana.)[15] Not only did he play extensively in the Astrodome, he also played in the similarly pitcher-friendly Dodger Stadium.[16] He did this while peaking in the offense-depressed late 1960s. He may have hit only .250 with a .436 slugging percentage for his career, but his tremendous plate discipline and context adjustments bring his Hall Rating all the way up to 109 (80 of that coming in his 11 seasons in Houston). Wynn ranks fourth in team history in WAR batting runs and home runs (and even tied for fifth in base-running) while placing third behind only Bagwell and Berkman in OPS+ (3,000+ plate appearances).

Larry Dierker, P (57): Dierker pitched 13 seasons for Houston and that is the only part of his career reflected in his Hall Rating. But he was also Houston's color commentator before and after a very successful five-year run as the club's manager. The Astros finished in first four times and Dierker was voted Manager of the Year in 1998.

As a pitcher, Dierker made his major league debut with the Colts on his 18th birthday in 1964. Since then, no player has debuted at a younger age.[17] Dierker's ERA+ of 104 is near the league average and only tenth in club history, but he threw more innings than any other Houston hurler. He is also third in wins and fourth in strikeouts. The two-time All Star was the first 20-game winner in Astros history and was worth over eight WAR in 1969.

Joe Morgan, 2B (55): Morgan is probably the best position player the Astros ever had. They just didn't have him long (or during his prime). Morgan is one of only 30 players with a 200 Hall Rating, but only 55 of it came before he was traded to the Reds following his age-27 season. Still, during his time as a Colt and Astro, Morgan was fifth (tied) in base-running runs (fourth in steals) and eighth in batting runs.

Joe Morgan

Bill Doran, 2B (52): Between Biggio, Morgan, and Doran, the Astros have some serious depth at second base on their All-Time Team. Doran rates as average defensively by WAR, but his plate discipline made him a slightly above-average hitter. He was also above-average on the bases, ranking seventh in club history in base-running runs. That combination is very valuable for a second baseman.

Don Wilson, P (50): Wilson was an erratic but electric pitcher who accumulated two no-hitters and a Hall Rating of 50 in his twenties. Tragically, he would never reach his 30th birthday, as he (and his five-year-old son) died of carbon monoxide asphyxiation. (See Clifford, this volume.) On the mound, Wilson was third in club history in ERA and fourth in ERA+.

Terry Puhl, RF (48): Puhl, a member of the Canadian Baseball Hall of Fame, spent 14 seasons with Houston and is the top right fielder in club history (by Hall Rating).[18] He was the type of player who didn't excel in any one area, but he was solidly above average in each WAR component: 78 runs batting, 17 runs between base-running and avoiding double plays, and 36 runs defensively. His 217 stolen bases rank fifth in club history.

Mike Scott, P (46): Scott's career highlights center around an absolutely brilliant 1986 season. Scott pitched a no-hitter that clinched the division for the Astros and led the league in ERA and strikeouts.[19] He was the National League's Cy Young Award winner and also captured the NLCS MVP Award, the first time the award went to a member of the losing club.[20] The three-time All Star led the NL in wins in 1989, but dropped off soon afterward. He is sixth in club history in ERA+, fourth in wins, and fifth in strikeouts.

Nolan Ryan, P (40): Ryan recorded 106 of his 324 wins, 1,866 of his 5,714 strikeouts, two of his eight All-Star appearances, and one of his seven no-hitters during his nine (of 27) seasons in Houston, the most seasons he spent with one club. Ryan leads all franchise pitchers in strikeouts and ERA (twice leading the National League in each), while ranking third in ERA+. (His tenure came during the relatively offense-depressed 1980s.) This past February, Ryan rejoined the Astros as an executive advisor.[21]

Bob Watson, 1B (39): Watson spent 45 years in the game, serving as a coach, general manager, and Major League Baseball's Vice President of discipline and Vice President of rules and on-field operations. Before that, he started an excellent playing career with 14 seasons as an Astro. He ranks among the club's best hitters, placing second in batting average (just behind Bagwell), fourth in OPS+, and seventh in WAR batting runs. He also ranks fifth in runs batted in.

J.R. Richard, P (39): Richard is one of three players (with Bagwell and Biggio) to spend his entire career (10 + seasons) with the Astros. Richard suffered a stroke during the 1980 season, tragically ending his career and threatening his life.[22] At the time, he had a 10–4 record with a 1.90 ERA. In the four preceding seasons, he won 20 games once, 18 three times, fanned 300 twice, and won an ERA title. Among Astros, he ranks behind only Ryan in ERA while placing fifth in ERA+, third in strikeouts, and fifth in wins.

Billy Wagner, P (37): When Wagner, a natural-born right-hander who pitched left-handed, struck out 14.4 batters per nine innings in 1997 (his first full season as a relief pitcher), it was the highest single-season strike-out rate of any pitcher in history (minimum eight innings). He proceeded to break the record in each of the next two seasons.[23,24] He would go on to save more games than any other Astro, securing 225 of his 422 saves in Houston. Wagner ranks 16th among Astros pitchers in strikeouts despite ranking 39th in innings. A three-time All-Star in Houston (seven times overall), Wagner's career Hall Rating is 65. While that isn't near the 100 Hall of Stats borderline, it is one of the better scores for a relief pitcher. Among pitchers with fewer than 150 starts, Wagner trails only Mariano Rivera, Hoyt Wilhelm, Rich Gossage, and John Hiller.

Roger Clemens, P (37): Clemens is the best pitcher the Astros ever had, but they only had him for three years. Unlike Joe Morgan, who spent his time in Houston at the beginning of his career, Clemens was with the team from age 41 to 43. Despite his advanced age, he led the league in winning percentage in his first year and in ERA (1.87) and ERA+ (226) his second year. He won the last of his seven Cy Young Awards and added a third place finish. His ERA and ERA+ are the best of any Astros pitcher with at least 150 innings pitched. (Clemens had 539.)

Joe Niekro, P (36): Despite ranking ninth among Houston pitchers by Hall Rating, Niekro was the winningest pitcher in Astros history (with one more victory than Oswalt). While the Astrodome suppressed his teammates' offensive numbers, it helped Niekro's. He was fifth among Astros in ERA, but ninth by ERA+. During his first two of 11 seasons in Houston he perfected his knuckleball.[25]

Shane Reynolds, P (34): Reynolds spent 11 of his 13 seasons in Houston. Like Niekro, he had some excellent seasons but overall was basically slightly better than league average. Despite an ERA of 3.95 with Houston (compared to 3.22 for Niekro), Reynolds ranks ahead of Niekro in ERA+ (placing eighth) because he pitched in the Steroid Era.

Ken Forsch, P (33): Forsch is another long-time Astro (11 seasons) who was a little better than league average. He spent quite a few seasons in relief, starting only 153 of his 421 Houston appearances. He was an All-Star as a reliever and later threw a no-hitter as a starter. Forsch ranks fourth among Astros in ERA and sixth in ERA+.

Ken Forsch

Richard Hidalgo, RF (32): Hidalgo was a cannon-armed outfielder who also had two excellent offensive seasons for the Astros. In 2000, he hit .314 and slugged .636 (with 44 home runs and 122 runs batted in), good for 38 WAR batting runs. In the outfield, he was also worth 13 fielding runs. In 2003, he recovered from a gunshot wound from an offseason carjacking in Venezuela to earn 30 batting runs (.309, 28 home runs, 88 RBIs) and 19 fielding runs.[26] He is fourth in fielding runs among Astros despite a short career.

Dickie Thon, SS (31): Thon, the Astros' top shortstop, is Houston's 23rd ranked player by Hall Rating. He was destined for stardom after posting 13.5 WAR at age 24 and 25, combining above average offense (27 batting runs) with dazzling fielding (32 fielding runs). He started hot in 1984 before taking a pitch in the eye, ending his season and threatening his career. Amazingly, Thon overcame depth-perception problems to eventually contribute a .271 average with 15 home runs for the Phillies in 1989. His talent before the incident, determination to work his way back, and later success lead some to speculate he was on a Hall of Fame track at the time of the injury.[27]

Dickie Thon

Glenn Davis, 1B (31): Davis was one of the most consistent power-hitting run producers of the late 1980s, totaling 166 home runs and 518 RBIs in 830 games as an Astro. He hit 20 or more home runs in six straight seasons and ranks fifth in club history in round-trippers. He is also fifth in OPS+ and ninth in WAR batting runs.

Steve Finley, CF (30): Finley—by far the least famous of the five players with 2,500 hits, 300 home runs, and 300 stolen bases—spent four seasons in Houston leading up to the 1994 strike. He was a much different player in Houston than he was later in San Diego or Arizona, relying mostly on speed (ninth among Astros in base-running runs) and fielding (seventh in fielding runs). While he didn't win a Gold Glove in Houston, he did start building the reputation that would win him five.

Turk Farrell, P (30): Farrell is the only player on this list who was selected by the Astros in the 1961 expansion draft.[28] He was the ace of the lowly 1962 club, making 43 appearances (29 starts) and throwing 241 innings with a 3.02 ERA (124 ERA+). The traditional metrics gave him 20 losses for his effort but WAR acknowledges his excellent pitching for a very weak defense and gives him a 7 WAR season. Farrell was an All Star that year and in two of the next three seasons. In all, he went 53–64 as an Astro with a league average 100 ERA+.

Ken Caminiti, 3B (30): If Finley changed when he went elsewhere, than Caminiti (who departed Houston in the same trade as Finley) takes that to a new level. In his 10 seasons with Houston (where he ranks first among Astros third basemen by Hall Rating), he was worth –6 WAR batting runs, 31 fielding runs, and a 30 Hall Rating. He also spent four seasons in San Diego where we was worth 134 batting runs, –31 fielding runs, and a 34 Hall Rating, winning the MVP award in 1996. Caminiti himself attributed the boost in offensive production to steroid use.[29] Caminiti's battle with drug addiction ended his life in 2004 at age 41.

WHO'S MISSING?

The Astros Hall of Stats features 27 players—12 pitchers (including one full-time reliever and one who filled multiple roles), three first basemen, three second basemen, one third baseman, one shortstop, and seven outfielders.

No catchers made the list. In fact, the best catcher in team history (by Hall Rating) is Biggio, simply based on his three-plus seasons behind the plate. After Biggio, there is Alan Ashby (11 seasons with Houston), Joe Ferguson (a mere 183 games with Houston with a 124 OPS+), Jason Castro (only 26 years old and with a chance to become the top Astros catcher sometime in 2014), and Brad Ausmus (45 fielding runs in Houston, but –177 batting runs over 10 seasons).

The left side of the infield is also light. Morgan Ensberg narrowly missed the cut, finishing a point behind Caminiti at 29. Doug Rader, Art Howe, and Denny Walling (13 years in Houston) aren't far behind. At shortstop, Thon is followed by Adam Everett (Astros leader in fielding runs) and Craig Reynolds (11 seasons as an Astro).

Among outfielders, Kevin Bass (10 years in Houston), Luis Gonzalez (third among Astros in fielding runs, long before his offensive outburst in Arizona), and Moises Alou (tenth in batting runs despite only three seasons in Houston) are next among retired players. The still-active Hunter Pence and Michael Bourne (fourth in base-running and eighth in fielding) even came close.

The top two pitchers to miss the cut were Mike Hampton (second among Astros in ERA+) and Wade Miller. They are followed by reliever Dave Smith, who spent 11 years in Houston and is second to Wagner in saves. While Bob Knepper ranks sixth in innings and ninth in wins, he didn't come particularly close in Hall Rating.

The Astros have retired nine numbers (not including Jackie Robinson's 42).[30] Pitcher Jim Umbricht is the only one of the nine not to be included in the Astros Hall of Stats. Umbricht's number 32 was the first number retired by the club in 1965. Umbricht was an excellent relief pitcher during the Colt .45s first two seasons before he died of melanoma six months after he pitched his final game.[31]

JUST A GUIDELINE

Should the Astros Hall of Fame perfectly mirror the Astros Hall of Stats? Of course not. But the Astros Hall of Stats does capture the contributions its inductees made to the franchise, and isn't that what a Hall of Fame (or Stats) should celebrate? I'm not advocating that the National Baseball Hall of Fame be replaced with the Hall of Stats, either. The Hall of Stats serves as an objective starting point and shows what a "default Hall" would look like if it were populated simply by context-adjusted run values. From there, adjustments can be made based on intangibles, narratives, and other subjective considerations. ■

Notes

1. Adam Darowski, "There's a Hall of Famer in Every Lineup", The Hall of wWAR, July 30, 2012, http://darowski.com/hall-of-wwar/hofpct/.
2. Team Halls of Fame come in many different varieties. The Cincinnati Reds Hall of Fame was established in 1958, and a physical museum opened in 2004. The New York Yankees do not have a Hall of Fame, but they do have Monument Park and a list of retired uniform numbers. The Boston Red Sox Hall of Fame wasn't established until 1995. It has a strong online presence and plaques of the Red Sox Hall of Famers are located inside Fenway Park. See Greg Rhodes, "The Reds Hall Finds a

Home," Cincinnati Reds, http://cincinnati.reds.mlb.com/cin/hof/about/index.jsp?loc=history, "Boston Red Sox Hall of Fame," Red Sox, http://boston.redsox.mlb.com/bos/fenwaypark100/halloffame.jsp.

3. Adam Darowski, Twitter post, January 10, 2014, 8:13PM, https://twitter.com/baseballtwit/status/421857473516294144.

4. "211 Hall of Fame Inductees," The Hall of Stats, www.hallofstats.com/#hof.

5. "69 Removed from the Hall," The Hall of Stats, www.hallofstats.com/#removed.

6. "69 Added to the Hall," The Hall of Stats, www.hallofstats.com/#added.

7. "The Formula," The Hall of Stats, www.hallofstats.com/about#formula.

8. "Position Player WAR Calculations and Details," Baseball-Reference, www.baseball-reference.com/about/war_explained_position.shtml.

9. "Hall of Fame Member Directory," Cincinnati Reds, http://cincinnati.reds.mlb.com/cin/hof/hof/directory.jsp.

10. "Red Sox Hall of Fame," Boston Red Sox, http://boston.redsox.mlb.com/bos/fenwaypark100/halloffame.jsp.

11. "200 Greatest Houston Astros," The Hall of Stats, www.hallofstats.com/franchise/hou.

12. "Houston Astros Attendance, Stadiums, and Park Factors," Baseball-Reference, www.baseball-reference.com/teams/HOU/attend.shtml.

13. "200 Greatest First Basemen," The Hall of Stats, www.hallofstats.com/position/1b.

14. Rob Neyer, "Big Game pitcher? How about the BIGGEST?," Baseball Nation, January 28, 2014, www.baseballnation.com/2014/1/28/5353248/big-game-pitchers-roy-oswalt-all-time.

15. Grant Brisbee, "Who is the best player to appear on a Hall of Fame ballot and not get a vote?," Baseball Nation, January 7, 2013, www.baseballnation.com/2013/1/7/3847354/hall-of-fame-voting-jimmy-wynn-no-votes.

16. "Los Angeles Dodgers Attendance, Stadiums, and Park Factors," Baseball-Reference, www.baseball-reference.com/teams/LAD/attend.shtml.

17. "Yearly League Leaders & Records for Youngest," Baseball-Reference, www.baseball-reference.com/leaders/Youngest_leagues.shtml.

18. "Terry Puhl," The Canadian Baseball Hall of Fame & Museum, http://baseballhalloffame.ca/museum/inductees/terry-puhl.

19. Roy S. Johnson, "What a Way to Win!," The New York Times, September 25, 1986, www.nytimes.com/packages/html/sports/year_in_sports/09.25.html.

20. "National League Championship Series," Wikipedia, http://en.wikipedia.org/wiki/National_League_Championship_Series#Most_Valuable_Player_Award.

21. "Astros name Nolan Ryan Executive Advisor," Houston Astros, http://houston.astros.mlb.com/news/article.jsp?ymd=20140211&content_id=67663704&vkey=pr_hou&c_id=hou.

22. William Nack, "Now Everyone Believes Him," Sports Illustrated, August 18, 1980, http://si.com/vault/article/magazine/MAG1123684/index.htm.

23. Frank Deford, "In Sports, Left-Handers Exploit Edge Every Day." National Public Radio, August 11, 2010, www.npr.org/templates/story/story.php?storyId=129109799.

24. Alan Schwartz, "Conversation with Billy Wagner," ESPN, June 12, 2003, http://sports.espn.go.com/mlb/columns/story?id=1566732.

25. Jordan Bastian, "Joe Niekro passes away at 61," MLB.com, October 28, 2006, http://mlb.mlb.com/news/article.jsp?ymd=20061028&content_id=1726132&fext=.jsp&c_id=mlb.

26. Jose de Jesus Ortiz, "Astros Richard Hidalgo shot in left arm during carjacking in Venezuela," The Houston Chronicle, November 22, 2002, www.chron.com/sports/astros/article/Astros-Richard-Hidalgo-shot-in-left-arm-during-2099084.php.

27. Jay Jaffe, "I Saw 'em When, Part 2," Baseball Prospectus, February 8, 2011, www.baseballprospectus.com/article.php?articleid=12892.

28. "1961 Major League Baseball expansion draft," Wikipedia, http://en.wikipedia.org/wiki/1961_MLB_expansion_draft.

29. Tom Verducci, "Totally Juiced," Sports Illustrated, June 3, 2002, http://sportsillustrated.cnn.com/vault/article/magazine/MAG1025902/index.htm.

30. "Retired Numbers," Houston Astros, http://houston.astros.mlb.com/hou/history/retired_numbers.jsp.

31. "Jim Umbricht," Astros Daily, www.astrosdaily.com/players/Umbricht_Jim.html.

Astrodome Proves to Be No Hitters Park

Paul Geisler

Long fences and "dead" indoor air gave Astrodome a reputation for being unfriendly to hitters. This analysis compares batting average, slugging percentage, and home run rate (home runs per 1,000 at-bats) for all Astros games at home (in the Dome) and on the road. The Astros played the same teams at home as they did on the road, and the same players were involved in all of the games, in a roughly equal spread of home and road games.[1] (see Table 1.)

We begin with the null hypotheses that batting average, slugging percentages, and home run rates have equal means, and seek to determine in each case if the category proves to be significantly lower at the Astrodome than at other parks.

A two-sample t-test of batting average, assuming unequal variances, produces a "p" value of 4.8E-05—indicating at well over the 99% level that batting averages prove significantly lower in the Astrodome.

A two-sample t-test of slugging percentage, assuming unequal variances, produces a "p" value of 1.22E-06—indicating at well over the 99% level that slugging percentages prove significantly lower in the Astrodome.

A two-sample t-test of home run rate, assuming unequal variances, produces a "p" value of 4.17E-09—indicating at well over the 99% level that the home run rate proves significantly lower in the Astrodome.

All three categories show strongly significantly lower numbers for the games played in the Astrodome, compared to games on the road in other National League ballparks.

The Astros moved the outfield fences several times. During "shorter" years (1972–76 and 1985–99), foul lines (left and right, symmetrical) were 325 to 330 feet, "power" alleys (left and right, symmetrical) 375 to 380 feet, and center field 400 feet. During "longer" years (1965–71 and 1977–84), foul lines were 340 feet, power alleys 390 feet, and center field 406 feet.[2] (See Table 2.)

Table 1.

Year	Astrodome BAVG	Astrodome SLG	Astrodome HR/1000AB	Other Parks BAVG	Other Parks SLG	Other Parks HR/1000AB
1965	0.236	0.329	10.3731	0.261	0.402	29.0553
1966	0.259	0.370	17.1032	0.258	0.391	26.5117
1967	0.253	0.357	11.3187	0.256	0.395	27.2381
1968	0.239	0.328	9.4580	0.240	0.336	15.3875
1969	0.245	0.356	16.6174	0.241	0.357	23.1396
1970	0.260	0.381	20.8825	0.265	0.404	25.4520
1971	0.235	0.318	8.3210	0.246	0.353	18.1361
1972	0.265	0.384	21.2607	0.248	0.379	25.9791
1973	0.244	0.360	20.2592	0.258	0.377	23.9842
1974	0.249	0.356	16.9492	0.269	0.380	18.4475
1975	0.254	0.360	15.1377	0.261	0.371	19.3280
1976	0.235	0.315	10.5751	0.270	0.375	16.6058
1977	0.247	0.349	13.3945	0.257	0.398	26.9354
1978	0.242	0.331	10.9259	0.262	0.379	17.7982
1979	0.235	0.317	8.5645	0.258	0.363	17.1587
1980	0.252	0.339	8.6941	0.254	0.359	17.0788
1981	0.228	0.299	7.5369	0.257	0.360	14.8994
1982	0.242	0.335	10.4953	0.251	0.358	19.1423
1983	0.237	0.324	9.8684	0.255	0.388	25.1792
1984	0.252	0.341	8.5315	0.260	0.377	22.4085
1985	0.254	0.364	16.8398	0.260	0.398	26.5551
1986	0.239	0.348	19.5676	0.241	0.377	25.0737
1987	0.248	0.350	17.6717	0.255	0.409	30.4475
1988	0.238	0.340	15.3024	0.248	0.376	24.2727
1989	0.246	0.354	16.2544	0.239	0.352	20.1946
1990	0.243	0.344	15.1403	0.254	0.383	26.0359
1991	0.243	0.346	12.8997	0.248	0.374	25.0916
1992	0.243	0.352	16.1204	0.255	0.386	22.1770
1993	0.253	0.377	21.9168	0.263	0.396	24.7426
1994	0.268	0.419	28.2077	0.275	0.427	28.0566
1995	0.256	0.366	17.7256	0.285	0.431	26.6667
1996	0.261	0.392	22.0628	0.275	0.425	28.7305
1997	0.248	0.379	21.1669	0.262	0.404	27.3529
1998	0.266	0.417	27.2971	0.269	0.413	28.2935
1999	0.257	0.386	21.3497	0.276	0.429	32.1068

Table 2.

Long Fences at the Astrodome				Short Fences at the Astrodome			
Year	BAVG	SLG	HR/ 1000AB	Year	BAVG	SLG	HR/ 1000AB
1965	0.236	0.329	10.3731	1972	0.265	0.384	21.2607
1966	0.259	0.370	17.1032	1973	0.244	0.360	20.2592
1967	0.253	0.357	11.3187	1974	0.249	0.356	16.9492
1968	0.239	0.328	9.4580	1975	0.254	0.360	15.1377
1969	0.245	0.356	16.6174	1976	0.235	0.315	10.5751
1970	0.260	0.381	20.8825	1985	0.254	0.364	16.8398
1971	0.235	0.318	8.3210	1986	0.239	0.348	19.5676
1977	0.247	0.349	13.3945	1987	0.248	0.350	17.6717
1978	0.242	0.331	10.9259	1988	0.238	0.340	15.3024
1979	0.235	0.317	8.5645	1989	0.246	0.354	16.2544
1980	0.252	0.339	8.6941	1990	0.243	0.344	15.1403
1981	0.228	0.299	7.5369	1991	0.243	0.346	12.8997
1982	0.242	0.335	10.4953	1992	0.243	0.352	16.1204
1983	0.237	0.324	9.8684	1993	0.253	0.377	21.9168
1984	0.252	0.341	8.5315	1994	0.268	0.419	28.2077
				1995	0.256	0.366	17.7256
				1996	0.261	0.392	22.0628
				1997	0.248	0.379	21.1669
				1998	0.266	0.417	27.2971
				1999	0.257	0.386	21.3497

COURTESY OF THE HOUSTON ASTROS

The Astrodome parking lot certainly had the capacity to handle almost any crowd, with 30,000 spaces.

The difference of ten feet at the foul lines and power alleys and six feet in center field made a significant difference in batting production. A comparison of shorter and longer years in a manner similar to that above (t-test, assuming unequal variances) shows home run rate to be strongly significantly lower during the long-fence years, with a "p" value of 6.47E-06. Slugging percentage was also significantly lower, but not as strongly, with a "p" value of 0.011. Batting average was also lower, but not as significantly, with a "p" value of only 0.03.

When compared with other parks in the league, even the shorter-fence version of the Dome still was significantly worse for hitters when compared with the other parks, "p" values of 0.0034 for batting average, 0.00094 for slugging percentage, and 1.43E-05 for home run rate. And in every case, the home run rate showed the most significant difference between the Astrodome and other ballparks. ■

Notes

1. Statistics gleaned from www.retrosheet.org/boxesetc/H/PK_HOU02.htm.
   NOTE: 1997–99 includes an uneven number of games involving AL clubs.
2. www.baseball-almanac.com/stadium/astrodome.shtml.

Dome Attendance Below League Average

Paul Geisler

Despite the phenomenal engineering feat and the novelty of the stadium, attendance at the Astrodome ranked significantly lower than the average attendance in the National League during the Dome's life, with a few notable exceptions.[1]

The Dome opened with strong attendance numbers in the inaugural season of 1965, with 2,151,470—158.4% of the league average. Once the honeymoon was over, totals declined each of next three seasons, yet remained above league average through 1969.

Ten years in, 1975 attracted the lowest number of fans in the Dome's 35-year tenure with an attendance of 858,002—less than 40% of the inaugural year, and only 62% of the league average for that year. They failed to reach the one million mark again the very next season with only 886,146.

Attendance numbers fell below the league average in 23 of the 35 years, including the 16-year stretch from 1982 through 1997.

Astrodome attendance surpassed the opening year total only three times: in 1980 (when the team won 93 games and finished first in their division) and in the final two years in the Dome—1998–99—when attendance bettered the league average. The Astros reached the two million mark two other times, 1993 and 1997.

Across the full 35-year term, Dome attendance ranks significantly lower than the league average, at the 96% level. A two-sample t-test, assuming unequal variances, produces a "p" value of 0.04. Excluding the high attendance total of the opening year, the level raises to the 98% level, with a "p" value of 0.02. ∎

Note

1. Attendance figures from www.baseball-almanac.com/teams/housattn.shtml.

Year	Astrodome Total	League Average
1965	2,151,470	1,358,114
1966	1,872,108	1,501,547
1967	1,348,303	1,297,143
1968	1,312,887	1,178,536
1969	1,442,995	1,257,912
1970	1,253,444	1,388,517
1971	1,261,589	1,443,738
1972	1,469,247	1,294,144
1973	1,394,004	1,389,610
1974	1,090,728	1,414,860
1975	858,002	1,383,374
1976	886,146	1,388,377
1977	1,109,560	1,589,186
1978	1,126,145	1,675,577
1979	1,900,312	1,764,868
1980	2,278,217	1,760,340
1981	1,321,282	1,039,866
1982	1,558,555	1,792,285
1983	1,351,962	1,795,774
1984	1,229,862	1,731,786
1985	1,184,314	1,857,680
1986	1,734,276	1,861,123
1987	1,909,902	2,061,180
1988	1,933,505	2,041,606
1989	1,834,908	2,110,320
1990	1,310,927	2,040,959
1991	1,196,152	2,058,014
1992	1,211,412	2,009,261
1993	2,084,618	2,637,470
1994	1,561,136	1,843,416
1995	1,363,801	1,793,589
1996	1,975,888	2,169,949
1997	2,046,781	2,277,526
1998	2,458,451	2,401,674
1999	2,706,017	2,380,436

Contributors

BRENDAN BINGHAM, was a contributing author to *Bridging Two Dynasties: The 1947 Yankees* and was a poster presenter at SABR43. He currently works in the medical device industry. During a 25-year career as a research scientist, Brendan has published original work in genetics, endocrinology and neuroscience.

STEPHEN D. BOREN MD, MBA, FACEP is an emergency medicine physician, Assistant Professor of Emergency Medicine at the University of Illinois College of Medicine, and was stationed in the U.S. Army in Korea where *M*∗*A*∗*S*∗*H* took place (but 20 years afterwards). In addition to multiple publications in the *Baseball Research Journal*, *The National Pastime*, and *Baseball Digest*, he has many medical publications.

RON BRILEY has taught history and film studies at Sandia Prep School in Albuquerque for 36 years. He is the author or editor of five books on baseball and sports history, including *The Baseball Film in Postwar America: A Critical Study, 1948–1962* (McFarland, 2011). He is a long-suffering fan of the Colt .45s and Astros.

MATTHEW M. CLIFFORD is a freelance writer from the suburbs of Chicago. He joined SABR in 2011 to enhance his research abilities and help preserve accurate facts of baseball history. His background in law enforcement and forensic investigative techniques aid him with historical research and data collection. He has reported several baseball card errors and inaccuracies of player history to SABR and the research department of the National Baseball Hall of Fame. He also writes for SABR's BioProject.

ADAM DAROWSKI is a front-end designer living in New England with his wife and three young children. He is the creator of the Hall of Stats: an alternate Hall of Fame populated by a mathematical formula. He serves as the chair of SABR's Overlooked Nineteenth Century Overlooked Base Ball Legends committee.

WILL FLAHERTY is a native Houstonian and life-long Houston Astros supporter. Will is a 2010 graduate in History and Political Science from Duke University. A SABR member since 2013, Will currently resides in New York City and works for SeatGeek, a search engine for live event tickets.

PAUL GEISLER, JR. grew up in San Antonio, Texas, and has been a Lutheran pastor for over 35 years. He lives in Lake Jackson, Texas, with his wife Susan and their three children: Sarah, Brydon, and Johanna. He loves anything baseball—playing, watching, coaching, researching, and writing.

CHARLES HARRISON was born in Bay City, Texas, and graduated Lamar University in 1964 (BSChe) and University of Missouri in 1966 (MSChE). He works for Bechtel and lives in Houston. Relatively new to SABR, he is a lifelong baseball fan and considers anything played in short pants to not be a true sport. Joe DiMaggio retiring in 1951 was first thing he saw on television.

MAXWELL KATES is a chartered accountant in Toronto. While Director of Marketing for SABR's Hanlan's Point Chapter, he helped organize several events to promote baseball research. One of these, a 2007 group interview of then-Blue Jays broadcaster Alan Ashby, served as the basis for this article.

JIMMY KEENAN has been a SABR member since 2001. His grandfather Jimmy Lyston and other family members were all professional baseball players. A frequent contributor to SABR publications, Keenan is the author of *The Lystons: A Story of One Baltimore Family and Our National Pastime* and a 2012 inductee into Baltimore's Boys of Summer Hall of Fame.

FRANCIS KINLAW has contributed to 14 SABR convention publications (the number of wild pitches thrown by J.R. Richard in the Astrodome in 1978) and attended 18 SABR conventions (the number of Astrodome starts for Larry Dierker in the 1968 and 1974 seasons). He resides in Greensboro, North Carolina, and writes extensively about baseball, football, and basketball.

BILL McCURDY holds degrees from Houston, Tulane, and Texas, but his baseball talent only made him a parochial school all-star. A member of SABR since 1992, Bill has served as Board Chair of the Texas Baseball Hall of Fame. He is co-author of *A Kid From St. Louis* with Jerry Witte, co-author of *Toy Cannon* with Jimmy Wynn, and initiator and co-author of *Houston Baseball: The Early Years, 1861–1961* with others from the Larry Dierker Houston Chapter of SABR, where he is historian.

JOHN McMURRAY is Chair of the SABR Deadball Era Committee. He contributed to *Deadball Stars of the American League* and is a past chair of SABR's Ritter Award subcommittee. He has contributed many interview-based player profiles to *Baseball Digest* and also writes a monthly column for *Sports Collectors Digest*.

ERIC ROBINSON, a graduate of the University of North Texas, currently works in elementary education in Austin. He focuses his research on pre-MLB baseball history, Texas baseball history, and Central Texas blackball history, on which he has presented to local schools. Eric recently discovered his grandmother had a neighbor who played for the 1933 Brooklyn Dodgers. His website is www.lyndonbaseballjohnson.com.

RICK SCHABOWSKI, a retired machinist from Harley-Davidson, is currently an instructor at Wisconsin Regional Training Partnership in the Manufacturing program, and is a certified Manufacturing Skills Standards Council instructor. He is also President of the Ken Keltner Badger State Chapter of SABR, Treasurer of the Milwaukee Braves Historical Association, President of the Wisconsin Oldtime Ballplayers Association, and a member of the Hoops Historians.

ERIC THOMPSON is a two-time presenter at SABR national conventions concerning baseball's first expansion between 1960 and 1962. A retired high school mathematics teacher, Thompson authored *Baseball's LOST Tradition: Two Eight-Team Leagues*. Today Thompson plays softball in The Babes of 1916 senior league in Solon, Ohio, where he lives with Colleen, his wife for 45 years. He has three grown children and five grandchildren.

DAN VanDeMORTEL became a Giants fan in Upstate New York and moved to San Francisco to follow the team more closely. He has written extensively on Northern Ireland political affairs, and his Giants-related writing has appeared in San Francisco's *Nob Hill Gazette*. He is currently writing a book on the 1971 Giants and welcomes feedback at giants1971@yahoo.com.